Beyond Philosophy

New Critical Theory
General Editors:
Patricia Huntington and Martin J. Beck Matuštík

The aim of *New Critical Theory* is to broaden the scope of critical theory beyond its two predominant strains, one generated by the research program of Jürgen Habermas and his students, the other by postmodern cultural studies. The series reinvigorates early critical theory—as developed by Theodor Adorno, Herbert Marcuse, Walter Benjamin, and others—but from more decisive post-colonial and post-patriarchal vantage points. *New Critical Theory* represents theoretical and activist concerns about class, gender, and race, seeking to learn from as well as nourish social liberation movements.

Beyond Philosophy

Ethics, History, Marxism, and Liberation Theology

Enrique Dussel

Edited by
Eduardo Mendieta

ROWMAN & LITTLEFIELD PUBLISHERS, INC.
Lanham • Boulder • New York • Oxford

ROWMAN & LITTLEFIELD PUBLISHERS, INC.

Published in the United States of America
by Rowman & Littlefield Publishers, Inc.
A Member of the Rowman & Littlefield Publishing Group
4501 Forbes Boulevard, Suite 200, Lanham, Maryland 20706
www.rowmanlittlefield.com

PO Box 317
Oxford
OX2 9RU, UK

British Library Cataloguing in Publication Information Available

Library of Congress Cataloging-in-Publication Data

Dussel, Enrique D.
  [Selections. English. 2003]
  Beyond philosophy : ethics, history, Marxism, and liberation theology
/ Enrique Dussel ; edited by Eduardo Mendieta.
     p. cm.—(New critical theory)
Includes bibliographical references and index.
  ISBN 978-0-8476-9777-9
  1. Liberation theology—Latin America—History. 2. Christian
ethics—Latin America—History. 3. Social ethics—Latin
America—History. 4. Latin America—Church history. I. Mendieta,
Eduardo. II. Title. III. Series.
  B1034.D874A25 2003
  199'.82—dc21

                                                          2003007759

Printed in the United States of America

♾ ™ The paper used in this publication meets the minimum requirements of
American National Standard for Information Sciences—Permanence of Paper for
Printed Library Materials, ANSI/NISO Z39.48-1992.

Contents

v

Acknowledgments

This book would not have been possible without the enthusiasm, support, and encouragement of Maureen MacGrogan. I simply cannot thank her enough for this and many other books, including those that are not my own, that she has so wisely, generously, and masterfully guided into existence. Enrique Dussel was my teacher at Union Theological Seminary in the late 1980s, that amazing institution of North American Religious Radical Thought (Dietrich Bonhoeffer, Paul Tillich, James Cone, and Cornel West, taught or were students there). Since then he has never ceased to amaze me both with his inexhaustible curiosity and ability to work and produce amazing books, but most importantly with his humanity and generosity. This volume is a very small sampling of his prodigious intellectual production, and I want to thank him for this gift as well as his friendship and guidance. I also want to express my gratitude to all the translators who have contributed to the dissemination of Dussel's work; their names are acknowledged on the pieces they translated. To the editors of the many journals where Dussel's essays first appeared, thank you. This book was conceived as a companion to the volume Linda Martín Alcoff and I co-edited under the title *Thinking from the Underside of History: Enrique Dussel's Philosophy of Liberation* (Rowman & Littlefield, 2000), so I want to thank Linda for all her support and encouragement. I want to thank John Wehmueller for his diligence and thoroughness, Eve de Varo for her patience and expert guidance of this manuscript through production, and of course Azucena Cruz who helped proofread the manuscript and produce the index. Finally, I want to thank Pedro Langé-Churion, Louis Ann Lorentzen, Gerardo Marin, and Martin Woessner—who have supported this work with their friendship.

Eduardo Mendieta
Stony Brook

Preface

As I find myself this fall at Harvard University to give some postgraduate seminars, I think that this book, edited by the "Latino" thinker Eduardo Mendieta, can be helpful in showing part of an unknown Latin-American intellectual production. The advantage of this work is that it gathers a set of works that are very difficult to read because they are extremely dispersed throughout many publications. This collection selects works that deal with theological, economic, and historical themes. They are all from a material and critical Latin-American perspective, and they all form part of an Ethics of Liberation.[1] This ethics takes into consideration as ultimate criteria of "content" the production and reproduction of human life. These chapters were elaborated in their majority during the eighties,[2] a period during which I began to write a complete commentary on Marx's "Four Redactions of *Capital*."[3] I think that the discourse developed in this book (theological, economic, historical) shows an explicit awareness of the importance that the reflection and critique carried out by liberation theology has for Latin America, especially given the state of exploitation and poverty. It is an awareness that is articulated from the critical economics that impregnated the entire theological and historical problematic.

In this sense, the second chapter ("The Bread of the Eucharist Celebration") already shows the perspective of the entire volume: a liturgical, religious act such as the Eucharist is essentially and critically related to the unjust economic and historical structures at the beginning of Modernity in the Caribbean, in 1514, before Erfurt's Luther and way before the future Northern Europe began an epoch properly industrial capitalist. If the

sacramental bread has been stolen from the poor, the liturgical celebration is idolatrous. Blood is life for the Hebrews (which is value for Marx:
coagulation and objectification of life); therefore, to pretend to offer to the
"gods" bread stolen from the poor, or not to pay the just wage, "is to kill
the son in the presence of the father." The structure of the biblical–symbolic text is economic, and only Marx has categories to hermeneutically
decipher it. Evidently, I belong to the group of thinkers who continue to
relate at the beginning of the twenty-first century the theology of liberation to Marx's thought, because I participated (and still participate to this
day) in a critical theoretical community that since the late seventies has
been rethinking Marx out of other suppositions than those of "Soviet
standard Marxism." I think that this Marx liberated of the Stalinist bal-
last will be the "classic" Marx of the twenty-first century, which is perfectly coherent with the Christian experience. I did not use the "standard
Marx" to then apply him "already done" to theology. Instead, I reconstructed Marx after a deconstruction of standard Marxism, which disappeared in 1989 with the Soviet Union. What I encountered was the profound, prophetic coherence of Marx with the critical positions of the
prophets of Israel, with Jesus, the founder of Christianity, who was crucified because of the accusations of the priests of the temple and by soldiers of the Empire ruling at the moment. The critical Christ victim of the
sacralized powers of his period has a lot to say in the beginning of this
twenty-first century, as do Marx, Freud, Levinas, and so many others,
and even still with greater reason. Christ does so, however, not as a fun-
damentalist Christ, conservative or liberal, but rather as a Christ who,
more critical than Nietzsche's Anti-Christ, is above all a testimony to the
life that loves and that does not accept the loss of assassinated lives of the
victims of history.

A careful reader can see how I made a transition from a theology that
used Marxist categories[4]—discretely and insofar as it was necessary—to
another that integrated the categories of an Apelian–Habermasian prag-
matics (for example, "Theology and Economy," chapter 9).

A reader can also discern the treatment of the theme that today we
would call globalization. Since the sixties, I have been formulating the
need of a reflection that takes into account the horizon of world history. It
is one that is not a mere chapter in empirical–historical science; instead, it
is a critical "location," or "point of departure," for a theoretical discourse
that knows its original "placement." To be born at the North Pole or in
Chiapas is not the same thing as to be born in New York City."[5] In the first
chapter, "Domination–Liberation," I show—next to the erotic (the problem of feminism) or the pedagogical (I had in mind Paulo Freire)—how

the categories "center" and "periphery" had already situated discourses within a differentiated world history, with a heterogeneous structure, which allowed the transfer of value from the colonies to the European metropolises (and today in terms of the postcolonial periphery and the North American centrality). The blood of the Amerindian Indians and African slaves was shed and transferred as silver or tropical produce to Europe, which accumulated it as capital: dead Mammon (as Domingo de Santo Tomás in the exploited Bolivia of 1550 already saw it). This whole topic of globalization was already an original epistemological horizon; in fact, in 1966, I gave a course (still unpublished) on "Latin America in Universal History" *(América Latina en la Historia Universal)*. My intention then was to discover the Latin-American epistemological "place" from whence a philosophy, theology, and even a non-Eurocentric historical interpretation could be elaborated.

Rereading these texts, some of which have more than thirty years, I am rejoiced at how following the sense of a straight and coherent line of the same type of discourse impregnates the entire path of my thinking, which furthermore, I believe, had the capacity to anticipate many contemporary themes. It was a thought borne in the "periphery," and as such, it has suffered in obscurity, in its skin, that of the living corporeal subject, but one also of the thinking subject, the experience of violence perpetrated by a national elite domesticated according to the dictates of metropolitan interests. In 1973, I suffered a bomb attempt in my house, with my wife and children, because I expressed opinions such as those expressed in the texts here collected; in 1975, I was expulsed from my university and from Argentina for criticizing a military dictatorship put in power by CIA recommendation, one placed under Kissinger's strategy, whom the Spanish judge Garzón does not judge, but who was the explicit and public inspiration for Pinoché, Videla, and so many dictators of the period. It was Kissinger who began the international politics and pure doctrine of the "defense of *North American interests*" without any reference to ethical principles.[6] Thus, I began my long exile in Mexico. I anticipated many intellectuals of the "center" not because of greater intelligence, but because I lived first the violence of the system. Many of these works have been written with blood, the blood of the Latin-American people still victimized, exploited, robbed, humiliated by the metropolitan power and its own national elites who turn their back to the pain of their compatriots and victims, habituated through centuries to see them as part of the landscape and not as human beings (much like how the white "coletos" in Chiapas see the Mayan Indians). These elites were the "Herodians," as they were called during the

decade of the sixties, and they were formed by the civilized metropolises, as Sartre described in the preface to Fanon's *Wretched of the Earth*.
Herodes killed the innocent children of Belen when he sought to kill the
legitimate successor of the kingdom that he usurped as collaborating
traitor with the Roman Empire. That empire spoke Latin; today's empire
speaks English. It would do well to recall that Jesus, son of Maria and
Jose, was departing for a "political" [7] exile in Egypt, to a country where
he learned a lot. Among many things, he learned about the content and
order of the criteria of the final judgment (Matthew 25), which is inspired in the Osiris' judgment in the great hall of Maat in *Book of the
Dead*, chapter 125, in Isaiah as well, whose content has to do with the *material* reproduction of life (to eat, drink, to dress, to have a roof, health,
and to be safe).

These works are testimonies of a path traveled together with a suffering people, during an extremely hard period in Latin-American history.
From 1968 to beginning of the 1980s, many more martyrs were in Latin
America than in the whole Mediterranean Christian church during its
first centuries of existence.

In 1983, the Latin-American people began to dismantle the dictatorships imposed by the empire, but these will last until the nineties when
they face their extinction, although they will continue in some way until July 2, 2000, in the debacle of the PRI (Institutional Revolutionary
Party; what Vargas Llosa called the "perfect dictatorship"). The PRI is
one of the most intelligent and long-lasting bureaucracies of the continent. It allows one to say that a situation of "formal" relative democracy
extends lugubriously over all of Latin America, because the freely
elected government does not cease to overburden and augment the economic misery of "Our America," as Martí called it. Could it be that the
great central power allowed "democracy" to exist in Latin America so
that the "legitimate" governments would pay back the immense and irresponsible[8] economic debt that the illegitimate military regimes contracted (but because of their illegitimacy, the peoples would not be disposed to pay back)?

History has not ended, and it continues its unfolding, right before our
eyes. These works are some expressions of the panorama that is observed through small windows in the transversal that never ceases its
development.

I am thankful to Eduardo Mendieta, colleague and friend, for the patience and perspicacity of having edited this book. With his work, this
book can be presented to the critical consideration of the communities of
English language, which also exist in the Caribbean, Africa, and Asia. I

wish to thank others, too, without which Latin-American thought would be even more unknown than it presently is.

Enrique Dussel
Robert Kennedy Visiting Professor
Harvard University

NOTES

1. *Ethics of Liberation in the Age of Globalization and Exclusion*, forthcoming from Duke University Press.

2. Except the article "From Secularization to Secularism," which is from 1969. For my intellectual biography, there is nothing better than the introduction to *Thinking from the Underside of History: Enrique Dussel's Philosophy of Liberation*, ed. Linda Martín Alcoff and Eduardo Mendieta (Lanham, Md.: Rowman & Littlefield, 2000).

3. The commentary on Marx's political–economic manuscripts of 1861 to 1863 has now appeared in English: Enrique Dussel, *Towards an Unknown Marx: A Commentary on the* Manuscripts of 1861–1863 (London: Routledge, 2001). On the four redactions of *Capital,* see my essay "The Four Drafts of Capital: Towards a New Interpretation of the Dialectical Thought of Marx" *Rethinking Marxism* 13, no. 1 (2001): 10–26.

4. See my book *Ethics and Community*, 2nd edition (Maryknoll, N.Y.: Orbis Books, 1993), where I develop a theological discourse using categories developed by Marx in the *Grundrisse*.

5. I wrote this in 1976, when I began my exile in Mexico. See paragraph 1.1.1.2 of *Philosophy of Liberation*, 2nd edition (Maryknoll, N.Y.: Orbis Books, 1990), 2.

6. For that reason my book *Philosophy of Liberation* began with the statement "From Heraclitus to Karl von Clausewitz and Henry Kissinger, 'war is the origin of everything' . . ."

7. I say "political" not metaphorically, but historically. If someone flees because they are persecuted as a member of a dynastic family with possibilities of one day occupying power, this persecution is only and strictly political; in no way is it religious.

8. The governments and the banks of the metropolitan countries never remember that the governments that took (and stole) the loans were illegitimate; they were not elected by the people. No plebiscite was ever convened in order to ask if the people were ready to take over as a state the debt of particular transnationals and private interests. The economic debt is "irresponsible" *(a)* on the side of those that grant loans to illegitimate and dictatorial governments and *(b)* on the side of the governments that contracted the debt, because they were never elected democratically by citizens (at least when the majority of the great debts were undertaken in the decades of the seventies and eighties).

Introduction

When the history of Latin-American philosophy in the twentieth century is written, Enrique Ambrosini Dussel will occupy a very prominent place in it. Dussel is, and has been, one of the most prolific Latin-American philosophers of the last half of the twentieth century. He has written over fifty books and over three hundred articles ranging over the history of Latin-American philosophy, political philosophy, church history, theology, ethics, and occasional pieces on the state of Latin-American countries. His work has been translated into Russian, Yugoslavian, Korean, Japanese, as well as German, Italian, French, Portuguese, Dutch, Polish, and English. Some of his works are classics of Latin-American philosophy and have had many printings; in fact, many of them have been pirated. Dussel's work, like Latin America itself, is marked by a tortuous and fractious history. While some of his work has appeared in some countries, others have not because of censorship or political persecution. In other instances, some of his work is known in some countries, but ignored in others for ideological and political reasons. And while he has lived in Mexico for over twenty-five years, he is treated like an outsider. Nonetheless, the corpus of Dussel's work is voluminous, prodigiously researched, and, most important, ecumenical, innovative, and systematic. Dussel has contributed substantively and decisively to such fields as the history of Latin-American church, of which he is probably one of the most important historians; the development of Latin-American liberation theology, one of the most important religious, popular, church, intellectual, and cultural movements in twentieth-century Latin America;

1

the history of Latin-American philosophy; and liberation philosophy, which is parallel but distinctive from liberation theology.

Within philosophy, Dussel has contributed most consistently and determinedly to the field of ethics. Indeed, Enrique Dussel is above all a moral philosopher, or a philosopher of the ethical. The core of his work is the ethical relation. Yet, Dussel's voluminous oeuvre might appear from the standpoint of the highly specialized and academicized North American academy as wildly frantic in its disciplinary irreverence or promiscuous in its appropriation of seemingly disparate currents and traditions. Indeed, an incredible urgency and disciplinary eclecticisms mark his works, written under the pressure of violent historical events. These aspects, however, are not the mark of superficiality or frivolous shopping around. They exhibit, above all, impatience with a narrowly conceived and defined philosophy; they exhibit how these narrow conceptions actually hinder most noxiously practical philosophy, thereby rendering it into an accomplice to the atrocities of dictators, technocrats, and anonymous CEOs of denationalized transnationals—that is, megacorporations who once had national headquarters, but that in the age of globalized finance capital have disavowed all relationship to national capitals. Enrique Dussel is a philosopher of liberation for whom philosophy must be liberated so that it may contribute to its task of social liberation. Here we find embedded the two meanings that can be extracted from the title of this book. "Beyond philosophy," means to go beyond contemporary, existing, academicized, professionalized, domesticated, and "civilized" philosophy by taking recourse to all that demystifies the autonomy of philosophy and that at the same time turns our attention to its sources. "Beyond philosophy," also means to go beyond philosophy in the Marxian sense of abolishing philosophy by realizing it. This realization takes form primarily through the transformation of a social situation in which the living human agent is enslaved and dehumanized. Dussel's "barbarian"—as he has often characterized his philosophy of liberation—and his antidisciplinary stand toward philosophy aim at going beyond "hegemonic" and "accepted" philosophy so as to reach back or down into the core of the philosophical, which is the ethical relation. At the same time, Dussel's work points in the direction of going beyond philosophy by transforming a growingly dehumanizing global order in which the rhetoric of inclusion is belied by a sharpening of the actual exclusion of most of humanity from the benefits of technological and social development. In light of Dussel's planetary, or global, intent, we can also discern in the title a third sense, namely of going beyond national and even civilizational philosophies, to put on the agenda a thinking about the whole earth, the whole planet, now so inextricably tied in its common fate by the ecological devastation unleashed by chaotic markets, local wars on the verge of turning global conflagrations, and the continuous threat of a unilaterally deployed devastating violence to put down the protests of those most affected by the excesses of the "first world." The planet has one fate, and humanity one same future, but all citizens of the earth do not suffer the inequities, miseries, tragedies, and catastrophes that rain upon them equally.

This work will allow the reader to get a good sense of the breath and depth of Dussel's work. Four major areas are covered: ethics, economics, history, and liberation theology. His contributions to these areas are also presented within a chronology. The works edited here have appeared in a variety of publications over the last three decades. During these thirty-plus years, Dussel's philosophical tools have undergone changes, although his focus on the ethical relationship has never wavered. In the next section, I will therefore turn to a general characterization of the three most significant stages in the evolutions of Enrique Dussel's thought. In the final section, I will briefly characterize what gives coherence to the pieces here collected.

FROM ONTOLOGY, THROUGH MARX, TO DISCOURSE

Enrique Dussel was born in Argentina in 1934. After receiving his B.A. in philosophy, he traveled to Europe, where he obtained advanced degrees in philosophy, history, and theology. He studied in France and Germany, but then lived in Israel for two years, earning his living as a day laborer. An intellectual itinerary that spans half a century, several continents, and many national as well as global crises—or as he puts it, the crises of the small (Argentina) and large (Latin America) fatherlands—cannot but have undergone several and severe transformations. Dussel's thought could be divided into at least six stages, all of them determined by biographical factors: studies, travel abroad, return to the homeland, the discovery of Latin-American political reality and the challenges to philosophy, exile, and so on.[1] I would like to suggest that from the perspective of philosophy, Enrique Dussel's thought comprises three significant intellectual stages. Each stage was characterized by a quest or philosophical project.[2]

The first stage is circumscribed by the trajectory: from ontology to metaphysics. This stage covers the earliest years of Dussel's philosophical production, the decade of the sixties. Dussel was trained in Europe, mostly France and somewhat in Germany. There he came under the influence of Ricoeur and Heidegger. Dussel's early work was therefore deeply influenced by hermeneutics and phenomenology. He related to them less as traditions and more as forms of philosophical analysis that he proceeded to deploy in the discovering and forging of a Latin-American philosophical project. From Heidegger, Dussel derived the idea that all world-views are manifestations of existential attitudes. In other words, ideas are not absolute and abstract categories; rather, they are coagulations of existential experience. Existence entails certain preunderstandings. We cannot comprehend the world without already having some pre-experience of it. Conversely, certain forms of existence, or forms of social relations (to put it in the language of sociology), entail certain conceptual schemas, or ways of making sense of the world. Our way of being with others and in relationship to the world result in particular ways of viewing those persons and things we are in relation with. Concepts and world-view are extensions of the web of existential relations. Another way of putting it would be to say that mind and world, ideas and things, consciousness and its other, are not ontologically different, but are part of a continuum.

From Ricoeur, Dussel learned that this continuum is always a circle of meaning: interpreted meaning and interpreting meaning. Everything is a crystallization of acts of interpretation. If we approach culture oriented by these intuitions, then culture is to be treated like geological sediment, accumulations of layers of meaning. With these two methods in hand, Dussel set out to discover and recover the symbolics of Latin-American culture that would yield to his investigations the layers of meaning accumulated by centuries of a unique Latin-American existential experience. Ontology, however, is totalizing, as is already intimated by the correspondences established by Heidegger's ontology: mind and world, consciousness and its other, I and Thou. In this ontological circle, the other of either an "I" or a consciousness (or self-consciousness) can only be but a shadow of the already same. The other is a pre-figured in the same, the "I," the self-enclosed hermeneutical world. There is no other; what is left is merely a refracted version of what an ontological horizon contains within itself.

In the late sixties and seventies, Dussel was challenged by the pedagogical inappropriateness of the methods he had learned in Europe; he was also urged on by the revolutionary fervor in Latin America and by the rise of populism in Argentina in particular. Dussel thus came to realize that existentially, hermeneutically, and culturally, Latin America occupied a place in world history that could not be assimilated to the European models of development, or even explanation. Biographically, the context was of political and cultural turmoil and ferment, as was the case for most world thinkers around the momentous years of the late sixties and early seventies. As Dussel undertook a massive philosophical work of ethics, *Towards an Ethics of Latin American Liberation*,[3] he discovered the work of the great Jewish thinker Emmanuel Levinas, in particular *Totality and Infinity* (1961).[4] This work produced in Dussel a "subversive disorientation"[5] that challenged all of his preunderstandings, in particular, his Heideggerianism. The discovery of Levinas allowed Dussel to develop his own unique philosophical methodology, one that he considered more appropriate to the task of the recovery of Latin-American symbolics and hermeneutics. He calls this method the *analectical method*, and sometimes, the *anadialectical method*.[6] Analectics, which comes from the Greek root *ano* (beyond), takes as its point of departure the unmitigated transcendence of the other. The other is never the mere shadow—a faulty, incomplete image or realization of the same, the I, the one. The other is beyond the horizon of what is already experienced and comprehended. The method of the self-mirroring (and self-projection of the same) is dialectics, and it is this method that has ruled all of Western philosophy at least since the pre-Socratics (Parmenides and Heraclitus). But dialectics is war, the war of the same and the I to affirm itself in and through the other, and to wrest from the other what makes the other inassimilable alterity. The horizon of comprehension and existence of the I is a totality. Dialectics is the production of the totality. The other is an exteriority that is irreducible to the totality of the self-same. As long as we subscribe to an ontological approach, the otherness of the other will remain inscrutable alterity. To open ourselves to the other requires that we destroy ontology and in its place institute a metaphysical approach, one that sets out from the fundamental principle that the truth of the world is always beyond what is never exhausted by the given. To put it formulaically, ontology is to dialectics as metaphysics is to analectics. The former is mobilized by exclusion and war, the later by expectant openness and solidarity.

In Dussel's works from the seventies, then, Western thought is seen as the succession of dialectically produced and maintained totalities, whose very constitution and preservation has been predicated on the exclusion of an abject alterity: a vilified, despised, exploited, annihilated other. Thus, the totality of the polis was predicated on the exclusion of women, slaves, and barbarians (those who did not speak Greek); the totality of Christendom was predicated on the exclusion of women, the infidel, the atheist, the heterodox; the totality of Modern Europe was predicated on the exclusion of the other of civilization and culture, namely the

Amerindian, the African, and Asian cultures. Every hermeneutical and existential, or *ontologological* (epitomized in Hegel, the high priest of self-referential totalities), totality is totalitarian, belligerent and martial. And as long as we approach them dialectically, we will remain within the domain of their domination. To break free of their coercion and subjugation, we must open ourselves to the other from the standpoint of the other. We must think, hear, see, feel, and taste the world from the standpoint of the other. This is the analectical moment. Thus, if dialectics is conditioned by magnanimity, analectics is conditioned by humility; if the one is conditioned by erotic love, the other by compassionate solidarity; if one is conditioned by quid pro quos, the other is conditioned by expectant solicitude; if one is about production and profit, the other is about service and gift. We approach the other in a reverent attitude, disposed to service and to empathic solidarity. The alternative is war, dispossession, occlusion, exclusion, and genocide. A philosophy that tries to think this alternative, from the standpoint of the alterity of the other, is a philosophy of liberation, and not just simply a radical hermeneutics or phenomenology. This is a philosophy at the service of liberation, and it is produced by the experience of liberation, of and about. It is this philosophy that Dussel has been working on since the late sixties and early seventies.

Politics, looked at from a metaphysical point of view and dealt with via the analectical methods, yields the insight that there is a politics of the totality and a politics of the other. The former is the politics of the status quo, of the established and ruling totality. This is a politics of fetishization and divinification, of enthronement and intolerant homogenization. In fact, ontological politics turn into the science of the smooth-functioning machine of power that assimilates otherness to the self-same, and it excludes the indissoluble alterity of the other. Politics becomes the craft of the production and the concentration of power with the telos of the control of the other within and outside the totality.

A political totality divides into the master and its oppressed as oppressed within that particular system, and the other of the totality, as political alterity. Every totality has its internal and exterior others. The politics of the other, then, is an anti-politics; it is a politics of de-legitimating, of subversion and contestation. It is a politics that challenges the established hierarchies and legal verities that justify and legitimized enforced exclusions. The politics of the other, the anti-politics of alterity, proclaims the injustice and illegitimacy of the present system, not in the name of chaos or lawlessness, but in the name of a new legality, a new lawfulness, one which will be generalized, more universalized, where these two terms refer to the point of view of the abjected and excluded other. In Dussel's view, then, metaphysical politics, the politics of the other, the anti-politics of alterity, is energized and made dynamic by the struggles of the excluded, exploited, and disenfranchised. Its determining virtues are neither equality nor justice, but respect and solidarity. At the core of the politics of antipolitics is the fundamental insight that all power struggles are predicated on asymmetries. What mobilizes us to shift the scales is not justice, which remains within the outlook of the totality that grants to similars the same; it is but respect and solidarity for him/her or it, whose interpellation remains incomprehensible lest we opt for utter gratuitous solidarity with they who clamor. The suffering of the other raises as a cry. This turns into an interpellation that challenges the verities and principles of the extant legal and political system. The more reticent a system is to the interpellation of its others, the more totalitarian, belligerent, and intolerant it turns. The intolerant homogenizing totalitarian totality is the ontological version of the annihilating terrorist state of the concentration camp, what Eugene Kogon called the *SS-Staat*. This dual view of politics will remain a constant in Dussel's thought.

The second stage in Dussel's philosophical itinerary is circumscribed by the trajectory: from metaphysics to Marxism. This stage overlaps partially with Dussel's exile in Mexico, which begins in 1975. Philosophically, Dussel is confronted with the challenge of the increasing importance of a historically specific analysis of the systematic exclusion not just of a group within a nation (class and *pueblo*, for instance), but also of even an entire continent within a world totality—more specific, Western culture. Evidently, such a historically specific analysis took Dussel to a critique of capitalism, which at that time was seen as the only cause of the increasing impoverishment of the Latin-American people. This critique could only be executed with the tools of Marxism. At the same time, however, this Marxism had to be wrested away from the entrenched and already solidified dogmatism of the Eastern Block nations.

Notwithstanding the shift from ontology to metaphysics we described earlier, Dussel had continued to read Marx as another functionary of the totality. As a child and follower of Hegel, Marx was thinker of the totality and an executor of dialectics. During the midseventies, Dussel began to revise his reading of Marx; but already skeptical of Western and, in particular, European philosophical readings, he realized that traditional approaches are insufficient for the task of the appropriation of Marx in a Latin-American context. In fact, he realized that he must read Marx himself. This meant reading the manuscripts that were being made available, too slowly for Dussel's interest and agenda, as the complete work of Marx and Engels were being published by the Marx–Lenin Institutes in Berlin and Moscow. Dussel immerses himself in a reading of the four redactions of *Capital*, as well as other manuscripts produced by Marx toward the end of his life. Out of this archival work, there emerged a three-volume commentary and analysis of the process and evolution of Marx's categories.[8]

Dussel's reading of Marx distinguishes itself by at least the following four unique aspects. First, Dussel's reading of Marx is based on an unparalleled and unprecedented knowledge of the trajectory of Marx's own intellectual development. Dussel not only read the recently published works, but also the preparatory notes and different drafts Marx worked on as he began to elaborate his *Capital*, of which he only saw volume one through print. Second, insofar as Dussel has studied, exegeted, and reconstructed for us an immense unknown corpus of theoretical productivity, Dussel discovered not only a Marx that was relevant to the project of Latin American liberation, but he also discovered a hitherto unknown Marx that has made it indispensable to begin a critical assessment of Marx's reception in the twentieth century. To this extent, Dussel might have discovered a Marx for the twenty-first century.

Third, Dussel's careful reconstruction of the emergence of certain key categories in the *Grundrisse* and *Kapital* lead Dussel to conclude that Marx in fact was not just a left Hegelian, but also even a Schellingian. What this means is that in Dussel's reconstruction, the fundamental method of Marx was not dialectics, but what he called *analectics*. Dussel thinks that the core philosophical and methodological insight in Marx's work is that the fountain of value—that which is appropriate as surplus value and that which gives the commodity its ability to generate value that is accumulated in capital—is living labor *(lebendige Arbeit)*. The capitalist system does not produce value. Value is extracted and appropriated from the living corporeality of the laborer. A commodity, then, is a coagulation, a crystallization, of living labor. In Dussel's view, such an analysis of the processes of commodity production and the accumulation of surplus value into capital correspond more to a late Schellingian metaphysical perspective than to a Hegelian dialectical perspective. For the late Schelling, specifically the one of the *Philosophie der Offerbarung (Philosophy of Revelation)* of 1941–1942, the ground of the world is the mystery of God's wholly otherness. What is, is revelation of the mystery of God. In terms of philosophy, Being is posterior to the non-Being of the wholly other. Or, to put in the terms of German idealism, the identity of the identical and the nonidentical is replaced in Schelling by the nonidentity of the identical and the nonidentical. There is always a surplus beyond the identical. The other is always the epiphany of an unsupersedeable alterity. In Dussel's view, this reverence and acknowledgement of the life of the other, as the living labor of the worker, is what makes Marx's method not Hegelian, but Schellingian, and one may add, Levinasian. The Marx Dussel discovered is what we would call today, of course anachronistically but entirely suggestively and appropriately, a Levinasian Marx.

Fourth, and consequently, Dussel's Marx is not one who is correctly read through the Althusserian distinction between the young and the late Marx, where the former is a humanist and dialectical Marx, while the latter is a scientific and materialist Marx. Nor is Marx correctly understood when we try to dissociate him from Engels' dialectical materialism and appropriately associate him with historical materialism. Instead—and here Dussel enunciates a challenge for the twenty-first century Marxists— Marx is to be read metaphysically, humanistically, and as a critic of Hegelian, Aristotelian, and Platonist totalities. Dussel thus calls us to dispense with the distorting reading of Marx executed by Western Marxism, as well as *diamat* (Soviet sanctioned and dogmatically thought in the socialist block dialectical materialism). In Dussel's view, the really humanist Marx is he whom we encounter in *Capital*, where we are confronted not with a science of economics, but a critique of the political economy that produces the system for the expropriation of life of the laborer. *Capital* is less a scientific treatise, and more an ethics. A nice parallel would be to say that *Capital* is not like Hegel's *Logic*, but more like Levinas' *Totality and Infinity*, which at root is a fundamental ethics, a metaethics. The first philosophy, *prima philosophia*, of all philosophical speculation, in Levinas' view—and here Dussel concurs unequivocally—is ethics. In this sense, for Dussel, *Capital* is a *prima philosophia* that describes an ethics. In summary, Dussel discovers an ethical Marx that has been betrayed and eclipsed by decades of the ontologizing and Hegelianizing of his fundamental option for the creativity of the living corporeality of the worker.

The metaphysically criticized totalities of the first stage of Dussel's thought turned into the Marxistically unmasked systems of exploitation. History is not just a succession of ontological totalities; it is also a succession of systems of the exploitation, expropriation, and extraction of value from the living labor of workers. This exploitation and expropriation has taken place at regional, national, and continental levels. It is in this way that totality and transcendentality (the alterity of the other) are translated in Dussel's Schellingian Marx into the categories of center and periphery. Of course, such a reinscription takes place against the background of the concepts developed by dependency and underdevelopment theory.[9] In the seventies and early eighties, the central question for Dussel became the *development of underdevelopment* on a global level. During this period, Dussel's analysis of politics turns more economicist, in the sense that his books and essays are now suffused by careful studies of the flow of capital (i.e., accumulated value) from one continent to another (from Latin America to Europe, and from Latin America to the United States). From this perspective, then, the analysis of politics turns into the critique not just of political totalities, but most specific, into the critique of the political economies of imperial systems of the transfer of life coagulated into commodities from a sphere or region of production to a region or sphere of consumption. Here, Dussel's critique of the imperial political economy of world-systems converges with those critiques developed by Immanuel Wallerstein[10] and Samir Amin.[11] During this second stage, Dussel adds to his analysis of antipolitical politics, the planetary and global perspective that he assimilated from a Marxism read and discovered from a third world perspective. In Dussel's view, whoever would like to speak of poverty and destitution—topics that are uncircumventable in the age of mass culture, world wars, and continental famines—must speak of global capitalism, imperialisms, and world accumulation of wealth for a minority and impoverishing expropriation of a majority. A nationalistic approach, an approach that only looks even at regions within continents and one that focuses only on the capitalist accumulation of certain "industrialized" Western nations contributes only to the distortion of the global nature of the capitalist system of production and accumulation of wealth. In short, during his second stage, the critique of Western philosophy as ontology has turned into a critique of the political and economic theories that misconstrued and contributed to the occlusion of the system of massive and global inequity.

The third stage of Dussel's philosophical development is traced by a trajectory: from Marxism to discourse. Biographically, this stage overlaps, more or less, with the fall of the Berlin Wall, the voting out of office of the Sandinistas in 1991, and the splitting apart of the Soviet Union. This stage could be said to begin in 1989, when Enrique Dussel began a decade long debate with Karl-Otto Apel, the founding father of discourse ethics.[12] As the first stage was summarized in his five-volume *Latin American Philosophical Ethics*[13] and as the second in his three-volume reconstruction and commentary on Marx's redactions of *Capital*, this third stage is summarized in the monumental *Ética de la Liberación en la edad de globalización y de la exclusión (Ethics of Liberation in the Age of Globalization and Exclusion)*, from 1998.[14] In this work, Dussel sets out to reformulate the foundations of a planetary ethics of liberation of the oppressed and excluded, but he now combines his particular brand of Levinasian and Ricoeurian phenomenology and hermeneutics with Apelian and Habermasian discourse ethics. Much of the preliminary work for the *Ethics of Liberation* fortunately has appeared in English under the title of *The Underside of Modernity: Apel, Ricoeur, Rorty, Taylor, and the Philosophy of Liberation*.[15] In this collection of essays, as well as in the ethics of 1998, Dussel confronts the challenges of the linguistic turn, and in particular, the challenge of how to ground an universalistic ethics in the face of the dismantling and critique of monological and logocentric philosophy of consciousness. While Dussel proceeds to offer a third way among abstract and universalistic (but now dialogically reconstituted) Kantianism, and particularistic and historicist Hegelianism, with already dialogically constituted agents, in debate with Rorty, Taylor, Ricoeur, Vattimo, it is clear that the central dialogue partners are Apel and Habermas.

At the center of the debates, summarily put, are three questions: first, whether the community of communication *(Kommunikationsgemeinschaft)* —which acts either as the a priori condition of possibility of all discourse or as a counterfactual idealization that is both precondition and telos of all communication, in Habermas' less strict formulation—is either prior or posterior to a community of life *(comunidad de vida)*. In Dussel's terms, before discourse, there must be life *(bios)*, in the sense that people must at the very least have secured the conditions for their survival and preservation. If these conditions are not met, then discourse, as conceived by both Apel and Habermas, becomes, at best, an empty idealization, or, at worst, a way to conceal the factual lack of the conditions for true discourse, in which the only coercion is the noncoercion of the better argument and in which the primary goal is agreement and not deception or determination by fiat. The second question is whether we can dichotomize in practice what both Apel and Habermas had distinguished as discourses of justification (or grounding) and discourses of application. Discourses of justification attend to the theoretical dimension of ethical questions, namely, whether we can offer rational and universal warrants that are not vitiated by their historical and local contexts of discovery. Discourses of application attend to the circumstantial, historicized, contextual, and very singular application of principles. Dussel thinks that this disjunction contributes to the misrepresentation of the very practical character of ethical questions—that is, that ethical questions emerge from very specific contexts and that universal principles are generalization of concrete problems. More concretely, Dussel thinks that the generalized principles of an ethics already anticipate their contexts of application, and vice versa, and that specific context of moral consideration becomes visible as such precisely because of certain ethical outlooks. A third bone of contention is the degree to which any ethics should refer its affirmations to neurobiology, or, philosophically articulated, to the fact that ethical entities are biological organisms: with needs, desires, and neurological systems that filter the world and process it into ideas and perceptions. As Kantians, neither Apel nor Habermas, are prepared to accept the empirical evidence or insights offered by neurobiology in their moral philosophies, despite Habermas' call for a deflationary philosophy that works in close cooperation with the fallible sciences.[16] Dussel, instead, thinks that such extreme Kantianism leads to the erasure of the body or sentient corporeality. Most important, such intellectual rigorism and asceticism lead to the foreshortening of the ethical outlook. In other words, the exclusion of the body, as orienting being-in-the-world corporeality, leads to the misrepresentation of not just the source of ethics, but also its goals.

A brief discussion of the *Ethics of Liberation* of 1998 will make it clear how Dussel has substantively replaced the philosophical infrastructure of his ethics while retaining its fundamental concern and motivating telos: the oppression, exclusion, and genocide of the poor, destitute, suffering, vulnerable living corporeality of the victim. After a lengthy introduction (which is a monograph on its own) traces the history of world ethical systems, the book is divided into two major sections. The first deals with what Dussel calls foundational ethics. The second deals with critical ethics. Each part is divided into three chapters, each dealing with a major foundational aspect of ethics: the material moment, the formal moment, and the feasibility moment of ethics. The first chapter of the first part deals with the material, or "content," moment of ethics. For Dussel, ethical questions have to do with our being in the world, not just in the Heideggerian sense of being interpreting entities whose world is always already interpreted, but also in the sense that we are in the world by virtue of our needs and desires. All ethics deals with specific choices and the principles that guided them, and these choices are "about" things and persons in the world. The second chapter of the first part deals with formal moralities, that is, with the question, or demand for, intersubjective validity. Validity remits us to the legitimation and application of the material principle. The next chapter deals with what Dussel calls "the good" (*das Gute*), or what he also calls *ethical feasibility*. From these considerations, three principles emerge: the practical principle of the preservation of life; the formal principle of the discursive legitimation of norms and principles; and the goodness, or feasibility, principle.

The second part of the *Ética de la liberación* develops the critical principles of his ethics of liberation in a negative vein; that is, if the foundational ethics, discussed in the first part, concerns the positive formulation of the principles that guide ethical action, then critical ethics concerns the formulation of the critical principles that guide all ethical critique. Thus, chapter 4, which is the first chapter of the second part, deals with the ethical critique of the ruling systems. This chapter concludes with the enunciation of the critical–material principle of ethics that commands that the affirmation of life calls for the critique of all systems in which the corporeality and dignity of the other is negated. All ethical critique emerges from the recognition of the suffering of the other. This suffering, however, is always material and bodily. The condition of possibility of all critique is the *recognition* of the dignity of the other subject, the cosubject, but from the perspective of their being seen and experienced above all as *human living beings*. The next chapter covers the antihegemonic validity of the community of victims. In this chapter, Dussel deals with the problem that the ethical critique of the victims of any system will always appear illegitimate from the standpoint of that system. To that extent, their critique turns into a delegitimizing critique of the legitimacy of the status quo. This chapter closes with the enunciation of the critical–discursive principle that commands that who *acts* ethically must participate in a community of victims, who (having been excluded) recognize themselves as such and thus issue a critique of the system. The closing chapter develops what Dussel has christened the "liberation principle." All ethics, worthy that name, must culminate in the imperative to liberate all victims from the system that turns them into victims. Evidently, the question arises: How, under what conditions, and by what means is this liberation to be pursued and achieved? This chapter, in parallel with the preceding chapters, concludes with the elaboration of the "liberation principle," which commands that who *acts* critically–ethically *ought* to, or is compelled to pursue, a feasible and performable *transformation* of the present system that is the cause of the suffering of the victims, while also being compelled to pursue the *construction* of a new order in which the life of the victim will be made possible.

BEYOND PHILOSOPHY: TOWARD THE ETHICAL THROUGH RELIGION, THEOLOGY, AND HISTORY

This collection of Dussel's essays seeks to give readers insight into the different areas to which he has contributed. It also seeks to give readers an insight into the generative core of his philosophical views, which, as we noted at the beginning, have primarily to do with the fundamental ethical relations that constitute all human interaction. The book has been organized in four major sections. In the first, I have gathered those texts that have a manifesto and formulaic character. The first essay lays out in the most explicit way the conceptual matrix of all of Dussel's thinking. Since this essay is from the early seventies, Dussel is still operating with a Levinasian framework here. The last piece in this section reproduces the same framework, but now from the perspective of a postmetaphysical and postlinguistic framework. Yet, while almost three decades separate these texts, the reader will appreciate their originating impetus, namely, the question of the liberation of the oppressed and the system of oppression that operates at different levels of human interaction. In between, but also possessing the same manifesto quality, we encounter a piece that exhibits Dussel's approach to religion. For him, religion has an essential liturgical character. A religious ritual, however, is not a mere public performance enacted to invest some with power and to cower others with the awe of sanctioned violence. As sacraments, the liturgical aspects of Christianity coagulate an ethical experience. A sacrament is to practice as a theological category is to theory, but the former has both temporal and phenomenological priority. The bread of the Eucharist embodies the promise and project of a justice that is not just formal but is also, and perhaps most important, material. It is the body of life, for all: Jew, slave, woman, gay, and old person.

The third piece in this section eventually became part of the second part of the introduction to the *Ethics of Liberation*. Beyond the obvious historiographical contributions this piece has made to the unmasking of the myth of modernity, Dussel offers also a metaphilosophical reading of this myth. The issue is the relationship between a philosopheme—in other words, a fundamental philosophical category or trope—and the geopolitics of knowledge. As Dussel shows, modernity has come to stand in for what has made the West different and unique from those cultures and societies that it has so assiduously pursued to dominate and exploit. Modern philosophy, from Descartes through Hegel and Kant up to Habermas, has labored at projecting a utopian land of universality while covering the historical tracks that have made such an ideal both possible and necessary. By uncovering the historical traces and by recovering the material conditions of philosophical production, Dussel has sought to provincialize an alleged universality, thus opening up a way to a transversality, or situated cosmopolitanism, that is attentive to its historical origin but which seeks dialogue across differences.[17] In these three pieces, we find gathered the nuclei of Dussel's work: the liberation of the oppressed, an oppressed that is not an abstract, metaphysical alterity, but someone who experiences exclusion as the negativity of a particular system. Every system, or totality, produces its excluded ones. But every totality or system is different. Religion is both memory and promise of a justice beyond all ethical systems, but this promise is anticipated in a liturgical enactment, praxis of sharing and inclusion. Philosophy has contributed to the concealment of the experience of catastrophe that history has been; to liberate philosophy to its critical function requires that we turn its gaze to its own history.

The section entitled "Liberating Theology" gathers texts dealing explicitly with central themes for liberation theology. The essays deal with liberation theology but also with the project of the liberation of theology. This liberation of theology, however, is not an extrinsic project; rather, it arises from the impetus and central experiences of Christianity itself. In this way, one may speak with Juan Luis Segundo of a *liberating dogma*, by which he meant that the liberation trust of liberation theology is intrinsic to both the theology and liturgy of Christianity.[18] At the root of the liberation of theology *by liberation theology* is the return to the sources of Christianity, namely, the promise of liberation of the people of God. This people are the poor. The poor are the chosen of God, not because they constitute an ethnos, or a people in the sense of a nation, but because they are in their condition of negativity and exclusion, of privation and penury, the mark of the very absence of God's love and will in the world. The poor are those whom God opts for because they are the forgotten ones, the despised ones, of a world that in rejecting and excluding them, exclude and reject God. The option for the poor is an option for God, an option to allow God's promise of justice, love, wholeness, and an upright and well-lived life to fully reign and shine. The "preferential option for the poor" is the preferential option of God's love, a love that is a project of redemption and salvation. God's love is an orthopraxis, and so the option for the poor must be also an orthopraxis—praxis of justice. The essays in this second section, then, focus on the relationship between the church, its dogma, and its relationship to popular religion.

The third section, entitled "Ethics and Economics," gathers those essays that exhibit one of Dussel's most fundamental philosophical lessons: that all economics is an ethics, even when it is anti-ethical, or refuses to assume an ethical position in the name of some sort of scientific objectivity. Economics is not an abstract, nomothetic science. It is a part of practical philosophy, or what the English moralists called *moral philosophy*. Conversely, all ethics entails an economic–political relationship, both as a telos and as a condition of possibility. Ethics is fundamental to human reality because this reality is of relationship, of being-with (*Mit-sein*), which is a solid, formal being, and not a fleeting, temporal being there (in Spanish, it is *ser* and not *estar*). "All being with" is mediated by practical relationships, and these practical relationships are what economics deals with. At the center of economics (as a form of moral philosophy) is the issue of the preservation and development of human life. This life, however, is always the organic, somatic, corporeal life of the human agent. Economics is not the science of the maximization of profit and the minimization of costs for the sake of the augmentation and accumulation of capital. Economics is the questioning about the means and ends for the distribution of the bread of life, the product of economic activity. In this section, I have included three essays in which Dussel specifically deals with the economic and political situation of Latin America, in general, and the Mayan Indians in Mexico, in particular. For Dussel, economic–political questions remit us to specific historical conditions that are in turn determined by geopolitics of global and imperialistic capitalism.

The fourth and final part of the book, entitled "History," gathers a meager but representative sampling of Dussel's work on history. The first essay in this section, the oldest in the book (dating from 1969), will be particularly relevant in contemporary times. Here Dussel sets out to unmask one of the most important myths of Western culture and its philosophical flag, namely, modernity. Modernity, and the West, is above all defined in terms of secularization, while the rest of the West is defined by their lack thereof. Dussel differentiates between secularism as an ideology and secularization as a societal and critical-enlightenment project. While the former has to be rejected, the latter remains a project that is not accomplishable yet it must not be abandoned. It is not that Dussel is an antisecularist, à la postsecularists or radical orthodoxy theologians in Cambridge (in the United Kingdom).[19] For Dussel, secular society has never become truly secular, for it is itself shot through with the rituals and idolatries of myths and religions. But the secular is not the opposite of the religious. The religious encompasses a truth that is neither exhausted by nor dispensable to secularizing society and defetishizing thinking. In tandem, Dussel differentiates between a Christianity that retains its prophetic faith and a Christendom that is Christianity as the ideology of empires and states. While Christianity stood on the side of the oppressed and the savage Amerindian, it was Christendom that urged their enslavement in the name of an imperial and sanctified project. The last essay in the book is particularly important because it allows us to trace two related topics in Dussel's oeuvre: the role of the Americas in global history, and the imperative to develop a planetary ethics in an age of the massive exclusion of the majority of humanity from even the poorest of human standards of living (discussed in chapter 3).[20] The so-called discovery of the New World, in Dussel's view, was an axial event, a pivot on which world history turned into truly global and planetary history. The universality that emerged, however, of the modernity inaugurated with this invasion and invention of the Americas has been but the projection of an ethnocentric and deeply devastating rationality. While the issue here is the understanding of globalization, the deep conceptual core and preoccupation are once again the liberation of suffering and starving humanity from an economic–political system that demands its allegiance in the name of a metaphysics of history: idolatry of progress and the so-called creative violence of allegedly free markets.

Eduardo Mendieta

NOTES

1. For a biographical sketch, see the introduction to Linda Martín Alcoff and Eduardo Mendieta, *Thinking from the Underside of History: Enrique Dussel's Philosophy of Liberation* (Lanham, Md.: Rowman & Littlefield, 2000), 13–26; see also Enrique Dussel, "Autopercepción intelectual de un proceso historico" *Anthropos* 180 (September–October 1998): 13–36.

2. In the following, I am drawing on my article "Politics in an Age of Planetarization: Enrique Dussel's Critique of Political Reason" in *The Political,* ed. David Ingram (Malden, Mass.: Blackwell, 2002), 280–97.

3. Enrique Dussel, *Para una ética de la liberación latinoamericana,* 5 vols. (Buenos Aires: Siglo XXI, 1973).

4. Emmanuel Levinas, *Totality and Infinity: An Essay on Exteriority* (Pittsburgh, Pa.: Duquesne University Press, 1969).

5. Enrique Dussel and Daniel Guillot, *Liberación y Emmanuel Levinas* (Buenos Aires: Editorial Bonum, 1975), 7.

6. Enrique Dussel, *Método para una Filosofía de la Liberación. Superación analéctica de la dialéctica hegeliana* (Salamanca, Spain: Sígueme, 1976).

7. Eugene Kogon, *The Theory and Practice of Hell: The German Concentration Camps and the System Behind Them* (New York: Berkeley Publishing, 1960).

8. See Enrique Dussel, *La producción teórica de Marx. Un comentario de los Grundrisse* (México: Siglo XXI, 1985); *Hacia un Marx desconcido. Un comentario a los Manuscritos del 1861–1863* (México: Siglo XXI, 1988) (This is now available in English as *Towards an Unknown Marx: A Commentary on the Manuscripts of 1861–1863* [New York: Routledge, 2001]); *El último Marx (1863–1882) y la liberación latinoamericana* (México: Siglo XXI, 1990); "Marx's Economic Manuscripts of 1861–1863 and the 'Concept' of Dependency," *Latin American Perspectives* 17, no. 2 (1990): 61–101.

9. Ander Gunder Frank, *Latin America: Underdevelopment or Revolution* (New York: Monthly Review Press, 1970).

10. Emmanuel Wallerstein, *The Capitalist World-Economy* (Cambridge: Cambridge University Press, 1979).

11. Samir Amin, *Accumulation on a World Scale; A Critique of the Theory of Underdevelopment* (New York: Monthly Review Press, 1974).

12. See my *Adventures of Transcendental Philosophy: Karl-Otto Apel's Transformation of Philosophy* (Lanham, Md.: Rowman & Littlefield, 2002), in which I offer a reconstruction of Karl-Otto Apel's philosophical itinerary and how he developed

discourse ethics. This book contains a chapter in which I study the debates between Apel and Dussel.

13. Enrique Dussel, *Para una ética de la liberación latinoamericana*, 2 vols. (Buenos Aires: Siglos XXI, 1973); *Filosofía ética latinoamericana*, vol. 3 (México: Edicol, 1977); *Filosofía ética latinoamericana*, vol. 4 (Bogotá: USTA, 1979); *Filosofía ética latinoamericana*, vol. 5 (Bogotá: USTA, 1980).

14. *Ética de la Liberación en la edad de globalización y de la exclusión* (Madrid: Editorial Trotta, 1998). See my review on this book, "Ethics for an Age of Globalization and Exclusion" in *Philosophy and Social Criticism* 25, no. 2 (1999): 115–21.

15. Enrique Dussel, *The Underside of Modernity: Apel, Ricoeur, Rorty, Taylor, and the Philosophy of Liberation*, trans. and ed. Eduardo Mendieta (Atlantic Highlands, N.J.: Humanities Press, 1996).

16. Jürgen Habermas, *The Theory of Communicative Action*, 2 vols. (Boston: Beacon Press, 1984–1987); *The Philosophical Discourse of Modernity: Twelve Lectures* (Cambridge, Massachusetts: MIT Press, 1987); *Vorstudien und Ergänzungen zur Theorie des kommunuitakiven Handelns* (Frankfurt: Suhrkamp, 1984); *Moral Consciousness and Communicative Action* (Cambridge: MIT Press, 1990).

17. See Lorenzo C. Simpson's discussion of situated cosmopolitanism in his *The Unfinished Project: Toward a Postmetaphysical Humanism* (New York: Routledge, 2001).

18. Juan Luis Segundo, *The Liberation of Dogma: Faith, Revelation, and Dogmatic Teaching Authority* (Maryknoll, N.Y.: Orbis Books, 1992)—the original title of the book in Spanish is *El Dogma que libera*.

19. See John Milbank, Catherine Pickstock, and Graham Ward, eds., *Radical Orthodoxy: A New Theology* (New York: Routledge, 1999).

20. In an earlier version of this manuscript, I had included more essays dealing with Dussel's interpretations of world history, globalization, and the world-system. Due to space constraints, I had to exclude these essays, but the reader is directed to Enrique Dussel, "Globalization and the Victims of Exclusion: From a Liberation Ethics Perspective," *The Modern Schoolman*, 75 (January 1998): 119–55; and "World-System and 'Trans'-Modernity" in *Nepantla: Views from the South* 3, no. 2: 221–44.

I

GENERAL HYPOTHESES

1

Domination—Liberation:
A New Approach

This chapter is divided into two parts. The first part consists of a detailed analysis of some of the themes currently prevailing in Latin American theology. This is followed, in part II, by a methodological analysis to show the relevance of this theology not only for our Latin America, but for all "peripheral" cultures—in fact for theology throughout the world, beyond the bounds, that is, of strictly European theology.

I. DOMINATION—LIBERATION

In this first section we shall examine in detail the trends taken by Latin American theology, which always starts, not from a theological position, but from the state of affairs as they actually exist. We start, therefore, not with what theologians have said about the situation, but with the situation itself. As we can indicate only some of the themes possible, we shall consider the three which tradition suggests should be the most important. In Semitic thought Hammurabi declared quite clearly in his *Code*: "I have defended them with wisdom, so that the strong shall not oppress the weak, and that justice be done to the orphan and widow." These political, sexual, and educational levels are also indicated in Isa. 1:17, "correct oppression; defend the fatherless; plead for the widow." The same three levels are also indicated by Jesus: "Truly I say to you, there is no man who had left house, or wife or

Enrique Dussel, "Domination—Liberation: A New Approach," *Concilium* 96 (1974): 34–56.

parents or children . . ." (Lk. 18:29). In the sixteenth century, Bartolomé de las Casas accused European Christians of injustice because "the men—for in battles normally only children and women are left alive—are oppressed with the hardest, most horrible and harshest servitude."[1] The brother-to-brother aspect (male, oppressed, weak) is the political level; the man-woman aspect (home, wife, widow) is the sexual level; the father-son aspect (orphan, child) is the educational level. Let us see how, on these three levels, an argument can be constructed from the situation as it actually exists.

1. The Political Starting-Point

The present world situation reveals in its structure an imbalance that is already five centuries old. Byzantine Christianity was destroyed in 1453 and, thanks to the experiences of Portugal in North Africa and the failure of its eastward expansion the conquest movement of the crusades in the Middle Ages which tried to reach the Orient by way of the Arab world, Latin Christianity began to expand in the North Atlantic, which has remained, up to the present day, the centre of world history, politically speaking. First Spain, then Holland and England, followed by France and other European countries, worked out the framework of a truly world-wide oikumene, for until the fifteenth century the Latin, Byzantine Arab, Indian, Chinese, Aztec, or Inca oikumenes were purely regional. The new oikumene had its centre in Europe and, since the end of the nineteenth and beginning of the present century, the United States, Russia, and more recently Japan. It also had a huge periphery—Latin America, the Arab world, Black Africa, South East Asia, India, and China.

European man first said, through Spain and Portugal, with Pizarro and Cortés: "I conquer"—and he said it to the Indian. With Hobbes he stated more clearly still: "Homo homini lupus." With Nietzsche he called himself "the will to power." Thus the political and economic structure of the world was unified into one all-powerful international market. Table 1.1 is an example that illustrates the profound moral injustice of this dehumanizing structure.

This dependence and colonial injustice was to last without interruption from the sixteenth to the twentieth century. Raul Prebisch tells us in 1964 that, between 1950 and 1961 in Latin America, "net remissions of foreign capital of all types reached the figure of 9,600 million dollars, while Latin American exports overseas amounted to 13,400 million dollars."[2] So far as the political situation is concerned (brother-to-brother) domination is now exercised by the centre over the periphery. This pattern is repeated when the capital city exploits the interior or the provinces,[3] or where an upper-

Table 1.1. Exports of Precious Metals from the Private Sector to Europe, with Corresponding Imports of Merchandise into Latin America (In maravedis, the currency of the period).

Period	Exports from the private sector	Imported goods	Balance in Spain's favour
1561–1570	8,785 million	1,565 million	7,220 million
1581–1590	16,926 ,,	3,915 ,,	13,011 ,,
1621–1630	19,104 ,,	5,300 ,,	13,804 ,,

(Source: Works of Alvaro Jara, Pierre Chaunu, and Osvaldo Sunkel.)

class minority dominates the working classes, and where bureaucracy directs the fortunes of the masses.

2. The Sexual Starting-Point

Interpersonal relations show that in the relationship of man to woman, injustice has existed for thousands of years—an injustice which reached its highest level in modern Europe. If it is true, as Freud so brilliantly revealed, that, in our male-dominated society, "the *libido* is generally masculine in nature,"[4] it was not so clearly seen that the colonizer was usually male and his victim in our case was the Indian woman. Bishop Juan Ramírez of Guatemala, wrote on March 10th, 1603: "The worst forms of force and violence, unheard of in other nations and kingdoms, are perpetrated upon the Indian women. The wives of Indian men are raped forcibly by order of the authorities and they are obliged to work in the homes of planters, on farms and in labour camps where they live in sin with the master of the house, with mestizos, mulattos, blacks, or with other cruel men."[5] The colonial male who lies illegally with the Indian woman is the father of the mestizo, and the Indian woman is the mother. The male conquistador—first the planters and colonial bureaucracy, later the native-born creole minority and finally the bourgeoisie of the dependent territories—sexually oppressed and alienated the Indian, the mestizo or the poor woman. The male from the national higher-class minority seized the local girl from the hands of the poor working man living on the outskirts of the big cities—a theme sung in the Tango "Margot" 1918, by Celedonio Flores—while demanding of his own high-born wife both purity and chastity. This particular piece of hypocrisy was pointed out by W. Reich and it can be observed extensively in the Third World.

The everyday "I conquer," the ontological *ego cogito*, comes from the oppressor male, who, as we see by psychoanalysis of Descartes, denies his mother, his lover, and his daughter. To borrow an expression from Maryse Choisy and Lacan, we might say that these days "phallocracy goes hand-in-hand with plutocracy."

3. The Educational Starting-Point

Political and sexual domination is completed through *education*: the child is conditioned within the family, and youth in society is moulded through the media. Since Aristotle[6] educators have maintained that "parents love their children because they regard them as they regard themselves (*heatous*), for they are in some sense one's self (*tauto*), yet divided into separate individuals" (Et. Nic. VIII, 12, 1161 b 27–34). Cultural conquest of other peoples is equally an expansion of the self. The conquistador or the propagandist achieves his aim by force of arms or by violently imposing on the other (the Indian, African, Asian, the community, the worker, the oppressed) so-called civilization, or his religion, or by exalting his own cultural system (the ideological closed system). Educational domination is dialectical (from the Greek *dia* = through)—a movement whereby the cultural boundaries of the father, the imperialist or the obligarchy extend so as to embrace the other (the son) within its self. The process of conquest and cultural assimilation in America, Africa and Asia and the education of the son into the self (as Socrates proposed in his mayeutica as a means of "being delivered of one's ideas") is a kind of inverted Passover, an ideological dialectic whereby the new being (the other, the young person) is eclipsed and domination made complete. Further, it is projected into the personal and social ego, so that the son or the oppressed culture even begins to sing the praises of his oppressor: "two different civilizations be seen side by side—the one belonging to the country itself and the other to European civilization."[7] Sarmiento spurns the culture of the periphery, the dependent nation, the *gaucho* and the poor; instead he exalts the culture of the "centre," which is a minority culture, élitist and oppressive.

4. Face-to-Face Encounter—the Closed System and the Outside

Starting-point of our argument was the "actual situation" or (reality) considered at three levels. But reality can have two different basic meanings. Anything within the world is real as having existence in the world[8] and in this sense the Indian was a real being assigned to a master and the Black was a real being, who was enslaved. On the other hand, something can also be real from a universal point of view[9] as constituted by its essential physical structure.[10] The political, sexual, and educational points we have made are events taking place within various situations, with men playing different roles, whether as dependent underdeveloped countries, as woman or as child. These situations are, however, distortions or denials of that very basic human (one might even say, sacred) quality—face-to-face encounter. The real situation of men *within* circumstances of oppression is a denial of the real nature of man as "another being"—which is the metaphysical meaning of reality.

Encounter face-to-face (Hebrew *pnîm'el pnim* of Ex. 33:11), person-to-person encounter (Greek *prosopon pros prosopon*, 1 Cor. 13:12), is a linguistic reduplication, common in Hebrew, used to convey the greatest nearness of comparison—the very closest in this case: closeness, the immediacy of contact between two mysteries each equally aware of meeting another. In sexual activity this encounter is mouth-to-mouth—i.e., the kiss: "Oh that you would kiss me with the kisses of your mouth!" (Song of Songs 1:1). This a fundamental truth, a *veritas prima*—to see the face of someone without oneself losing the quality of someone; to see the face of the other, and yet to remain oneself; to encounter the mystery which opens out, incomprehensible and sacred beyond the eyes that I actually see and which actually see me in the closeness of encounter.

There was a day when the conquistador stood face-to-face with the Indian, the African, and the Asian. The boss stood face-to-face with the unemployed who came to seek work. The man was face-to-face with the helpless woman begging for mercy. The father stood before his new-born son, face-to-face, as a man talking to his intimate friend. With its closed system (the ontological), Europe opened itself as the male and the father was open to the otherness (the metaphysical if *physics* is "being" in the sense of the world's horizons) of the peripheral cultures, to the woman and child, or, we might say, to the "stranger, the widow and the orphan," as the prophets had it.

The other is primary (the parents who beget the son, the society which admits us into its traditions or the Creator who gives us real being). Man, rather than relate to nature (the economic level), chooses to expose himself to another man. We are born in the womb of a someone (our mother); in our first waking moments we eat that someone (we suckle at the breasts of our mother). We ardently want to remain face-to-face ever afterwards. After the closeness of face-to-face relationship the separation necessitated by economic dealings is a painful alternative.

5. The Oppressor Praxis—Sin and the Poor

Biblical symbolism shows us through the prophetic tradition an argument or line of thought which we shall here set out briefly. In the first place "Cain rose up against his brother Abel, and killed him" (Gen. 4:8), and Jesus adds the comment "innocent Abel" (Mt. 23:25). To say "no" to my neighbour is the only possible sin, it is the "sin of the world" or the fundamental sin. The same "no" to my neighbour is said by the priest and the levite in the parable of the Samaritan (Lk. 10:31–32). Augustine, in his political interpretation of original sin, says clearly that "Cain founded a city, while Abel the wanderer did not."[11] Historically and actually sin since the fifteenth century has taken the form of a "no" on the part of the North Atlantic centre to the Indian, the African, the Asian and to the worker, the peasant and the outcast. It has been a "no" to the woman in patriarchal families, and a "no" to the child in the oppressor's educational system.

"No" to my neighbour (anthropologically speaking) or fratricide leads to maximizing the reign of the "flesh" (*basar* in Hebrew; *sarx* in Greek). The device of *temptation* (and not of Prometheus bound to the *ananke*) is the one proposed by the closed system in the words, "You shall be as gods" (Gen. 3:5). Sin, beginning as "no" to my neighbour, takes the form of self-deification, the exalting of self as an object of worship, and leads to idolatry—"no" to the Creator. To be able to say with Nietzsche "God is dead" it was necessary first of all to kill his manifestation of himself to the Indian, the African and the Asian.

Idolatrous exaltation of the *flesh*, in this case as seen in the modern structure of European Christianity, produces within the closed system as separation between the one who dominates "the world" (a new term for "*flesh*," but now completely deified) and the oppressed. On the one side stand "the rulers" (*archontes*) of the nations (who) lord it over them (*katakyrieousin*) and the great men (who) exercise authority" (Mt. 20:25). These are the "angels" (sent by) the "Prince of this world" and the Pilates who "ask for water and wash their hands" (Mt. 27:24). The present world order (economic, cultural, sexual and aesthetic) is the prevailing rule of sin, inasmuch as it oppresses the poor. The "rulers" have their group projection which they objectivize as the projection of the whole system and which expands as an imperialist projection by means of conquest in Latin America, Africa, and Asia. The "self" remains the "self." The "praxis of domination" of those who ursurp the position of God and exalt themselves is sin in a very real and strict sense. This is the praxis of "no" to my neighbour, spoken to the oppressed brother, to woman as a sexual object, to the child as the unthinking reproducer of traditional ways of life.

The oppressed one is Job. He suffers because sin (the praxis of the great one acting as *oppressor*) alienates him, but he is not aware of having committed any sin at all. The wise men in his situation, speaking for the system (Bildad and Sophar), try to convince the oppressed one in the name of Satan, that he is a sinner. By so doing they maintain the innocence of the real sinner—of the oppressors.

The oppressed one humanly speaking is not the poor (the oppressed as an other). The "poor" in the words "Blessed are the poor" (*ptochoi*) (Lk. 6:20), or better still in the words "The poor you shall have with you always" (Mt. 26:11) is the other in that he does not share the supreme value of the socio-political system. The "poor" are just as much a category— they are the oppressed nation, class, person or woman in that these are outside the structure of the oppressor. In this sense the "poor" (in the biblical sense) are not the same as the alienated oppressed living *within* the system, but they do share many of the characteristics of the poor socially and economically speaking.

6. The Praxis of Liberation—Redemption and the Prophet

To make the contrast with the "praxis of sin" set out in the previous section, we can now look at the praxis of liberation, of anti-sin or the direct opposite of the negation of the other.[17] The Bible speaks, in the story of Moses (Ex. 3 ff.) or in the parable of the Samaritan, of a direct "yes" to my neighbour when he is still oppressed within the system. The prophetic light of faith permits us to see through the outward surface of the oppressed and to see the other within. Behind the slave of Egypt lies man, liberated. Behind the beaten, robbed traveller lying at the roadside is the otherness of the human *persona*. This is not a turning aside (*aversio*) from the other, but a turning towards (*conversio*) the other as a fellow citizen of the City of God. As we see in the case of Bartolomé de las Casas, that ardent anti-conquistador and modern European, the righteous man discovers the other as he really is. "God made these people (the Indians) the simplest of men, without guile or cunning, not quarrelsome, riotous or rowdy. They bear no ill-will or hatred, and they seek no revenge."[13]

To say "yes" to my neighbour, the system first has to be broken into, opened up. We have, in other words, to cease to believe in the system. The Virgin of Nazareth, the flesh, opens us to the spirit (otherness). Jesus said that we should "render to Caesar that which is Caesar's, and to God that which is God's" (Mt. 22:21). Like the prophets before him, he thus did not believe in Caesar, the flesh, and the closed system. When Feuerbach and Marx said they did not believe in the "god" of Hegel and of the European bourgeoise (the only god they knew), they set out along the correct and orthodox path.[14]

To achieve the breakdown of the closed system of sin, otherness has to attack it subversively. The ana-lectic (what is outside the system), the absolute Other, the Word (in Hebrew *dābhār*, which has nothing to do with the Greek *logos*) breaks into the closed system and becomes flesh: ". . . in the form of God . . . he emptied himself (*ekenosen*) and took the form of a servant" (*doulou*) (Phil. 2:6–7). Christ, the Church, the prophet must assume within the system the position of the oppressed. The servant (*'ebhedh* in Hebrew, *doulos* or *pais* in Greek) really assumes the position of the oppressed, whether socially, politically, culturally or economically. In their alienated position they become like the Indian, African or Asian, the worn-out woman, the educationally manipulated child. They immerse themselves in the prison of sin (the system), but do not obey its rules.

The servant, the prophet or the poor in spirit[15] acting from amongst the ranks of and together with the oppressed, carry out the praxis of liberation (Hebrew *'ᵃbôdhāh*; Greek—*diakonia*) which is the work of righteousness and worship performed by the saving God. This service performed by the Samaritan or by Moses for the sake of the poor or the slaves as members of the outside, is a subversive praxis, both historical (and hence socio-political, cultural, economic, and sexual) and eschatological. To this end he is called (Lk. 4:18; Is. 61:1) to undermine the system and direct history along a new path[16] and to liberate the poor in a year of festival or rejoicing.[17]

The liberator or the servant prophet, by responding to the cry of the poor (as other), discloses himself as the herald of the new system over against the old system of sin, imperialism and oppression, whether international or national, economic, political, cultural or sexual. Hence he announces the dispossession of the ruler and the end of him as an oppressor. The closed system or the flesh transforms mere domination into repression, violence, and persecution. So the liberating servant is the first to die: "Jerusalem, Jerusalem! killing the prophets and stoning those who are sent to you!" (Mt. 23:37). In such a case the liberator becomes a redeemer—the one who, by a truly expiatory sacrifice (Hebrew—*kibburîm*), pays in his own flesh for the liberation of the other: "Whoever would be great among you must be your servant (*diakonos*), and he who would be first among you must be your slave (*doulos*); even as the Son of man came not to be served but to serve (*diakonesai*) and to give his life as a ransom for many" (*luton anti pollon*—Mt. 20:26–28).

There are many examples of this praxis of liberation—the prophets and Jesus, the Christians persecuted under the Roman Empire, Bishop Valdivieso (murdered in 1550 by the governor for defending the Indians in Nicaragua), Pereira Neto in Brazil in 1969 or Mahatma Gandhi or Patrice Lumumba in the non-Christian Third World—we see how the liberator, when he announces the end of the old system, is assassinated violently and in cold blood by the angels of the Prince of this Word, that is, by the conquistadors, the imperialist armies, the capitalist bankers or the "herodian" governments of the dependent nations themselves. The closed system spells death for itself. The death of the liberator is, on the other hand, the death of death and the beginning of a new birth (Jn. 3:5–8).[18]

7. Towards an Ecclesiology of Redemptive Liberation

All the foregoing is constantly lived out in the actual historical context of the community of the "called," that is the Church or even world history itself.

Since the liberating and redemptive death of Christ, world history has been living under a new order of reality, since any man of good will receives enough grace for salvation. However, because of sin, historical institutions (social, political, economic, sexual, and educational) tend to close in on themselves, petrify and become self-perpetuating. They have to be given new impetus, be opened to new influence, and be given dialectical flexibility in the direction of the parousia. God, from the creative outside, has founded the Church at the very heart of the flesh, of the world, of the closed system (an alienating or kenotic movement). The Church, his gift, is the becoming flesh of the spirit. By baptism, the Christian is consecrated to the liberating service of the world, and received into the community. The earthly phenomenon of the Church, an institutional community, was born, geopolitically speaking, in the western Mediterranean and reached maturity in Latin and Germanic Christianity, in other words in Europe, which together with the United States and Russia is the geopolitical centre of our modern world. On the other hand, since it was born, socially speaking, among the oppressed people of the Roman Empire, today it finds itself part of those nations that oppress the dependent peripheral nations and frequently finds itself compromised with the ruling classes (at national level) or with the ruling culture.

Thus, the Church which has become flesh in the world (like the leaven in the dough in the parable) comes to be identified with the flesh and the closed system. This self-identification with the Prince of this World is the sin of the Church, which petrifies the system and even sanctifies it. The terms *Holy* Roman Empire, *Christian* countries, Western *Christian* civilization, and so on, bear witness to this.

But the essential nature of the Church as the liberating community and institution requires it to identify itself with the oppressed so as to "break down the barriers" of the systems which have become closed by the work of sin, or by injustice, whether political—at national or international level—economic, social, cultural, or sexual. The sign (*semeion* of St. John's Gospel) of the Church, its proclamation, can only be effected by involving the community in the movement of liberation (Hebrew—*pāsāh* means moving, march or flight), to move a system which acts oppressively towards becoming a new system which acts to liberate. And this, in its turn, is, so far as the Church is concerned, the sign of the eschatological forward movement of the Kingdom. The Eucharist is a foretaste, in the forward movement of the Kingdom; it is a feat of liberation from sin (from slavery in Egypt). The liberation of Latin America is, therefore, the compelling call to the Church in Latin America (a dependent and to some extent oppressed sector of the world Church). At the same time, liberation of oppressed classes—women, children, and the poor—is also the basis of evangelization.

II. APPLICATION OF THE THEOLOGICAL ARGUMENT

We must now turn our attention to the theological argument itself, first of all as we see it in Europe. (We shall therefore be looking at what might be called the white theology of North America.) This may lead us to define the theology that emerges as a theology of oppression—whether applicable on a world-wide scale (coming from the peripheral nations), a national scale (coming from the oppressed classes), to sex (a theology of woman) or to education (from the point of view of the younger generation).

1. Conditioning of Theological Thinking

It is widely accepted by critical thinkers in Latin America today that all political expansion soon comes to be based on an ontology of domination (an ad hoc philosophy or theology). Modern European expansion had as its ontological foundation the *ego cogito*[19] preceded by the actual fact of "I conquer." For Spinoza, in his *Ethics*, the *ego* is a fragment of the unique substance of God—a position which the young Schelling and Hegel were to adopt later—the European *ego* had been deified. Fichte shows us that in the "I am that I am," the "I" is absolutely fixed.[20] It is an "I" that is natural, infinite and absolute (and in Hegel definitely divine). In Nietzsche, the "I" becomes a creative power ("I" as the "will to power"), while in Husserl it becomes the most abstract *ego cogito cogitatum* of phenomenology.[21] The most serious effect is that *the other* or the neighbour (the Indian, the African, the Asian or the woman) is reduced to the level of an idea. The meaning of the other is formulated in terms of the "I" who dreamed it into existence. The other is made a separate entity, becomes a thing, is abstracted into a *cogitatum*.

Similarly, European theology or the theology of the centre cannot escape from this reduction. The expansion of Latin-German Christianity gave rise to its own theology of conquest. Semitic and Christian thought of the Old and New Testaments was reduced to a process of Indo-European Hellenization from the second century onwards. Medieval European theology was able to justify the feudal world and the *ius dominativum* of the lord over the serf. Tridentine and Protestant theology had nothing to say about the Indian, the African, or the Asian (except the Salamanca School and that only for a few decades). Finally the expansion of capitalism and neo-capitalism allowed Christians of the centre to formulate a theology of the status quo and the ecumenism of peaceful coexistence between Russia, the United States, and Europe so as to dominate the "periphery" more effectively. The other—the poor—was once again defined in terms of the European "I": *Ego cogito theologatum*. With the basis of theological thinking so reduced, a parallel reduction occurs in the whole field of theology. Sin is reduced so as to apply only to intra-national injustice; it is exclusivized, allowed to have no political application, shown to have nothing to do with sex (or at other levels, shown to have an excessive relation to sex). But more seriously the limits and meaning of salvation and redemption are equally reduced to the narrow bounds of the Christian experience of the *centre*. We have an individual salvation, interiorized and other-worldly, resorting frequently to some painful masochistic experience at a given time and place, whereas the true cross of real history demands our life at the least expected moment.

This theology suffers from many unconscious limitations. Firstly, the limitations of the religiosity of German-Latin-Mediterranean Christianity which was accepted without hesitation as real simply because it was Latin. Then there are liturgical limitations, in which the Latin-type liturgy is regarded as the only one acceptable for the Christian religion and which still prevents other cultures having their own liturgies. There are also cultural limitations, in that theology is the province of an intellectual élite, university professors in well-paid and secure posts, a situation far removed from, and unhelpful to the study of Tertullian and St. Augustine. There are political limitations, for it is a theology adjusted and compromised by its closeness to the metropolitan power of the world. There are also economic limitations, for this theology finds favour for the most part among upper-class minorities in the bourgeoisie and in the neo-capitalist world (although sometimes there may be poor monks, they belong to "rich" orders). Finally, there are sexual limitations, because those who think theologically are celibates and have been unable to formulate an authentic theology of sexuality, marriage, and the family. For all these reasons, modern European theology from the sixteenth to the twentieth centuries is unconsciously compromised by its connection with the praxis of oppression in the political, educational and sexual fields.

It would be no exaggeration to say that in many respects it is really a theological ideology in that many of its facets remain unseen by virtue of its origins, just as we are unable to see the further side of the moon simply because we are inhabitants of planet earth. And what is still worse, in Latin America there are many progressive theologians who simply repeat the theology of the centre and by so doing they obscure their own message and, to their shame, become just as much advocates of oppression.

2. Revelation and Faith—the Anthropological Epiphany

Western theology has for centuries taken certain presuppositions for granted as unquestionably correct. Kant's ontology (which postulates a rational faith), Hegel's (which sees faith as within the bounds of reason) or Heidegger's (the comprehensiveness of Being) admit the Wholeness of being as the only frontier of thought. Being-in-the-world is the fundamental fact, original and primary.[22] Existential theology starts from the basis of the world as the Whole. The fault lies in that, in fact, the Whole is always mine, ours, the European's or the centre's. What passes unnoticed is that I am thereby denying other Christian worlds and other equally valid experiences. I am denying anthropological otherness as a possible starting-point for theological thought. [23]

As the older Schelling so clearly saw in his *Philosophie der Offenbarung*, faith in the Word of the Other lies beyond ontological reason (the Hegelian *Sein*), an argument that Kierkegaard carried forward (e.g., in the *Postscriptum*). Faith stands upon the revelation of the Other. Revelation is only the out-going message of God, existentially speaking, which sets out the guidelines for interpreting the reality of Christ. In everyday life (existentially), [24] God manifests the hidden secret (the fact of redemption in Christ) by means of an interpreting light (a classicist would put it: *ratio sub qua*), or by supplying guidelines (categories) for all mankind and for all history. God gives not only a specific revelation, but more importantly, the categories[25] which permit us to interpret it. Revelation comes to a peak in Christ with the New Covenant, but it unfolds it potentialities throughout the course of history. What we are trying to stress here is that this revelation is not effected in history by human words alone, but through man himself (as exterior to the flesh or the system), the poor and the Christ-man.

Faith, which accepts the Word of the Other, becomes Christian faith when the divine Word in Christ is accepted through the mediation of the poor man in history, who actually lives in a concrete situation. The true showing forth of the Word of God is the word of the poor man who cries "I hunger." Only the man who hears the word of the poor (beyond the system, and therefore ana-lectic, which presupposes that he does not believe in the system) can hear it as the Word of God. God is not dead. What has been assassinated is his self-manifestation—the Indian, the African, and the Asian—and because of this God cannot reveal himself any more. Abel died in the self-deification of Europe and the centre, and therefore God has hidden his face. The revealed category is clear enough: "I was hungry and you gave me no food. . . . They also shall ask, Lord, when did we see you hungry?" (Mt. 25:42–44). [26] Following the death of the "divine" Europe, there can rise the faith in the poor of the periphery, faith in God as mediated by the poor. The new manifestation of God in history (not a resurrection, for he never died) will be brought about by righteousness and not by endless theological treatises on the death of God. [27]

3. The Praxis of Liberation and Theology

Given the data of revelation and by virtue of living faith, theology is a reflection of reality. Recently there has been much talk of theologies of earthly realities or doubt, leading eventually to a theology of revolution[28] or development. [29] In European circles, to take just the term political theology[30] the matter has sterner implications. But Latin America detects in the theologico-political argument an attempt to restrict the prophetic voice of protest to the narrow national sphere. From this narrow viewpoint the fact of international, imperialist injustice passes unnoticed. But eschatological, undiscriminating protest must reach out not only to the constituent parts of the system, but to the system as a whole.[31]

In the same way the provocative theology of hope[32] betrays the limitations of the critical theory of the Frankfurt School (which influences Metz) and the works of Ernst Bloch (who inspires Moltmann). Both these philosophical hypotheses have failed to overcome ontology and dialectic, and they consider the future as a development of the Self. Although Moltmann understands the future as otherness, he still has difficulty in finding beyond the projection of the system (but this side of the *eschaton*) an historical projection of political, economic, cultural and sexual liberation. Hope extends as far as an historical change in the pattern of life,[33] but not to a radical renewal of the present system with a view to an historical liberation movement as a true sign of eschatological advance. Without this concrete mediation their hopes reaffirm the status quo and constitute a false dream.

On the other hand, a European theology of liberation will bring out clearly the question of Christianity and the class struggle, [34] but within the limits of a national Marxism and before moving on to the theory of dependence. It has not yet seen that the struggle of the proletariat within the centre itself, that is, in the metropolitan powers, can be oppressive in

terms of the colonial proletariat of the periphery. Classes have been
thinking double and may often oppose their own interests at international level. National liberation of the dominated countries goes hand in
hand with the social liberation of oppressed classes. Hence the category
known as the people takes on a special significance as opposed to the category of class. [35]

Latin American theology derives, by contrast, from the thinking of many
politically involved Christians about the praxis for liberating the oppressed. This theology-ethic is a product of the periphery, coming from the
outsiders, from the *lumpen* of this world. Their inspiration is not only sheer
necessity (the existence within the system of matters needing attention),
but also the desire to liberate (Hebrew *'ᵃbôdhâh'*; Greek—*diakonia*), that is a
ministry of liberation beyond the limits of ontology. And the sphere of liberation is not only political, but also sexual and educational. In fact, this is
a theology of the poor, woman as a sexual object and the child.

4. Towards a Theology of Liberation

After the great theology of Christianity from the fourth to the fifteenth
centuries and modern European theology from the sixteenth to the twentieth centuries, the theology of liberation of the periphery and of the oppressed is in fact the whole of traditional theology set into redemptive
motion from the point of view of the poor. The theology of Christianity
(the old model) almost identified the Christian faith with Mediterranean
Latin or Byzantine culture, subsequently halting progress. The argument
over Latin in Vatican II itself is an obvious recent demonstration of this.
Modern European theology, individualized and imperialistic, is reproduced in the colonies as progressive theology by those who operate as an
oppressive colonial minority and take as the scheme of salvation a theology which for the periphery is meaningless and therefore uncritical. The
status quo is once again supported. By contrast, the theology of liberation
(where a theology of revolution is only a first stage, political theology is
just one of the possible applications and the theology of hope looks to the
future) is based on the praxis of liberation, or on moving from sin as the
dominating influence exerted by the various systems (political, sexual,
and educational) to irreversible salvation in Christ and his Kingdom (the
eschaton). This movement is accomplished by every man, all people, and
every age—in short, by the whole of human history. However, there are
certain critical periods (*kairos*) in history and Latin America is living
through one such period now, [36] when complete eschatological liberation
can be more clearly indicated by the prophets, Christians or the Church.
Thus the theology of liberation gradually becomes an African or black

theology, though to date there has been no response from Asia,[37] and finally a theology of the whole world and of all the oppressed.

The theology of liberation which is coming from Latin American thinkers[38] can be distinguished when its dependence as a theology is realized in the same way as economy or culture is realized to be dependent (the culture of oppression as Salazar Bondy said in Peru in 1968). Gradually this theology discovers its own methods which I have defined as analectic and not only dialectic, [39] in that it is listening to the trans-ontological voice of the other (*ana-*) and is interpreting its message by means of analogies. (The other, however, remains mysteriously distinct from us, until such time as the progress of the movement towards liberation allows us to enter upon its world.) It adds an entirely new dimension to the question of analogies.

For its own part the theology of liberation favours the interpretation of the voice of the oppressed as the basis for its praxis. This is not a private departure within the unified Whole of universal abstract theology, neither is it an equivocal, self-explanatory theology.

Starting from a unique position of difference, each theologian, and indeed the whole of Latin American theology, takes a fresh look at traditional themes passed down through history, but enters the interpretative process from the distinct emptiness of his new found liberty (that is, with a blank sheet). The theology of a true theologian or a people like the Latin Americans is analogically similar, yet at the same time distinct, and hence unique, original and completely individual. If what is similar becomes univocal, the history of theology will remain European. On the other hand, if difference is made absolute, theologies become equivocal. The aim is not Hegelian identity, nor yet Jasperian equivocation, but analogy. The theology of liberation is a new focus in the history of theology, an analogical focus which has come to the fore after modern developments in Europe, Russia and the United States, and predating to some extent the most recent African and Asian theology. The theology of the poor nations, the theology of world-wide liberation is not easily acceptable to Europeans, who believe too passionately in their own invariable world-wide acceptance. They will not listen to the voice of the other (the barbarians, non-being if we define Being as the European way of thought), the voice of Latin America, the Arab World, or South-East Asia and China. The voice of Latin America is no longer a mere echo of European theology. It is a barbarians' theology— as the apologists would say, making the contrast with the "wise according this world." But we know that we have taken up our stand on the farther side of the modern, oppressive, European closed system. Our minds are set upon the liberation of the poor. We point towards the world-man of the future—man who shall be eternally free.

NOTES

This selection was translated by J. D. Mitchell.

1. *Brevísima relación de la destrucción de las Indias* (Buenos Aires, 1966), p. 36. For an historical insight into the argument of this present article, see my *Historia de la Iglesia en América Latina. Coloniaje y liberación (1492–1972)* (Barcelona, 1972); for the theological matter see *Caminos de liberación latino-americana*, two volumes (Buenos Aires, 1972–1973); for the philosophical background, *Para una ética de la liberación latino-americana*, three volumes (Buenos Aires, 1973–1974).

2. *Nueva política comercial para el desarrollo* (Mexico, 1966), p. 30. If to this is added the deterioration in price-ratios between raw materials and manufactured products, the so-called under-developed countries have been simply exploited, expropriated, and robbed. From this bulletin of CEPAL (UNESCO) came the so-called social economy of dependence based on the works of Celso Furtado, Jaguaribe, Cardoso, Faletto, Theotonio dos Santos, Gunter Frank, or Hinkelammert in Latin America or of Samir Amin in Africa, with the European position given by Arghiri Emmanuel or Charles Bettelheim. See also a bibliography on the subject in *Desarrollo y revolución (Bibliografía)* produced by CEDIAL, Bogotá, Parts 1 & 2 (1971–1973).

3. In the presidential elections in Argentina on 23 Sept. 1973, the Federal Capital (Buenos Aires) awarded the working/peasant class candidate 42% of the votes, while the poorest provinces in the north-east awarded more than 75% (Jujuy, Salta, Tucumán, Santiago del Estero, Catamarca, La Rioja). The big Latin American capitals provide evidence of internal dependence.

4. *Three Contributions to the Theory of Sex*, III, 4. Freud's error consists in confusing "the reality of masculine domination" in our society with the "reality of sexuality" as such. See my "Para una crótica latinoamericana" (chapter VII in *Para una ética de la liberación latinoamericana*, III, pp. 42–47).

5. *Archivo General de Indias* (Seville), Audiencia de Guatemala 156.

6. See my *Para una ética de la liberación*, op. cit., pp. 137 ff.

7. Domingo F. Sarmiento, *Facundo* (English trans.)

8. This is the meaning of reality for Heidegger, *Being and Time* (New York, 1962).

9. Expression used by the older Schelling (*Einleitung in die Philosophie der Mythologie*, XXIV); *Werke*, V (Munich, 1959), p. 748; *transmundan*, though not with the same meaning. Beyond being and beyond the world, is the Lord of being (ibid.).

10. Xavier Zubiri, *Sobre la escencia* (Madid, 1963), p. 395: "Reality is the object as something in its own right. The object is actualized in the mind and presents itself to us intellectually as existing in its own right before (prius) we actually see it." In the same sense the other for Levinas is the reality beyond the closed system and beyond being (cf. *Totalité et Infini*, The Hague, 1961). See also my *La Dialectica hegeliana* (Mendoza, 1972), pp. 141 ff.

11. *Civ. Dei*, XV, 1. Civ. Dei expounds the two basic biblical categories: the "closed shop" founded on self-seeking love (*libido*), and openness which lies open to the future in loving concern for others (*caritas*). See *Para una ética de la liberación latinoamericana*, Chap. IV, §§ 20–23, and Chap. V, §§ 26–28, volume II, pp. 13–88.

12. In Hegel this is the negation of distinction and the object, which for its part

has been the negation of Being in itself or Totality taken as the originating and divine Identity. On the other hand, in our case it is a matter of denying the alienation of the other (reduced to the level of an object), that is to say, to affirm (say "yes" to) the other who is distinct. (See my *Para una ética de la liberación*, chap. III, § 16, vol. I, pp. 118 ff.; chap. IV, § 23, and chap. V, §§ 29–31, vol. II, pp. 42–127); thus this is a negation of what Hegel affirmed coming from an Outside unknown to him.

13. *Brevísima relación*, p. 33.

14. See my paper "Atheism of the prophets and Marx," delivered to the 2nd Argentine Theologians Week, Guadalupe (Buenos Aires, 1973), and "Historia de la fe cristiana y cambio social en América latina," in *América latina, dependencia y liberación* (Buenos Aires, 1973), pp. 193 ff. There I show that the prophets begin their attack on the system of sin with a criticism of the idolatry and fetishism of that system. Would it not be both truly Christian to attack the fetishism of money (Marx, *Das Kapital*, I, chap. XXIV, 1: "Das Geheimnis der ursprünglichen Akkumulation")? Is it perhaps not correct that Hegelian theology should be denied in order to affirm instead an anthropology of the Thou (Feuerbach, *Grundsätze der Philosophie der Zukunft*), especially if we remember that Christ is the Other made man and mediator with God and the Father and Creator? We might say that Latin American theology of liberation is non-believing when it comes to the religion of oppressionist Europe (not to confuse religion with Christianity) see my article, "From Secularization to Secularism," in *Concilium*, September 1969 (American edn., Vol. 47). See chapter 2 in this book, p. 187 ff.

15. I may be permitted this translation of *hoi ptokhoi to pneumati* (Mt. 5:3), to distinguish between the "poor" as the outsider (the sense in which I use it in § 5), and the "poor in spirit," i.e., the actively involved liberator, the prophet. See in my *El humanismo semita* (Buenos Aires, 1969), the footnote on "Universalismo y misión en los poemas del Siervo de Yahueh" (pp. 127 ff.).

16. "He has put down the mighty from their thrones, and exalted those of low degree; he has filled the hungry with good things, and the rich he has sent empty away" (Lk. 1:52–53). *Sub-vertere* in Latin is to make low what was high and vice versa.

17. Lev. 25:8–12 "Jubilee" comes from the Hebrew *yôbhēl*, the horn-shaped trumpet which announced the liberation of the slaves (Ex. 21:2–6).

18. "That which is born of the flesh (the closed system) is flesh. That which is born of the spirit (the other, the outsider) is spirit" (ibid.).

19. "*Je pense, donc je suis*" was a statement so firm and confident that the most determined contradictions of the sceptics were not enough to shake it;" see *Discours de la méthode*, IV (Paris, 1953), pp. 147–48.

20. "Ich bin Ich. Das Ich ist schlechthin gesetzt" (*Grundlage der gesamten Wissenschaftslehre* (1794), § 1 (Berlin, 1956), I, 96). He still says that "the essence of critical philosophy is the absolute position of an 'I', absolute and unconditioned, and not to be defined in terms of any higher order." For the only translation in German: "Darin besteht nun das Wesen der kritischen Philosophie, dass ein absolutes Ich als schlechthin unbedingt und durch nichts Höheres bestimmbar aufgestellt werde). (Ibid. I, § 3; 1, 119).

21. See my *La dialéctica hegeliana*, 4–9 (pp. 31–121) and *Para una destrucción de la historia de la ética*, §§ 11–21 (Mendoza, 1972), pp. 75–162.

22. The theology of Karl Rahner comes from Heidegger's philosophy (also influenced by Maréchal) and is set out in *Spirit in the World* (London and Sydney, 1968), or in *Hearers of the Word* (London and Sydney, 1969). Quite rightly Eberhard Simons, *Philosophie der Offenbarung. Auseinandersetzung mit K. Rahner* (Stuttgart, 1966), demonstrates that the *Mit-Sein* has not been brought out sufficiently in Rahner's thinking. It is not a matter of mentioning the other as a mere aside, but of making it the starting-point of theological argument, but not merely of the *divine* Other.

23. For a philosophical point of view see the works of Levinas (op. cit.), and Michael Theunissen, *Der Andere* (Berlin, 1965), and chap. III of my *Para una ética de la liberación*, vol. I, pp. 97 ff.

24. As Yves Congar so well shows, the locus theologicus is everyday events ("the history of the Church, in a certain sense, embraces all of it," see his "Church History as a Branch of Theology" in *Concilium*, September 1970 (American edn., Vol. 57). Revelation is mediated by historical otherness—God reveals himself in history. In the same sense Edward Schillebecckx, *Revelation and Theology* (London and Melbourne, 1967), offers us the "Word as the medium of revelation." However, in both cases, as with Schelling and Kierkegaard, the mediatory function of the anthropological outsider is not grasped. It is not enough to say that revelation is possibly effected in the form of human speech, as Rahner does in his *Hearers of the Word*, but we must go on to say that the poor, like the metaphysical other is the mediator chosen by God for his revelation. As a fact of history (not just of myth as in Exodus 3) Moses heard the word of God through the mediation of the poor (Ex. 2:11–15), as Schillebeeckx says in his *Revelation and Theology*.

25. These categories are flesh (Totality), the poor (the human outsider), God as creator and redeemer, the Word, the Spirit (outreaching modes of the divine in face-to-face encounter) and service *'abodhāh* or *diakonia*). See my *Caminos de liberación latinoamericana* II, VI. The category is what is revealed in Christ as essential revelation. What is interpreted by these categories is the Christian meaning of event, the fruit of faith.

26. In *Concilium*, February 1973 (American edn. vol. 82), much was said about liturgy, Scripture, poetry, but almost nothing about the privileged place of faith in the other—the poor; without him faith becomes ideology, mere doctrine, obscurity.

27. See *Caminos de liberación latinoamericana* I, §§ 1–7; *Para una ética de la liberación latinoamericana*, §§ 31 and 36.

28. From Latin America see Hugo Assmann, *Teologla desde la praxis de la liberación* (Salamanca, 1973), pp. 76 ff. A bibliography on *Desarrollo y revolución*, CEDIAL, II, pp. 73–95. This idea and the one that follows are inspired in part by the Christian praxis in Latin America.

29. Cf. Bibliography in CEDIAL (op. cit.), II, 31–47.

30. The works of Johann Baptist Metz is of importance: starting with "Friede und Gerechtigkeit. Ueberlegungen zu einer 'politischen Theologie,'" in *Civitas* VI, (1967), pp. 13 ff.; then *Theology of the World* (London, 1969), and "The Problem of a Political Theology," in *Concilium* June, 1968 (American edn., Vol. 36); and finally the colourless "Erlösung und Emanzipation," in *Stimmen der Zeit* 3 (1973), pp. 171 ff. (where the word "Befreiung" is avoided in its ambivalent sense of "cross." The "cross" of the murdered prophet is not the same as the "pain" of the oppressed poor.

31. Liberation protest as a function of the Church (see J. B. Metz, *Theology of the World*, op. cit.) is very different if it's concerned with international political protest (pointing out the unjust acquisitiveness of the centre), and with social protest (pointing out the oppression of the ruling classes). In this situation we still look for a concrete programme of action to make the protest really mean anything. Theology is essentially an ethic, and most important, a political ethic.

32. Cf. Jürgen Moltmann, *Theology of Hope* (London, 1969); idem, *Perspektiven der Theologie* (Mainz, 1968) and *Diskussion über die 'Theologie Hoffnung'* (Munich, 1967).

33. See J. Moltmann, *Theology of Hope*, op. cit. Something in the nature of a reactionary professional ethic, but not a subversive movement to oppose the closed nature of the system, and which knows it has to initiate a programme of historical liberation as a sign of the coming Kingdom.

34. Cf. Jules Girardi, *Christianisme, libération humaine et lutte des classes* (Paris, 1972).

35. See my *De la dialéctica a la analéctica*, general conclusions (to be published in Salamanca, 1974).

36. Bear in mind that Latin America is the only continent, culturally speaking, which has been both Christian and colonial. Europe has been Christian, but was not colonized. Other colonial peoples have not been Christianized. This places Latin America in a unique position in world and ecclesiastical history. From our unique experience must come, of necessity, a theology which must be different to be authentic.

37. In Africa, such authors as V. Mulango, A. Vanneste, H. Burkle; the "black theology" of J. Cone, A. Hargreaves, Th. Ogletree, Ch. Wesley point to this line of thought; see also J. Peters, "Black Theology as a Sign of Hope," *Concilium*, November 1970 (American edn., Vol. 59); G. D. Fischer, "Theologie in Lateinamerika als 'Theologie der Befreiung,'" in *Theologie und Glaube* (1971), pp. 161–78; R. Strunk, "Theologie and Revolution," in *Theologische Quartalschrift*, 1 (1973), pp. 44–53; and CEDIAL, op. cit., II, pp. 58–72). Some European opinions, for example, Vancourt, "Thélogie de la libération," in Esprit et Vie 28 (1972), pp. 433–40, & 657–62, who thinks that this theology is inspired solely by the Marxist method, are very biased.

38. G. Gutiérrez wondered in his short work "Hacia una teología de la liberación" (Montevideo, 1969) whether beyond a theology of development we ought to formulate a specific theology of liberation. The previous year Rubem Alves in *Religíon: opio o instrumento de liberación?* (Montevideo, 1968) had already gone some way with this idea. Also Methol Ferré in his article "Iglesia y sociedad opulenta. Una crítica a Suenens desde América latina," in *Víspera* 12 (1969), pp. 1–24, points to a "struggle of two theologies," since "all theology one way or another has political implications," and in fact, "within the Catholic Church itself there exists oppression by the richer local churches of the poorer ones." Thus there arose a new theological argument.

39. See my *Para una ética de la liberación latinoamericana*, § 36, vol. II. Pp. 156 ff. I would define theology as *"an analectic pedagogy of historical and eschatological liberation."* A pedagogy, for the theologian, is a teacher and not a politician, nor is he involved sexually; analectic because the method is neither purely epistemological nor dialectic. For this definition see my *Caminos de liberación* II, lecture XII.

2

✝

The Bread of the Eucharist Celebration as a Sign of Justice in the Community

A year has passed since the tragic death of Archbishop Romero, that zealous pastor who was murdered on 24 March 1980, *while he was celebrating Holy Mass.* He crowned his ministry, devoted particularly *to the poorest* and most marginalised, with his blood. It was a supreme witness, which has become the symbol of the tribulations of a whole people; but also a motive of hope for a better future.

—Pope John Paul II, 24 March 1981

This chapter seeks to explore the links between bread as the fruit of common human labour, exchanged among those who produce it, and bread as the substance of the Eucharistic offering. On a deeper level, the bread of the sacrifice also has to be linked to the body of the prophet offering himself throughout history in struggles for justice, for the building of the kingdom. Bread of labour; bread of the offering; the body of the martyr as Eucharistic bread. That is, how to link *economy* and *Eucharist*, the essence of Christianity.

As I have done elsewhere, I would like to take a particular episode in the history of the Church as a starting-point.[1] Here it will be the prophetic conversion of Bartolomé de las Casas in April 1514, an episode related in the *Historia de las Indias*, Book III, ch. 79.[2] Bartolomé had reached America on 15 April 1502, nearly ten years after Columbus discovered the continent, and had taken part with Ovando in the violent conquest of the Tain Indians. He was the first priest to be ordained in the New World, saying

---

Enrique Dussel, "The Bread of the Eucharist Celebration As a Sign of Justice in the Community," *Concilium* 152 (1982): 56–65.

his first Mass in 1511, having been sponsored by Diego de Colón, son of the *conquistador*. In Hispaniola he became acquainted with the Dominicans Pedro de Córdoba and Antón de Montesinos. In January 1513, he accompanied Pánfilo de Narvaez in the conquest of the island of Cuba, where European, Christian, domination was imposed "with blood and fire." In recompense for his services, he was given a band of Indians to work for him (the "sharing-out" system). He had spent twelve years as a participant in the violence in the Caribbean.

"The cleric Bartolomé de las Casas," he wrote of himself, "was very concerned and busy with his harvests, as were others, sending his "shared-out" Indians to work in the mines, to dig for gold, and to sow the crops, taking as much advantage of them as he could." When Diego Velázquez came to the "villa of the Holy Spirit," and since there was "no other priest or friar" on the island, he asked Bartolomé to say Mass and preach the gospel to him and his companions. So Bartolomé decided to "leave the house he had beside the river Arimao" and began "to consider some authorities on Holy Scripture" in preparation. The biblical text that became the prop for the prophetic conversion of this great sixteenth-century fighter is important:

The first and main passage he considered was this, from the Book of Ecclesiasticus, chapter 34:

> A sacrifice derived from ill-gotten gains is contaminated,
> a lawless mockery that cannot win approval.
> The Most High is not pleased with the offering of the godless,
> nor do endless sacrifices win his forgiveness.
> To offer a sacrifice from the possessions of the poor
> Is like killing a son before his father's eyes.
> Bread is life to the destitute,
> And it is murder to deprive them of it.
> To rob your neighbour of his livelihood is to kill him,
> and the man who cheats a worker of his wages sheds blood.

"And he began (writes Bartolomé of himself) to consider the misery and slavery those people (the Indians) were suffering. Applying the one (the biblical text) to the other (the economic conditions in the Caribbean), he decided in himself, convinced of the very truth, that everything that was being committed against the Indians in these Indies was unjust and tyrannical."

Bartolomé found himself unable to celebrate his Mass, his Eucharistic offering. First he freed his Indians ("he agreed to let them go completely free"), and began his prophetic career, first in Cuba, then in Santo Domingo, later in Spain, and finally throughout the West Indies, "while all were amazed and even horrified by what he said to them."[3] "Dealing with contemplative and active life, which was the subject-matter of the gospel for that Sunday, and touching on the works of mercy, he has obliged to show them the obligation they had to fulfill and carry them out with those people they were using so cruelly." The text of Ecclesiasticus 34:18–22 is indeed striking in its structure.

1. "BREAD"

The text Bartolomé re-read in Cuba says: "Bread is life to the destitute."[4] In the Mediterranean, a corn-growing region, "bread" is the symbol and the reality of the product of human labour. That is, it is the basic fruit of the man-nature relationship of work. This relationship belongs to the productive order (the *ordo* of *factibilia*)[5] referred to the Offertory prayer of the Catholic Mass: "this *bread* . . . which *earth* has given and human hands have *made*." (The phrase used of the wine, "*work* of human hands" must be substituted here to follow the author's argument.—*Trans.*) So let us examine these three elements: earth, bread, work.

This subject-nature relationship through work is a *material* relationship. Earth becomes the material (*in quo* and "with which") of work. Without work, there is the earth and the cosmos, but there is no "material." This "material" (the materialism of the sacrament) is constituted by and is *a posteriori* to the human and subjective *a priori* of work. Cosmological materialism ("everything is matter") is ingenuous and easily refuted. Productive materialism is irrefutable and sacramental: earth is the *material* of work. Without earth and work there is no bread. Without bread, there is no Eucharist. But what is *bread*?

Bread is a *pro-duct*, it is that which comes forward (*pro-*) to our view as a phenomenon in the world. It is human creation; it is an extension of the divine creation. It is an exteriorization, distancing, and objectivation of human subjectivity. It is the cultivation of the earth. It is culture, and technique, technology. It is the products that surround us as a system, as a civilization. Above all this "bread" is the fruit of what is more worthy than bread itself: work. In the Hebrew of the Bible, *habodah*.[6] It is a manual work (but it is also, as we shall see in section 7, the work of the temple, divine "service").[7] The "servant" (*hebed*) of Yahweh is the "worker" of the Lord. The prophets work, so do the Pharisees, the Apostles, and Jesus himself. Work is the worthy human activity par excellence which objectivizes human dignity in nature. Without work, man would be a mere fruitless subjectivity without "bread" for the sacrifice: his hands would be empty.

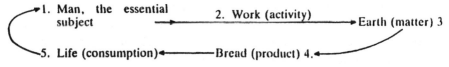

Figure 2.1.   The Circle of Production

2. BREAD IS "LIFE"

The text that brought about Bartolomé's prophetic conversion says that "bread is life."[8] What lives is what is "other" than any other; that is free; that is self-determining; that is autonomous in its existence; that moves itself in its corporeality in order to accomplish its aims, that enjoys, that is satisfied; that adores; that as a living thing offers homage to the living God.

Life is opposed to death. Any *necessity* is a sort of death (see level 1 of figure 2.1). "I was hungry . . ." is the first necessity. Hunger is lack of food. Bread is food of the first order. That is, while bread is a product of work, it is first the requirement of a necessity; we produce bread because we need to eat. Bread is a sustenance of life before it is a product of work (the 1–5 relationship in figure 2.1 is still more basic than 2–4). The consumption of the product is the denial of denial; it brings death to death; gives life to life. Therefore "I was hungry and you gave me to eat" is, in its sacramental materialism, the *absolute* criterion of the Last Judgment.

Therefore Jesus says, in the Eucharistic and so productive sense, "I am the bread of life" (John 6:35). The bread that feeds, before being a product (Manna was a "bread from heaven"[9] and so a free gift from the pre-economic God: bread without work), is satisfier, enjoyment, life, and the Kingdom brought about.[10]

To "eat" ("take and *eat*: this is my body": Matt. 26:26). The bread is to destroy it, to break it up, chew it, deny it. The death of the bread is life to life. Bread was a sort of death to man in his work, in a mysterious and sacred dialectic of death-life, destruction-resurrection. What is certain is that life is the original and final cause of bread. The "bread of life" that feeds and dies as it gives life.

3. "BREAD IS LIFE TO THE DESTITUTE"

The biblical text does not say: "Bread is life to man," but "to the destitute," the poor. "Man" would include us all: the "poor" are only some of us.

If we are to understand "poor" in the biblical sense, we need to make some prior distinctions. For there to be poor people, there needs to be more than one person. Robinson Crusoe quite alone would be neither poor nor

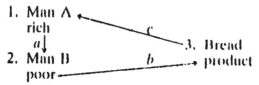

Figure 2.2. The Practical-Productive Circle: Economics

rich, but simply "a man." To be poor means occupying a precise place in the man-man relationship. If the man-nature relationship is *productive*, the man-man relationship is *practical* (*operabilia*). The interpersonal relationship is *ethical*; the man-nature relationship is *technical*. Ethical relationships concern good and evil, virtue and vice. Technical relationships deal with efficiency or productivity. The relationship between persons is one of service to or respect for the other or of domination or alienation of the other. Sin is a *practical*, ethical relationship. If there are to be "poor," there must be "rich." Without the poor, there are no rich and vice-versa. It is a dialectical concept: it includes its opposite. But the two terms are not interchangeable: one cannot be both poor and rich in the same relationship *hic et nunc*. The rich man is the dominator, the sinner; the poor man is the dominated, who suffers the sin of the sinner (so, in this relationship, he is the just man, the present subject of the kingdom of Heaven). The practical or ethical rich-poor relationship is one of dominator-dominated (arrow *a* in figure 2.2). A rich man poor in intention cannot be "poor in spirit" or "spiritual." Intention is not the Holy Spirit.[11] The "poor in spirit" are those who make a prophetic option for the condition of dominated: "though he was in the form of God . . . emptied himself, taking the form of a servant" (Phil. 2:7). But this is not all.

The poor are those who produce or labour their product to satisfy their own needs (arrow *b* in figure 2.2). The "bread" (3 in figure 2.2), however, does not come back to the producer in the form of consumption, but, by a process of alienation (arrow *c*) goes to the dominator. In practice, the dominator becomes "the rich man" (there can be a dominator who does not become rich because, for example, he frees those whom he dominates immediately after his act of domination) when he appropriates to himself the product of others' work. In this way he accumulates the fruit of his own work and of other people's. "Rich," as a biblical category, means not simply the sinner, but the structural, historical, economic sinner:[12] that is, he who enjoys and consumes, utilises the product of others' work as an instrument of domination over them.

So that when the Bible speaks of the "poor," it does not mean simply those who have no goods, or who take a free "take it or leave it" attitude to goods. This is not enough: for there to be poor, there have also to be rich, there has to be domination, production, product, alienation from it

and productive structuration of the domination. The poor are the dominated; those who are structurally alienated from the fruits of their work.

Now we can understand the biblical phrase: "Bread is life to the destitute." Bread is the product-food for the alienated-poor who are forced to
work but do not consume, their life is objectivized in the product but it
does not come back to them in the form of life-consumption. When bread
is not life to the poor, the poor die.

4. "IT IS MURDER TO DEPRIVE THEM OF IT"

When someone dominates another person it is a practical, ethical sin, like
striking another person with no regard for his sacred dignity as a person. But
when someone deprives another of the product of his work, the relationship
is not only practical (man-man), not only productive (man-product), but
practical-productive: economic. Another person is dominated, but by means
of the product of his work. "Thou shalt not steal" operates on a practical-
productive level: an economic level. But in the last analysis, it refers back
to "thou shalt not kill." The text Bartolomé read made this plain: "Bread is
life to the destitute and it is murder to deprive them of it. To rob your
neighbour of his livelihood is to kill him, and the man who cheats a worker
of his wages sheds blood." The logic of Hebrew theology is coherent: if the
bread consumed is life, the bread that is not consumed leaves the subject
who works (and who un-lives by objectivising his life in the product of his
work) in the state of pure negativity of necessitating need: death. The
bread that is produced and not consumed is "bread of death"—and he
who eats this "eats damnation to himself" as St. Paul said.

This is why death is the fruit of sin—in its original, radical meaning:
those who dominate their neighbours and deprive them of the fruit of their
work leave them hungry: "I was hungry and you did not feed me" is the
absolute criterion of Eternal Damnation. Leaving the producer without his
product is murdering, killing, destroying the epiphany of God: as much of
his revelation as of his worship;[13] the dominated "other," the poor.

The Indians of the Arimao river had to hand over to Bartolomé part of
the crops they grew and part of their working day, as a form of tribute and
under the violence of domination, according to the economic system of
"sharing-out." Bartolomé then came to understand "the misery and slavery (of) those peoples," and to discover "the blindness, injustices and
tyrannies" of the *conquistadores*. He suddenly discovered that the "bread"
he was about to offer had been snatched from the poor; that it was uncon-
sumed bread; that it was murdering the Indians to deprive them of the
fruits of their work. And as he was "about to say Mass" he told the Euro-

peans there that they "could not be saved" if they treated the Indians in this way. He saw the relationship between the Eucharistic liturgy and the economic system of oppression. He saw the bread stained with blood. There is a story about St. Francisco Solano, OFM, a holy preacher in Peru and Argentina in the sixteenth century. When he was invited to eat by some *conquistadores*, he said the blessing and took a piece of bread, which he squeezed in his hands and blood began to ooze out of it. He then said: "This is the blood of the Indians," and went back to his convent without touching a mouthful, leaving the rich Europeans amazed and dismayed.[14]

5. THE BREAD OF THE ECONOMY IS THE BREAD OF THE EUCHARIST

The first thing to realize is that the bread of the Eucharist, the bread prepared for the sacrifice, is *real* bread; it is *really* the product of someone's work, in time, specific, human work. This means that offering something to God not only has a sacramental meaning (if by sacrament we understand an "outward—material—sign of grace" indicating the man-nature relationship—water, oil, salt, bread . . .) but also an economic meaning. Giving, offering, presenting something to someone, or exchanging it with him, or stealing it from him is an economic relationship. Offering God a piece of bread ("We have this bread to offer, which earth has given and human hands have made") is an act of worship, of *theologal economy*.[15]

Bartolomé, the *conquistador* (A in figure 2.3), had dispossessed the Indian (the exploited poor man, B) of the fruit of his work. The Indian's work (arrow *a*) does not come back to him as life, but goes to the dominator by a process of alienation (arrow *c*). This stolen bread, the *same* bread, is now placed on the altar as "Eucharistic bread." The prophet of Latin America understood the economic-Eucharistic dialectic in the text of Ecclesiasticus:

"To offer a sacrifice from the possessions of the poor
is like killing a son before his father's eyes.
Bread is life to the destitute,
and it is murder to deprive them of it."

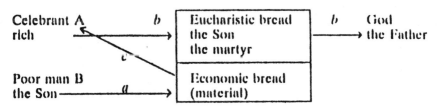

Figure 2.3. Productive-Practical Relationships of Worship: the Eucharist

And the immediately preceding phrase:

"The Most High is not pleased with the offering of the godless."

What he saw was the identity between the bread-product of everyday work, changed and exchanged, respected or stolen, and the bread on the altar. The bread contains the objectivized life of the worker, his blood, his intelligence, his efforts, his love, his enjoyment, his happiness, the kingdom. And what was being done was taking this bread unjustly from him and offering it to God. For this bread to become the very "body" of the "lamb that was slain" it has to be bread of life, bread that has satisfied, fed, deigned the denials of death, need, domination, sin: the bread of justice.

6. IDOLATRY IS NOT EUCHARIST

So those who offer God bread stolen from the poor give God the life of the poor as their offering. The poor is "the Son" (the Indian) and the celebrant (Bartolomé, the "rich man") who offers this bread unjustly snatched from the poor is offering the "Father" (God) the very life of his Son: "kill—a *son* before his *father's* eyes." The father who perversely desires the sacrifice of his son, who wants his blood, cannot be a loving father, but only a blood-thirsty idol—Moloch, Mammon, Money.

This is why the text says: "The Most High is not pleased with the offering of the godless." How could he accept such an offering, which is sacrifice to the Idol, the Fetish, Satan? God does not want the life of his Son to be offered by killing him in his presence. God wants the life of his Son to be a free existence; what he justly wants in sacrifice is the denial of the death of the dead, which death is the need of the poor, the oppressed. Giving the hungry to eat, giving life back to the dead, giving life to those who lack life is the worship required by the Most High. Fetishistic worship offers the idol stolen bread, the blood of the poor; Eucharistic worship offers the Father of goodness the bread of justice, the bread that has satisfied hunger: "All whose faith *had drawn them together* held everything *in common*: they would sell their property and possessions and make a general distribution as the *need* of each required. With one mind they kept up their daily attendance at the temple, and, *breaking bread* in private houses, shared their meals with unaffected joy, as they praised God . . ." (Acts 2:44–46).

The Eucharistic bread of those "whose faith had drawn them together" was bread that had satisfied *need*, in justice ("made a general distribution . . .) in the joy of consuming, of eating, of satisfaction. It was a bread of life, of the community, of love. It is the Utopia of primitive Christianity and the Utopia of the final kingdom; it is the horizon of critical understanding of every economic system in history: justice as the *practical condition* which *makes possible* the Eucharistic celebration which saves.

7. THE "BODY" OF THE MARTYR AND FETISHISTIC WORSHIP

The bread that is eaten gives life by being destroyed, consumed, negated. The death of the bread is the beginning of life for those who receive it. Jesus is "the bread of life." "The Son of Man did not come to be served, but to serve, and to give up his life as a ransom for many" (Matt. 20:28). Serving (the Greek *diakoneín* translates the Hebrew *habodāh*) means working and offering worship. The "servant" (deacon and worker) struggles on God's behalf and thereby offers worship to Yahweh. Christ's historical "work" was not merely that of an artisan producing products (houses, tables, chairs, as he would have done in Nazareth), but making his own body the product offered to God so that the "many"[16] would become "a people."[17] Giving life involves death. Jesus himself is life (John 11:25), and is the bread (John 6:35) offered in sacrifice: "Take and eat; this is my body" (Matt 26:26). His "body," his very martyr's "flesh" becomes historically "the lamb that is slain." Now the corporeality, the carnality, the very being of the prophet, in history, in the class contradictions between rich and poor, in political events, in the struggle for the oppressed, in opposition to the dominators, their armies, their armaments . . . now the flesh of the Redeemer is offered on the altar of history: "There they crucified him, and with him two others, one on the right, one on the left, and Jesus between them" (John 19:18). His hanging body is now the "bread" of the sacrifice so that many will *live*.

The "body" of the poor man is killed when bread is snatched from him: hunger is the alienation of the bread of work. Interposing one's own "body" (material) between the poor and the rich, against the dominator and in favour of the dominated, is making one's own "body" the object of the brutal act of domination, the mortal act, the very Satanic action of the Fetish, the Idol. The Fetish lives off the blood of the poor. The life of the Idol is the death of the poor. To take the Fetish's life for justice's sake kills him. But before dying, the Fetish kills. He kills the martyr (he who shows the poor the possibility of consuming the bread he produces: the kingdom as a feast of justice) who fights for the life of the poor. The life of the poor is bread; struggling for them to have this bread is offering one's own "body" as an object of the violence of sin, of the domination of the Idol. The Idol seeks to take the life of the Son, wants him to die. The Son offers the life taken by the Idol to the Father—who does not wish his death but accepts it because the death of the just man, the poor, the Son, is the passage from death to life; passage through the desert of the slavery in Egypt to the promised land, the land of this earth and the eschatological land of the kingdom, which has already begun when the poor eat, satisfy their hunger, in history.

Christ identified himself with the material body, the suffering and needy carnality of the poor: "As often as you did it to one of the least of my brethren, you did it to me" (Matt. 25:40). But Christ became the "bread" of history and offered up his body for the liberation of the poor. As did Mgr. Antonio de Valsivieso in Nicaragua in the sixteenth century, and Mgr. Oscar Romero in El Salvador in the twentieth. As Pope John Paul II says, his body was martyred "while he was celebrating Holy Mass. He crowned his (priestly) ministry with his blood." The bread of justice made Mgr. Romero identify himself with the struggle of the people of El Salvador, the struggle to give the poor back the fruits of their work. But the Idol and his forces took life away from the body of the prophet just as they had previously taken life away from the poor by stealing their bread. Well could Mgr. Romero celebrate the Eucharist, because his Eucharistic bread was economic bread in justice! He had preached to the military and the Christian Democrat Junta, asking them to stop squeezing the poor body of his people. In reply, they murdered his martyr's body. And so once again Jesus' prophecy, which links the martyr's death with the liturgy, was fulfilled: "Indeed the time will come when anyone who *kills* you will suppose that he is performing a *religious duty (latreían)*" (John 16:2). Those who deprive the martyr's body of life—having previously deprived the body of the poor of life through domination and theft—are offering homage to the Fetish. That is why Christ said "will suppose," that is, will think they are performing a duty to God whereas in fact they are performing it to the Fetish. And this brings us to the basic question: By what criterion can we distinguish between idolatrous worship and Eucharistic worship?

8. THE "PRACTICAL CONDITIONS" THAT MAKE EUCHARISTIC WORSHIP "POSSIBLE"

The same group of people, around the same priest, can offer breads that are alike in their real structure. But some will be paying homage to the Idol and "eating damnation to themselves" while others will be communing in the life of the lamb that is slain. How do we discern the righteousness of those who make the offering (*ex opere operantis*)?

After all that has been said. I think the conclusion is clear enough. God cannot accept bread that is stolen from the poor, the bread of injustice. But it is not just a question of personal, individual, occasional injustice. How do we see structural injustice, the historical sin of systems? Can the fruit stolen from the poor, the oppressed classes, the exploited nations, be offered as Eucharistic bread? Have the practical conditions for Eucharistic bread which can be offered to God been met in a system where the wage-earner under capitalism (the successor of the "shared-out" Indian of the sixteenth century) is structurally deprived of part of the fruits of his work? Does the structural sin not stain the bread and prevent one from having a bread that can be offered in justice? How can those who live in dividends from the multinationals in the rich countries (such as Nestlé with its campaigns in the Third World to encourage mothers to use industrial "powdered milk" instead of their own milk) offer the Eucharist?

When Bartolomé worked all this out—the relationship between work, life, the products of work, the offering of the sacrifice, the poor, the alienation of the fruits of work as a death, offering the stolen fruit as an offering by the son to the father. . . . When he found that the poor were the Indians. . . . When he realised that he was the one who was exploiting the Indians. . . . When he saw that he as a priest was thinking of offering the bread stolen from the Indians under the system in the Eucharist. . . . When he perceived the relationship between Eucharist, liturgy, and economy, the unjust system of distribution and exchange. . . . He could not celebrate the Eucharist! Rather, he set his Indians free, on 15 August 1514, and "decided, as best he could, though he had not a single cent to his name, nor any means of earning, apart from a mare that he could sell for a hundred gold *pesos*, to go to Castile and give the King an account of what was going on."[18]

So he began his struggle for justice which was to occupy the rest of his life, fifty-two long years of much persecution. But of course he could go back to celebrating his Eucharist . . . because he had bread that was not snatched from the poor. He had the bread of justice, the *manna* from heaven, bread kneaded in his commitment to the interests of the poor, to the development of juster economic structures, the *practical conditions* that make it *possible* to offer the Eucharistic bread, the "bread of life."

NOTES

This selection was translated by Paul Burns.

1. See "Christian Art of the Oppressed in Latin America" in *Concilium* 132 (1980), sec. 1, "Economic status of the Eucharist," 40–41; "Analysis of the Final Document of Puebla: The relationship between economics and Christian ethics" in *Concilium* 140 (1980) 101ff.; on Bartolomé de las Casas, see ch. 1 of the collective work being produced by CEHILA, *Historia General de la Iglesia en América Latina* (1982) I.

2. BAE, II (Madrid 1961) pp. 356ff.

3. Ibid. p. 358.

4. See Kittel, art. ártos in *TWNT* I. 475–76 (biblio. brought up to date in vol. X, 2, p. 993).

5. "Ordo quem ratio considerando facti in rebus exterioribus constituit per rationem humanam, pertinet ad artes mechanicas," Th. Aquinas, *In Ethic. Expos.*, L. 1, lect. 1 (Turin 1949) p. 3.

6. See Bertam, art. *égon* in *TWNT* II, 631–53 (biblio. in X, 2, 1084–85); also Various, art. *paîs*, in ibid. V, 636–712. The art. by Bornkamm, *latreúo*, in IV, 58–68 is important, showing that the Greek *latreîa* and *latreúein* indicate the Hebrew *habodah* and *habad* (p. 59, 1. 45; p. 61, II. 27–28).

7. See my art. "Domination-Liberation: A New Approach" in *Concilium* 96 (1974), sec. 6, "The Prayers of Liberation-Redemption and the Prophet" 42–45. It is suggestive that *látris* (from which "worship" comes in Greek) means "worker's wages" to offer worship is to pay the worker his wages (see Kittel in *TWNT* IV, 59).

8. See Bultmann, arts. *záo, zoé* and *thánatos* in *TWNT* II, 834–874 and III, 7–21. Life (*Jalim*) is the supreme good (Prov. 3:16; Mac. 8:36).

9. The "bread of heaven" (*ártos ek toû ouránou*), John 6:31, referring to Exod. 16:4; Neh. 9:15; Wis. 16:20, etc. See *Dict. de la Bible* VI (1960) cols. 965–76.

10. "Happy the man who shall sit at the feast in the kingdom of God" (Luke 14:15). The kingdom is described from the experience of eating and being filled, satisfied.

11. The "spiritual" (*pneumatikós*; see art. pneûma in *TWNT* VI, 330–453) should not be confused with something purely "mental" in intention. As though it were an act of an anthropological faculty (intelligence in action). This confuses *intentio* with the Holy Spirit. The *psikhikós* (animic or human) must be distinguished from the *pnuematikós* (which proceeds from the Holy Spirit), as in Matt. 5:3, where the Spanish translator Juan Mateos gets it right; "Blessed are those *who choose* to be poor," in contrast to, e.g., the French *Bible de Jérusalem*.

12. See my remarks on "Social sin" in *Concilium* 140 (1980) 104 and 106.

13. See art. in *Concilium* 96 (1974) 49–51, on the poor as the "epiphany." But the poor are equally the epiphany of religious duty: to serve the poor is to serve God; giving the hungry food is offering the same bread to God himself. God reveals himself to us *through* the poor and we worship him *through* the poor (the practical circle of revelation-worship).

14. The saint said afterwards: "I cannot eat bread kneaded with the blood of the humble and the oppressed at this table": E. Vidal de Battini, "Leyendas de San Francisco Solano," in *Selecciones folklóricas Codex*, V (Buenos Aires 1965) 78.

15. See the article cited in *Concilium* 132 (1980) diagram on p. 41.

16. See Mever-Katz, art. *okhlós* in *TWNT* V, 582–89. This is the theme of the *ham haarets*, the "mass" (Mac. 3:20; Luke 5:1; Acts 7:9, etc.). It means a group of people without organisation, without a future, without consciousness, without historical memory.

17. See Strathmann, art. *laós* in *TWNT* IV, 29–57. The Hebrew word *ham* appears more than 2,000 times in the text of the Bible, *goi* only forty times, and *thom* only eleven. The "people" already conveys a community with unity, in alliance, with a historical memory, a future, hope. It is a positive category, as is "holy people" (*ham gadosh*) in Rabbinic theology.

18. The *Historia*, referred to at the beginning of the article, and cited in note 2, at p. 359.

3

The "World-System":
Europe as "Center" and Its
"Periphery" beyond Eurocentrism

In this chapter, we will study the question of Modernity, which comprises two paradigms. In the following passages, we will characterize both of them.

The first paradigm is from an Eurocentric horizon, and it formulates that the phenomena of Modernity is *exclusively* European; that is, it develops from out of the Middle Ages and later diffuses itself throughout the entire world.[1] Max Weber situates the "problem of universal history" with the question that is thus formulated:

> . . . to what combination of circumstances the fact should be attributed that in *Western civilization*, and in Western civilization only,[2] cultural phenomena have appeared which (as *we*[3] like to think) lie in a line of development having *universal* significance and value.[4]

Europe had, according to this paradigm, exceptional *internal* characteristics that allowed it to supersede, through its rationality, all other cultures. Philosophically, no one else better than Hegel expresses this thesis of Modernity:

> The German Spirit is the Spirit of the new World. Its aim is the realization of absolute Truth as the unlimited self-determination *(Selbstbestimmung)* of Freedom—*that* Freedom which has its own absolute form itself as its purport.[5]

Enrique Dussel, "The 'World-System': Europe As 'Center' and Its 'Periphery' beyond Eurocentrism," in *Latin America and Postmodernity: A Contemporary Reader*, ed. Eduardo Mendieta and Pedro Lange-Churión (Atlantic Highlands, N.J.: Humanities Press, 2001), 93–121. This version is the complete translation of the original manuscript.

What calls attention here is that the Spirit of Europe (the German spirit) is the absolute Truth that determines or realizes itself through itself without owing anything to anyone. This thesis, which I will call the "Eurocentric paradigm" (in opposition to the *"world* paradigm"), is the one that has imposed itself not only in Europe and the United States, but also in the entire intellectual world of the world periphery. As we have said, the "pseudo-scientific" division of history into Antiquity (as antecedent), the Medieval Age (preparatory epoch), and the Modern Age (Europe) is an ideological and deforming organization of history. Philosophy and ethics need to break with this reductive horizon in order to open themselves to the "world," "planetary" sphere. This problem is already an ethical one with respect to other cultures.

Chronology has its geopolitics. Modern subjectivity develops spatially, according to the "Eurocentric paradigm" from the Italy of the Renaissance to the Germany of the Reformation and the Enlightenment, toward the France of the French Revolution.[6] This paradigm concerns central Europe.

The second paradigm is from a planetary horizon, and it conceptualizes Modernity as the culture of the *center* of the "world-system,"[7] of the first "world-system"—through the incorporation of Amerindia[8] and as a result of the *management* of said "centrality." In other words, European Modernity is not an *independent*, autopoietic, self-referential system, but, instead, it is "part" of a "world-system": its *center*. Modernity, then, is planetary. It begins with the *simultaneous* constitution of Spain with reference to its "periphery" (the first of all, properly speaking, Amerindia: the Caribbean, Mexico and Peru). *Simultaneously*, Europe, as a diachrony that has its premodern antecedents (the Renaissance Italian cities and Portugal), will go on to *constitute* itself as "center"—as superhegemonic power that passes itself from Spain to Holland, to England, to France, and so on—over a growing "periphery": Amerindia, Brazil, and slave-supplying coasts of Africa; Poland in the sixteenth century;[9] consolidation of Latin Amerindia, North America, the Caribbean, Eastern Europe in the seventeenth century;[10] the Ottoman Empire, Russia, some Indian reigns, sub-Asian, and the first penetration to continental Africa until the first half of the XIX century.[11] Modernity, then, would be for this planetary paradigm a phenomenon proper to the "system" "center-periphery." Modernity is not a phenomenon of Europe as *independent* system, but of Europe as "center." This simple hypothesis absolutely changes the concept of Modernity, its origin, development and contemporary crisis; thus, it also changes the content of the belated Modernity or post-Modernity.

Furthermore, we sustain a thesis that qualifies the prior: the centrality of Europe in the "world-system" is not sole fruit of an internal superiority accumulated during the European Middle Age over against other cultures.

Instead, it is also the effect of the simple fact of the discovery, conquest, colonization, and integration (subsumption) of Amerindia (fundamentally). This simple fact will give Europe the determining *comparative advantage* over the Ottoman–Muslim world, India, or China. Modernity is fruit of this happening, not its cause. Subsequently, the *management* of the centrality of the "world-system" will allow Europe to transform itself in something like the "reflexive consciousness" (Modern Philosophy) of world history, and the many values, discoveries, inventions, technology, political institutions, and so on that are attributed to itself as its exclusive production are in reality the effect of the *displacement* of the ancient center of the third stage of the interregional system toward Europe—that is, following the diachronic way of the Renaissance to Portugal as antecedent, toward Spain, and later toward Flanders, England, and so on. Even capitalism is fruit, and not cause, of this juncture of European planetarization and centralization within the "world-system." The human experience of forty-five hundred years of political, economic, technological, cultural relations of the "interregional system," will now be hegemonized by Europe—which had never been "center," and that during its best times only got to be a "periphery." The slipping takes place from central Asia toward the Eastern and Italian Mediterranean, more precisely toward Genoa and toward the Atlantic. With Portugal as an antecedent, it begins properly in Spain and in the face of the impossibility of China's even attempting to arrive through the Orient (the Pacific) to Europe and thus to integrate Amerindia as its periphery. Let us look at the premises of the argument.

DEPLOYMENT OF THE "WORLD-SYSTEM"

Let us consider the deployment of world history's departing from the rupture, due to the Ottoman–Muslim presence, of the third stage of the interregional system, which in its classic epoch had Baghdad as its center (from A.D. 762 to 1258), and the transformation of the "interregional system" into the first "*world*-system," whose "center" would situate itself up to today in the North of the Atlantic. This change of "center" of the system will have its prehistory from the eighth through the fifteenth century A.D., but before the collapse of the third stage of the interregional system, with the new fourth stage of the "world-system" *originating* properly with 1492. This change of "center" of the system will have its prehistory from the eighth through the fifteenth century A.D., before the collapse of the third stage of the interregional system, but with the new fourth stage of the "world-system," it *originates* properly with 1492. Everything that had taken place in Europe was still a moment of *another* stage of the interregional system, yet the question remains: Which state originated the deployment of the "world-system?" Our answer is that it could annex Amerindia, from which it will go on to accumulate a prior nonexisting superiority toward the end of the fifteenth century as a springboard, or "comparative advantage."

But why not China? The reason is very simple, and we would like to define it from the outset. For China,[12] it was impossible to discover Amerindia (nontechnological impossibility, that is to say, empirically factual, but historical or geopolitical), for it had no interest in attempting to arrive at Europe because the "center" of the interregional system (in its third stage) was in the East, either in Central Asia or in India. To go toward completely "peripheral" Europe? This could not be an objective of Chinese foreign commerce.

In fact, Cheng Ho, between 1405 and 1433, was able to make seven successful voyages to the "center" of the system; in fact, he arrived at Sri Lanka, India, and even to Eastern Africa.[13] In 1479, Wang Chin attempted the same, but the archives of his predecessor were denied to him. China closed upon itself and did not attempt to do what precisely at that very same moment Portugal was undertaking. Its internal politics—perhaps the rivalry of the Mandarins against the new power of the merchant eunocos[14]—prevented its exit into foreign commerce. Had China undertaken it, however, it would have had to depart *toward the West* in order to reach the "center" of the system. The Chinese went toward the East, and they arrived at Alaska. It appears that they even arrived as far as California and even still more to the South. But when they did not find anything that would be of interest to its merchants and as they went farther away from the "center" of the "interregional system," they most probably abandoned the enterprise altogether. China was not Spain for geopolitical reasons.

However, to refute the old "evidence," which has been reinforced since Weber, we still need to ask ourselves: Was China culturally *inferior* to Europe in the fifteenth century? According to those who have studied the question,[15] China was not inferior, neither technologically,[16] nor politically,[17] nor commercially, not even because of its humanism.[18] There is a certain mirage in this question. The histories of Western science and technology do not take strictly into account that the European "jump" (the technological *boom*) begins to take place in the sixteenth century, but that it is only in the seventeenth century that it shows its multiplying effects. The *formulation* of the modern technological paradigm (eighteenth century) is confused with the origin of Modernity, without leaving time for the crisis of the Medieval model. No notice is taken that the scientific revolution—to talk with Kuhn—departs from a Modernity that has already begun, antecedent, as fruit of a "modern paradigm."[19] It is for that reason that in the fifteenth century (if we do not consider the posterior European inventions) Europe does not have any superiority over China. Needham even allows himself to be bewitched by this mirage, when he writes:

> The fact is that in the spontaneous autochthonous development of Chinese society did not produce any drastic change paralleling the *Renaissance and the scientific revolution* of the West.[20]

To place the Renaissance and the scientific revolution[21] as being *one and the same event* (one from the fourteenth century and the other from the seventeenth century) demonstrates the distortion of which we have spoken. The Renaissance is still an European event of a peripheral culture of the third stage of the interregional system. The "scientific revolution" is fruit of the formulation of the modern paradigm, which needed more than a century of Modernity to attain its maturity. Pierre Chaunu writes:

> Towards the end of the XV century, to the extent to which historical literature allows us to understand it, the far East as an entity comparable to the Mediterranean . . . does not result under any inferior aspect, at least superficially, to the far West of the Euro-Asiatic continent.[22]

Let us repeat: Why not China? Because China found itself in the farthest East of the "interregional system," because it looked to the "center": to India in the West.

So why not Portugal? For the same reason. That is, because it found itself in the farthest point of the West of the same "interregional system," and because *it also looked, and always did so, toward the "center"*: toward the India of the East. Colon's proposal (i.e., the attempt to reach the "center" through the West) to the king of Portugal was as insane as it was for Colon to pretend to discover a new continent, since he *only and always* attempted yet could not conceive another hypothesis, to reach the "center" of the third stage of the interregional system.[23]

As we have seen, the Italian Renaissance cities are the farthest points of the West (peripheral) of the interregional system that articulated a new continental Europe with the Mediterranean after the Crusades failed in 1291. The Crusades ought to be considered as a frustrated attempt to connect with the "center" of the system, a link that the Turks ruptured. The Italian cities, especially Genoa (which rivaled Venice, which had a presence in the Eastern Mediterranean), attempted to open the Western Mediterranean toward the Atlantic to reach once again through the south of Africa the "center" of the system. The Genoese placed all their experience in navigation and the economic power of their wealth at the service of opening for themselves this path. It was the Genoese who occupied the

Canaries in 1312,[24] and it was they who invested in Portugal to help them develop their navigational power.

Once the Crusades had failed, they could not count on the expansion of Russia through the steppes, who advanced through the frozen woods of the North in the seventeenth century to reach the Pacific and Alaska[25]; therefore, the Atlantic will be the only European door *to the "center" of the system*. Portugal, the first European nation already unified in the eleventh century, will transform the reconquest[26] against the Muslims into the beginning of a process of Atlantic mercantile expansion. In 1419, the Portuguese discover the Madeiras Islands; in 1431, the Azores; in 1482, Zaire; and in 1498, Vasco de Gama reaches India, the "center" of the interregional system. In 1415, Portugal occupies the African–Muslim Ceuta; in 1448, El-Ksar-es-Seghir; in 1471, Arzila. But all of this is the *continuation* of the interregional system whose connection is through the Italian cities:

> In the twelfth century when Genoese and the Pisans first appeared in Catalonia, in the thirteenth century when they first reach Portugal, this is part of the efforts of the Italians to draw the Iberian peoples into the international trade of the time. . . . As of 1317, according to Virginia Raus, "the city and the part of Lisbon would be the great centre of Genoese trade. . . ."[27]

Portugal—with contacts in the Islamic world, with numerous sailors (farmers expelled from an intensive agriculture), with a money economy, in "connection" with Italy—opened once again peripheral Europe to the interregional system. But because of this, it did not stop being a "periphery." Not even the Portuguese could pretend to have abandoned this situation, since Portugal could have attempted to dominate the commercial exchange in the sea of the Arabs (the Indian sea),[28] but never pretend to produce the commodities of the East (e.g., silk fabrics, tropical products, the sub-Saharan gold). In other words, it was an intermediary and always peripheral power of India, China, or the Muslim world.

With Portugal we are in the anteroom, but we are still neither in Modernity, nor are we in the "world-system," that is, the fourth stage of the system, which originated, at least, between Egypt and Mesopotamia.

So why does Spain begin the "world-system," and with it, Modernity? For the same reason that it was prevented in China and Portugal. Since Spain could not reach the "center" of the "interregional system" that was in Central Asia or India, it could not go toward the East since the Portuguese had already anticipated them and thus has exclusivity rights. Spain could not go through the South of the Atlantic as well, around the Coasts of Western Africa, until the Cape of Buena Esperanza was discovered in 1487. Spain only had one opportunity left: to go toward the "center," to India, through *the Occident*, through the West, by crossing the Atlantic Ocean.[29] Because of this, Spain "bumps" into, "finds without looking," Amerindia, and with it the entire European "Medieval paradigm" enters into crisis, which is the "paradigm" of a peripheral culture—that is, the Western furthest point of the third stage of the "interregional system." Thus, it inaugurates slowly but irreversibly the first *world* hegemony. This "world-system" is the only one that has existed in planetary history, and it is the modern system, European in its "center" and capitalist in its economy. This *Ethics of Liberation* pretends to situate itself explicitly within the horizon of this modern "world-system." (Is it perhaps the first practical philosophy that attempts to do so "explicitly"?) It takes into consideration not only the "center"—as has been done *exclusively* by Modern philosophy from Descartes to Habermas, thus resulting in a *partial*, provincial, regional view of the historical ethical event—*but also* its "periphery," and with this one, obtains a *planetary* vision of the human experience. This historical question is not informative or anecdotal. It has a philosophical sense that is *strictu sensu*! I have already treated the theme in another work.[30] In that work, I showed Colon's existential impossibility, a Renaissance Genoese, of convincing himself that what he had discovered was not India. He navigated, according to his own imagination, close to the coasts of the fourth Asiatic peninsula (which Heinrich Hammer had already drawn cartographically in Rome in 1489),[31] always close to the "Sinus Magnus" (the great gulf of the Greeks, territorial sea of the Chinese) when he traversed the Caribbean. Colon died in 1506 without having superseded the horizon of the third stage of the "interregional system."[32] He was not able to subjectively supersede the "interregional system"—with a history of forty-five hundred years of transformations, beginning with Egypt and Mesopotamia—and thus open himself to the new stage of the "world-system." The first one who suspected a *new* (the *last* new) continent was Amerigo Vespucci, in 1503, and therefore, he was existentially and subjectively the first "modern," the first to unfold the horizon of the "Asian-Afro-Mediterranean system" as "world-system," which incorporated for the first time Amerindia.[33] This revolution in the *Weltanschauung*, of the cultural, scientific, religious, technological, political, ecological and economic horizon, is the *origin* of Modernity, seen from the perspective of a "world paradigm" and not solely from an eurocentric perspective. In the "world-system," the accumulation in the "center" is for the first time accumulation in a world scale.[34] Within the new system, everything changes qualitatively or radically. The very Medieval European "peripheral subsystem" changes internally as well. The founding event was the discovery of Amerindia in 1492.[35] Spain is ready to become the first modern state;[36] through the discovery, it begins to become the "center" of its first "periphery" (Amerindia), thus organizing the beginning of the slow shifting of the "center" of the older third stage of the "interregional system" (Baghdad of the thirteenth century), which had from peripheral Genoa (but from the western part of the "system") began a process of reconnection—first with Portugal and now with Spain, with Seville to be precise. Genoese, Italian wealth suddenly flows into Seville. The "experience" of the Eastern Renaissance Mediterranean (and through it, of the Muslim world, of India and even China) are thus articulated with the imperial Spain of Carlos V—who reaches to the central Europe of the bankers of Augsburg; to the Flanders of Amberes; and later, to Amsterdam, with Bohemia, Hungary, Austria and Milan, and especially the kingdom of the Two Sicilies[37] of the south of Italy, namely Sicily, Cerdeña, the Balareares, and the numerous islands of the Mediterranean. But because of the economic failure of the political project of the "world-empire," the emperor Carlos V abdicates in 1557: the path is thus left open for the "world-system" of mercantile, industrial, and, today, transnational capitalism.

As an example, let us take a level of analysis amongst the many that may be analyzed—we would not want to be criticized as being a reductive economicist because of the example that we have adopted. It is not coincidence that twenty-five years after the discovery of the silver mines of Potosí in the high Peru and the mines in Zacateca in Mexico (1546)—from which a total of eighteen thousand tons of silver arrived to Spain between the years of 1503 and 1660[38]—and thanks to the first shipments of this precious metal, Spain was able to pay, among the many campaigns of the Empire, the great armada that defeated the Turks in 1571 in Lepanto. This lead to the dominion of the Mediterranean as a connection with the "center" of the older stage of the system. However, the Mediterranean had died as the road of the "center" toward the "periphery" on the West because now the Atlantic was structuring itself as the "center" of the new "world-system"![39]

Wallerstein writes:

> Bullion was desired as a preciosity, for consumption in Europe and even more for trade with Asia, but it was also a necessity for the expansion of the European economy.[40]

I have read, amongst the many unpublished letters of the General Indian Archive of Seville, the following text of July 1, 1550, signed in Bolivia by Domingo de Santo Tomás:

> It was four years ago, to conclude the perdition of this land, that a mouth of hell[41] was discovered through which every year a great many people are immolated, which the greed of the Spaniards sacrifice to their god that is gold,[42] and it is a mine of silver which is named Potosí.[43]

The rest is well known. The Spanish colony in Flanders will replace Spain as a hegemonic power in the "center" of the recently established "world-system"—that is, it liberates itself from Spain in 1610. Seville, the first modern port (in relations with Amberes), after more than a century of splendor, will cede its place to Amsterdam[44] (the city where Descartes will write *Le Discours de la Méthode* in 1636 and where Spinoza will live);[45] it will cede naval, fishing, and crafts power, where the agricultural export flows; it will cede the great expertise in all the branches of production; it will cede to a city that will, among many aspects, bankrupt Venice.[46] After more than a century, Modernity already showed in this city a metropolis with its definitive physiognomy: its port; the channels, which as commercial ways reached to the houses of the bourgeoisie; the merchants who used their fourth and fifth floor as cellars, from which boats were directly loaded with cranes; a thousand details of a capitalist metropolis.[47] From 1689 on, England will challenge and eventually end up imposing itself over Holland's hegemony, of which it will always have to share with France, at least until 1763.[48]

Amerindia, meanwhile, constitutes the fundamental structure of the first modernity. From 1492 to 1500, about fifty thousand square kilometers are colonized in the Caribbean and on firm land: from Venezuela to Panama.[49] In 1515, this number will reach three hundred thousand square kilometers with about three million dominated Amerindians. Until 1550, more than two million square kilometers, which is an area greater than the whole of Europe of the "center," and up to more than twenty-five million (a low figure) indigenous peoples[50] are also colonized, many of which are integrated to a system of work that produces value (in Marx's strict sense) for the Europe of the "center"—that is, in the "encomienda," "mita," haciendas, and so on. We would have to add, from 1520 onward, the plantation slaves of African provenance, about fourteen million until the final stage of slavery in the nineteenth century, including Brazil, Cuba and the United States. This enormous space and population will give to Europe, "center" of the "world-system," the *definitive comparative advantage* with respect to the Muslim, Indian, and Chinese worlds. It is for this reason that in the sixteenth century:

> The periphery (Eastern Europe and Hispanic America) used forced labor (slavery and coerced cash-crop labor [of the Amerindian]). The core, as we shall see, increasingly used free labor.[51]

For the goals of this philosophical work, it is of interest to indicate solely that with the birth of the "world-system," the *"peripheral* social formations"[52] were also born:

> The form of *peripheral* formation will depend, finally, at the same time on the nature of the accumulated pre-capitalist formations and the forms of external aggression.[53]

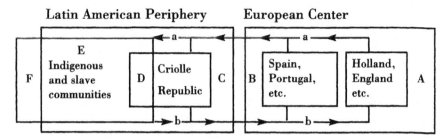

Figure 3.1.   An Example of the Center-Periphery Structure in the "Center" and Colonial "Periphery" of the XVIII Century
Arrow a: domination and export of manufactured goods. Arrow b: transfer of value and exploitation of labor. A: power of the "center." B: semiperipheral nations. C: peripheral formations. D: exploitation of Amerindian labor or slaves. E: indigenous communities. F: ethnic communities who retained a certain exteriority to the "world-system."[56]

These will be, at the end of the twentieth century, the Latin-American peripheral formations,[54] those of the African bantu, the Muslim world, India, the Asian Southeast,[55] and China, to which one must also add part of Eastern Europe before the fall of existing socialism.

MODERNITY AS "MANAGEMENT" OF THE PLANETARY "CENTRALITY" AND ITS CONTEMPORARY CRISIS

We have thus arrived at the central thesis of this chapter. If Modernity were, and this is our hypothesis, fruit of the "management" of the "centrality" of the first "world-system," we would now have to reflect on what this scenario implies.

First, one must be conscious that there are at least, in its origin, two Modernities. In the first place, Hispanic, humanist, Renaissance Modernity are still linked to the old interregional system of Mediterranean and Muslim Christianity.[57] In this, the "management" of the new system will be conceived from out of the older paradigm of the old interregional system. That is, Spain "manages" "centrality" as domination through the hegemony of an integral culture, a language, a religion (and thus, the evangelization process that Amerindia will suffer); it also dominates via military occupation, bureaucratic–political organization, economic expropriation, demographic presence (with hundreds of thousand of Spaniard or Portuguese who will forever inhabit Amerindia), ecological transformation (through the modification of the fauna and flora), and so on. This is the matter of the "Empire–World" project, which, as Wallerstein notes, failed with Carlos V.[58]

In the second place, the Modernity of Anglo-Germanic Europe begins with the Amsterdam of Flanders, and it frequently passes as the *only* Modernity—that is, according to the interpretation of Sombart, Weber, Habermas, or even the postmoderns, who will produce a "reductionist fallacy" that occludes the meaning of Modernity and, thus, the sense of its contemporary crisis. To be able to "manage" the immense "world-system"—which suddenly opens itself to the small Holland[59] and which, from being a Spanish colony, now places itself as the "center" of the "world-system"—this second Modernity must accomplish or increase its efficacy through *simplification*. It is necessary to carry out an abstraction that favors the *quantum* to the detriment of *qualitas;* that *leaves out* many valid variables, such as cultural, anthropological, ethical, political, and religious (aspects that are valuable even for the European of the sixteenth century); and that will not allow an adequate "factual,"[60] or technologically possible, "management" of the "world-system."[61] This *simplification* of complexity[62] encompasses the totality of the "lifeworld" (*Lebenswelt);* of the relationship with nature, the new technological and ecological positions that are no longer teleological; of subjectivity itself, the new self-understanding of subjectivity; of community, the new intersubjective and political relation; thus, as synthesis, a new economic attitude will establish itself (practico-productive).

The first Hispanic Renaissance and humanist Modernity produced a theoretical, or philosophical, reflection of the highest importance, and it has gone unnoticed to the so-called modern philosophy, which is only the philosophy of the "second Modernity." The theoretical–philosophical thought of the sixteenth century has contemporary relevance because it is the first, and only, that lived and expressed the original experience during the period of the constitution of the first "world-system." Thus, out of the theoretical "recourses" that were available (i.e., the scholastic–Muslim–Christian and Renaissance philosophy), the central philosophical ethical question that obtained was the following: "What right has the European to occupy, dominate, and 'manage' the recently discovered, militarly conquered, and currently-being-colonized cultures?" From the seventeenth century on, the "second Modernity" did not have to question the conscience (*Gewissen)* with these questions that had already been answered in fact: From Amsterdam, London, or Paris, in the seventeenth century and through the eighteenth century onward, "Eurocentrism" (superideology that will establish the valid legitimacy, without falsification, of the domination of the "world-system") will *no longer* be questioned until the end of the twentieth century. At that time, it will then be questioned by liberation philosophy as well as other movements.

In another work we have touched on this question.[63] Today we will only remind ourselves of the theme in general. Bartolomé de las Casas demonstrates in his numerous works—using an extraordinary bibliographical apparatus, grounding rationally and carefully his arguments—that the constitution of the "world-system" as European expansion in Amerindia (anticipation of the expansion in Africa and Asia) does not have any right; it is an unjust violence, and it cannot have any ethical validity:

> The common ways mainly employed by the Spaniards who call themselves Christian and who have gone there to extirpate those pitiful nations and wipe them off the earth is by unjustly waging cruel and bloody wars. Then, when they have slain all those who fought for their lives or to escape the tortures they would have to endure, that is to say, when they slain all the native rulers and young men (since the Spaniards usually spare only the women and children, who are subjected to the hardest and bitterest servitude ever suffered by man or beast), they enslave any survivors. . . . Their reason for killing and destroying such an infinite number of souls is that the Christians have an ultimate aim, which is to acquire gold, and to swell themselves with riches in a very brief time and thus rise to a high estate disproportionate to their merits. It should be kept in mind that their insatiable greed and ambition, the greatest ever seen in the world, is the cause of their villanies.[64]

Posteriorly, philosophy will no longer formulate this problematic, which showed itself unavoidable at the origin of the establishment of the "world-system." For the ethics of liberation, this question is today still fundamental.

In the sixteenth century, then, the "world-system" in Seville is established, as are philosophy questions from out of the old philosophical paradigm, including the praxis of domination; but it does not reach the formulation of the *new paradigm*. However, the origin of the new paradigm ought not to be confused with the origin of Modernity. Modernity begins more than a century before (1492) the moment in which the paradigm, adequate to its very own new experience is formalized—that is, to speak again with Kuhn. If we note the dates of the formulation of the new modern paradigm, we can conclude that it takes place in the first half of the seventeenth century.[65] This new paradigm corresponds to the exigencies of *efficacy*, technological "factibility," or governmentality of the "management" of an enormous "world-system" in expansion; it is the expression of a necessary process of *simplification* through "rationalization" of the lifeworld, of the subsystems (economic, political, cultural, religious, etc.). "Rationalization," as indicated by Werner Sombart,[66] Ernst Troeltsch,[67] or Max Weber,[68] is *effect* and not cause. On the other hand, to *manage* the "world-system," the effects of that *simplifying rationalization* are perhaps more profound and negative than Habermas or the postmoderns imagine.[69]

The corporeal Muslim–Medieval subjectivity is *simplified*: subjectivity is postulated as an *ego*, an I, about which Descartes writes:

> Accordingly this 'I'—that is, the soul by which I am what I am—is *entirely* distinct from the body, and indeed is easier to know than the body, and would not fail to be whatever it is, even if the body did not exist.[70]

The body is a mere machine, *res extensa*, entirely foreign to the soul.[71] Kant himself writes:

> The human soul should be seen as being linked in the present life to two worlds at the same time: of these worlds, inasmuch as it forms with the body a personal unity, it feels but only the material world; on the contrary, as a member of the world of the spirit [mind] *(als ein Glied der Geisterwelt)* [without body] it receives and propagates the pure influences of immaterial natures.[72]

This dualism—which Kant will apply to his ethics, inasmuch as the "maxims" ought not to have any empirical or "pathological" motives—is posteriorly articulated through the negation of practical intelligence, which is replaced by instrumental reason, the one that will deal with technical, technological "management" (i.e., ethics disappears before a *more geometric* intelligence) in the *Critique of Judgment*. It is here that the conservative tradition (such as that of Heidegger) continues to perceive the *simplifying* suppression of the organic complexity of life, which is now replaced by a technique of the "will to power" (via critiques elaborated by Nietzsche and Foucault). Galileo, with all the naive enthusiasm of a great discovery, writes:

> Philosophy is written in this grand book, the universe, which stands continually open to our gaze. But the book cannot be understood unless one first learns to comprehend the language and read the letters in which it is composed. It is written in the *language of mathematics*, and its characters are triangles, circles and other geometric figures, without it is humanly impossible to understand a single word of it; without these, one wanders about in a dark labyrinth.[73]

Heidegger already said that the "*mathematical* position"[74] before entities is to have them already know "ready-to-hand" (e.g., in the axioms of science) and to approach them only in order to use them. One does not "learn" a weapon, for instance; instead, one learns to make "use" of it, because one already knows what it is:

> The *mathemata* are the things insofar as we take cognizance of them as what we already know them to be in advance, the body as the bodily, the plant-like of the plant, the animal-like of the animal, the thingness of the thing, and so on.[75]

Examples of the diverse moments that are negated by the indicated *simplification* include the "rationalization" of political life (bureaucratization), the capitalist enterprise (administration), the daily life (Calvinist asceticism or Puritanism), the decorporalization of subjectivity (with its alienating effects on living labor, as criticized by Marx, as well as on its drives, as analyzed by Freud), the nonethicalness of every economic or political gestation (understood only as technical engineering, e.g.), the suppression of practical–communicative reason (which is now replaced by instrumental reason), and the solipsistic individuality that negates the community. They are all apparently necessary for the "management" of the "centrality" of a "world-system" that Europe found itself in the need of perpetually carrying out. Capitalism, liberalism, dualism (without valorizing corporeality), and so on are *effects* of the management of this function that corresponded to Europe as "center" of the "world-system." They are effects constituted through mediations in systems that end up totalizing themselves. Capitalism, mediation of exploitation and accumulation (effect of the "world-system"), is later on transformed into an *independent system* that, from out of its own self-referential and autopoietic logic, can destroy Europe and its periphery, and even the entire planet. And this is what Weber observes, but he does so reductively. That is to say, Weber notes part of the phenomenon but not the horizon of the "world-system." In fact, the formal procedure of *simplification* (that turn *manageable* the "world-system") produces formal rationalized subsystems that later on do not have internal standards of self-regulation within its own limits of Modernity and that could only be redirected at the service of humanity. It is in this moment that there emerge critiques from within the "center" (and from out of the "periphery," such as is mine) against Modernity itself. Now one attributes to *ratio* all culpable causality (as object 'understanding,' which is set through disintegration) from Nietzsche to Heidegger, or with the postmoderns; this culpability will be traced back as far as Socrates (Nietzsche) or even Parmenides himself (Heidegger). In fact, the modern *simplifications*—the dualism of an *ego*-alma without a body, the teleological instrumental reason, the racism of the superiority of one's own culture, and so on—have many similarities with the *simplification* that Greek slavery produced in the second interregional system. The Greek *Weltanschauung* was advantageous to the Modern man; however, not without complicity does the Modern man resuscitate the Greeks, as was done through the German romantics.[76] The subsumptive superseding *(Aufhebung)* of Modernity will mean the critical consideration of *all* these simplifying reductions produced since its origin—and not only a few ones, like Habermas imagines. The most important of said reductions, next to the one of the solipsistic subjectivity (i.e., without community), is the negation of the corporeality of said subjectivity, to which are related the critiques of Modernity by Marx, Nietzsche, Freud, Foucault, Levinas, as well as the ethics of liberation, as we will see throughout the length of this work.

Because of all of this, the concept that one has of Modernity determines, as is evident, the pretention to its realization, such as is Habermas, or the type of critiques one may formulate against it, such as that of the postmoderns. In general, every debate between rationalists and postmoderns does not overcome the Eurocentric horizon. The crisis of Modernity (already noted, as we have remarked frequently, by Nietzsche and Heidegger) refers to internal aspects of Europe. The "peripheral world" would appear to be a passive spectator of a thematic that does not touch it, because it is a "barbarian," a "premodern," or it may simply still be in need of being "modernized." In other words, the Eurocentric view reflects on the problem of the crisis of Modernity solely with the European–North American moments (or even now Japanese), but it minimizes the periphery. To break through this "reductivist fallacy" is not easy. We will attempt to "indicate" the path toward its surmounting.

If Modernity begins at the end of the fifteenth century, with a Renaissance premodern process and if, from there, a transition is made to the properly Modern in Spain, then Amerindia forms part of "Modernity" since the moment of the conquest and colonization (the mestizo world in Latin America is the only one that has as a much age as Modernity),[77] since it was the first "barbarian" that Modernity needed in its definition. If Modernity enters into crisis at the end of the twentieth century, after five centuries of development, it is not a matter only of the moments detected by Weber and Habermas, or by Lyotard or Welsch,[78] but we will have to add the very ones of a "planetary" description of the phenomenon of Modernity.

To conclude, if we situate ourselves, instead, within the planetary horizon, one can distinguish at least the following positions in the face of the formulated problematic. In the first place, the "substantialist"–developmentalist[79] (quasi-metaphysical) position on the one hand conceptualizes Modernity as an *exclusively European* phenomenon that had *expanded from the seventeenth century on* throughout all the "backward" cultures (i.e., the Eurocentric position in the "center," or the one modernizing in the "periphery"). Modernity is therefore a phenomena that must be concluded. Some of the ones who assume this first position (e.g., Habermas and Apel), defenders of reason, do so critically, since they think that European superiority is not material, but formal—thanks to a new structure of critical questions.[80] However, the conservative "nihilist" position negates to Modernity's positive qualities (of a Nietzsche or Heidegger, for instance) and thus proposes practically an annihilation without exit. The postmoderns take this second position in their frontal attack to "reason" *as such*, with differences in case of Levinas[81]— although, paradoxically, they also defend parts of the first position from the perspective of a developmentalist Eurocentrism.[82] The postmodern philosophers are admirers of postmodern art, of the *Media*. Although they affirm theoretically *difference*, they do not reflect on the origins of these systems that are fruit of a rationalization proper to the "management" of the European "centrality" in the "world-system," before which they are profoundly uncritical. Because of this position, they do not have possibilities of attempting to contribute valid alternatives (cultural, economic, political, etc.) for the peripheral nations, for the peoples, or for the great majorities who are dominated by the center and/or the periphery.

In second place, we defend another position, from out of the periphery, one that considers the process of Modernity as the already indicated rational "management" of the "world-system." This position intends to recuperate the redeemable of Modernity and to negate the domination and exclusion in the "world-system." It is then a project of liberation of a periphery negated from the very beginning of Modernity. The problem is not the mere superseding of instrumental reason (as is for Habermas) or of the reason of *terror* of the postmoderns; instead, it is the question of the overcoming of the "world-system" itself, such as it has developed until today for the last five hundred years. The problem is exhaustion of a civilizing system that has come to its end.[83] What presuppose the liberation of diverse types of oppressed and/or excluded populations are the overcoming of *cynical-managerial reason* (planetary administrative) of capitalism (as economic system), of liberalism (as political system), of Eurocentrism (as ideology), of machismo (in erotics), of the reign of the white race (in racism), of the destruction of nature (in ecology), and so on. It is in this sense that the ethics of liberation defines itself as trans-Modern (since the postmoderns are still Eurocentric). The end of the present stage of civilization shows itself some limits of the "system of 500 years"—as Noam Chomsky[84] calls it.

These limits are, in first place, the ecological destruction of the planet. From the very moment of its inception, Modernity has constituted nature as an "exploitable" object, with the increase in the rate of profit of capital[85] as its goal:

> For the first time, nature becomes purely an object for humankind, purely a matter of utility; ceases to be recognized as a power for itself.[86]

Once the earth is seen constituted as an "exploitable object" in favor of *quantum* (of capital) that can defeat all limits, all boundaries, there by manifesting the "great civilizing influence of capital," it now reaches finally its unsurmountable limit, where itself is its own limit, the impassable barrier for ethical-human progress, and we have arrived to this moment:

The universality towards which it irresistibly strives encounters barriers in its own nature, which will, at a certain state of its development, allow it to be recognized as being itself the greatest barrier to this tendency, and hence will drive towards its own suspension.[87]

Given that nature is for Modernity only a medium of production, it runs out its fate of being consumed and destroyed; in addition, it accumulates geometrically upon the Earth its debris, until it jeopardizes the reproduction or survival of life itself. Life is the absolute condition of capital; its destruction destroys capital. We have now arrived at this state of affairs. The "system of 500 years" (Modernity or Capitalism) confronts its first absolute limit: the death of life in its totality through the indiscriminate use of an anti-ecological technology constituted progressively through the sole criteria of the *quantitative* "management" of the "world-system" in Modernity: the increase in the rate of profit. But capital cannot limit itself. There thus comes about the utmost danger for humanity.

The second limit of Modernity is the destruction of humanity itself. "Living labor" is the other essential mediation of capital as such; the human subject is the only one that can "create" new value (i.e., surplus value, profit). Capital that defeats all barriers requires incrementally more absolute time of work: When it cannot supersede this limit, then it augments productivity through technology; but said increase decreases the importance of human labor. It is thus that there is *superfluous humanity* (i.e., displaced humanity). The unemployed does not earn a salary or any money, but money is the only mediation in the market through which one can acquire commodities to satisfy needs. In any event, work that is not employable by capital therefore increases (i.e., there is an increase in unemployment). It is thus the proportion of needing subjects who are not solvent, clients, consumers, or buyers—as much in the periphery as in the center.[88] It is poverty, poverty as the absolute limit of capital. Today we know how misery grows in the entire planet. It is a matter of a "law of Modernity":

Accumulation of wealth at one pole is, therefore, at the same time accumulation of misery, the torment of labour, slavery, ignorance, brutalization and moral degradation at the opposite pole. . . .[89]

The modern "world-system" cannot overcome this essential contradiction. The ethics of liberation reflects philosophically from out of this planetary horizon of the "world-system;" from out of this double limit configures a terminal crisis of a civilizing process: The ecological destruction of the planet and the extinguishing in misery and hunger of the great majority of humanity. Before these two co-implicating phenomena of such planetary magnitude intersect, the project of many philosophical schools would seem

naive, even ridiculous, irresponsible, irrelevant, cynical, and yet even com-
plicitous (as much in the center, but even worse yet in the periphery, in
Latin America, Africa, and Asia); yet these schools are closed in their "ivory
towers" of sterile Eurocentric academicism. Referring to the opulent counties of late capitalism, Marcuse had already written in 1968:

> . . . why do we need liberation from such a society if it is capable—perhaps in
> the distant future, but apparently capable—of conquering poverty to a greater
> degree than ever before, or reducing the toil of labour and the time of labour,
> and of raising the standard of living? If the price for all goods delivered, the
> price for this comfortable servitude, for all these achievements, is exacted from
> people far away from the metropolis and far way from its affluence? If the af-
> fluent society itself hardly notices what it is doing, how it is spreading terror
> and enslavement, how it is fighting liberation in all corners of the globe?[90]

The third limit of Modernity is the impossibility of the subsumption of
the populations, economies, nations, and cultures that it has been attack-
ing since its origin and since it has excluded from its horizon and thus cor-
nered into poverty. This is the whole theme of the exclusion of African,
Asian, Latin-American Alterity and their indomitable will to survive. I
will return to the theme, but for now I want to indicate that the globaliz-
ing "world-system" reaches a limit where the exteriority of the Alterity of
the Other, the locus of "resistance," and from whose analectical affirmation there departs the process of the negation of negation of liberation.
That is, liberation is launched from the Alterity of the Other, whose negation ("no" to oppression) rejects the negation of oppression (exploitation)—a formulation based on Marxian dialectics.

REFERENCES

Abu-Lughod, Janet. *Before European Hegemony: The World System A.D. 1250–1350.*
    New York: Oxford University Press, 1989.
Amin, S. *El desarrollo desigual. Ensayo sobre las formaciones sociales del capitalismo per-
    iférico.* Barcelona: Fontanella, 1974.
Amin, Samir. *L'accumulation à l'échelle mondiale.* Paris: Anthropos, 1970.
Bary, William Th. de. *Self and Society in Ming Thought.* New York: Columbia Uni-
    versity Press, 1970.
Bernal, Martin. *Black Athena. The Afroasiatic Roots of Classical Civilization.* Vol. 1.
    New Brunswick, N.J.: Rutgers University Press, 1989.
Bertaux, Pierre. *Africa: Desde la prehistoria hasta los Estados actuales.* Madrid: Siglo
    XXI, 1972.
Blaut, J. M., ed. *1492. The Debate on Colonialism, Eurocentrism and History.* Trenton,
    N.J.: Africa World Press, 1992.

Braudel, F. "Monnaies et civilisation: de l'or du Soudan à l'argent d'Amérique." *Annales ESC* 1, no. 1 (1946): 12–38.

Brenner, Robert. "Das Weltsystem. Theoretische und Historische Perspektiven." In *Perspektiven des Weltsystems*, edited by J. Blaschke, 80–111. Frankfurt: Campus Verlag, 1983.

Cardoso. *Historia económica de América Latina*, edited by Ciro F. S. Cardoso-Héctor-Brignoli. Vols. 1, 2. Barcelona: Crítica, 1979.

Casas, Bartolomé de las. *Obras escogidas de Fray Bartolomé de las Casas.* Vol. 1 (1957)–vol. 5 (1958). Madrid: Biblioteca de Autores Españoles, 1957.

Chaunu, P. *Conquête et exploitation des nouveaux mondes (XVIe. siècle).* Paris: PUF, 1969.

Chaunu, Pierre. *Séville et l'Atlantique (1504–1650).* Vol. 1 (1955)–vol. 8 (1959). Paris: SEVPEN, 1955.

Chaudhuri, K. N. *Trade and Civilisation in the Indian Ocean: An Economic History from the Rise of Islam to 1750.* Cambridge: Cambridge University Press, 1985.

Chomsky, N. *Year 501: The Conquest Continues.* Boston: South End Press, 1993.

Derrida, J. *De la Grammatologie.* Paris: Minuit, 1967.

———. *L'Ecriture et la Différence.* Paris: Seuil, 1967.

Descartes, René. *Oeuvres et Lettres de Descartes.* La Pléiade Series. Paris: Gallimard, 1953.

———. *The Philosophical Works of Descartes.* Vol. 1, *Discourse on the Method*, part 4, 127. Cambridge, U.K.: Cambridge University Press, 1985.

Drake, Stillman. *Discoveries and Opinions of Galileo.* New York: Doubleday, Anchor Books, 1957.

Dussel, E. *1492: El encubrimiento del Otro. Hacia el origen del mito de la modernidad.* Madrid: Nueva Utopía, 1993.

———. *El dualismo en la antropología de la Cristiandad.* Buenos Aires: Editorial Guadalupe, 1974.

———. "General." In *Historia General de la Iglesia en América Latina*, vol. 1, 1–724. Salamanca, Spain: Sígueme, 1983.

———. *Método para una Filosofía de la Liberación.* Salamanca, Spain: Sígueme, 1974.

———. *Para una de-strucción de la historia de la ética.* Mendoza, Argentina: Ser y Tiempo, 1973.

———. *Philosophy of Liberation.* Maryknoll, N.Y.: Orbis, 1985.

Frank, A. G. "A Theoretical Introduction to 5,000 years of World System History." *Review* (Binghamton), 13, no. 2 (1990): 155–248.

Galilei, Galileo. *Il Saggiatore.* Vol. 6 of *Le opere di Galileo Galilei.* Firenze, Italy: Tip. di G. Barbèra, 1933.

Godinho, V. M. "Création et dynamisme économique du monde atlantique (1420–1670)." *Annales ESC* 5, no. 1 (enero–marzo, 1950): 10–30.

Habermas, J. *Der philosophische Diskurs der Moderne.* Frankfurt: Suhrkamp, 1988.

———. *Theorie des kommunikativen Handelns.* Vols. 1, 2. Frankfurt: Suhrkamp, 1981.

Hall, A. R. *The Scientific Revolution.* London: Longman, 1983.

Hammarström, D. Ingrid. "The Price Revolution of the Sixteenth Century." *Scandinavian Economic History* 5, no. 1 (1957): 118–54.

Hegel, G.W.F. *Hegel Werke in zwanzig Bänden. Theorie Werkausgabe.* Vols. 1 (1971)–20 (1979). Frankfurt: Suhrkamp, 1971.

———. *The Philosophy of History*, translated by J. Sibree, 341. New York: Dover Publications, 1956.

Heidegger, Martin. *Die Frage nach dem Ding.* Tübingen, Germany: Niemeyer, 1963.

———. *What Is a Thing?*, translated by W. B. Barton et al., 73. Chicago: Henry Regnery Company, 1967.

Hinkelammert, F. *Crítica a la razón utópica.* San José de Costa Rica: CEI, 1984.

———. *Dialéctica del desarrollo desigual. El caso latinoamericano.* Santiago, Chile: Centro de Estudios de la Realidad Nacional, 1970.

———. *Ideologías del desarrollo y dialéctica de la historia.* Santiago de Chile: Ediciones Nueva Universidad, 1970.

Hodgson, Marshall. *The Venture of Islam.* Vols. 1–3. Chicago: University of Chicago Press, 1974.

Human Development Report 1992. Development Programme, United Nations. New York: Oxford University Press, 1992.

Jameson, Fredrick. *Postmodernism or the Cultural Logic of Late Capitalism.* Durham, N.C.: University Duke Press, 1991.

Kant, Immanuel. *Kant Werke.* Vols. 1–10. Darmstadt, Germany: Wissenschaftliche Buchgesellschaft, 1968.

Kennedy, Paul. *The Rise and Fall of the Great Powers.* New York: Random House, 1987.

Kuhn, Thomas. *The Structure of Scientific Revolutions.* Chicago: University of Chicago Press, 1962.

Lattimore, Owen. *Inner Asian Frontiers of China.* Boston: Beacon Press, 1962.

Luhmann, Niklas. *Soziale Systeme: Grundriss einer algemeinen Theorie.* Frankfurt: Suhrkamp, 1988.

Lyotard, Jean-François. *La condition postmoderne.* Paris: Minuit, 1979.

McNeil, William. *The Rise of the West.* Chicago: University of Chicago Press, 1964.

Mann, Michael. *The Sources of Social Power. A History of Power from the Beginning to A.D. 1760.* Vol. 1. Cambridge: Cambridge University Press, 1986.

Marcuse, Herbert. "Liberación respecto a la sociedad opulenta." In *The Dialectics of Liberation,* edited by David Cooper. London: Penguin Books, 1968.

———. "Liberation from the Affluent Society." In *To Free a Generation: The Dialectics of Liberation,* edited by David Cooper, 181. New York: Collier Books, 1967.

Marquard, Odo. *Abschied vom Prinzipiellen.* Stuttgart: Reclam, 1981.

Marx, K. *Grundrisse,* translated by Martin Nicolaus, 410. New York: Penguin Books, 1973.

———. *Grundrisse der Kritik der politischen Oekonomie* (1857). Berlin: Dietz, 1974.

———. *Das Kapital,* vol. 1 (1867) *MEGA* 2, no. 6 (1987).

McNeil, William. *The Rise of the West.* Chicago: University of Chicago Press, 1964.

Modelski, George. *Long Cycles in World Politics.* London: Macmillan Press, 1987.

Needham, J. "Commentary on Lynn White *What Accelerated Technological Change in the Western Middle Ages?*" in *Scientific Change,* edited by A. C. Crombie, 117–53. New York: Basic Books, 1963.

Needham, Joseph. "The Chinese Contributions to Vessel Control." *Scientia* 96, no. 98 (1961): abril, 123–28; mayo, 163–68.

O'Gorman, Edmundo. *La invención de América*. México: FCE, 1957.

Paz, Octavio. *El laberinto de la soledad*. México: Cuadernos Americanos, 1950.

Rossabi, Morris. *China among Equals: The Middle Kingdom and Its Neighbors, 10–14th Centuries*. Berkeley: University of California Press, 1982.

Rorty, Richard. *Philosophy and the Mirror of Nature*. Princeton, N.J.: Princeton University Press, 1979.

Sombart, W. *Der Bourgeois*. München: Duncker, 1920.

Sombart, Werner. *Der moderne Kapitalismus*. Leipzig, Germany: Duncker, 1902.

Stavarianos, L. S. *The World to 1500: A Global History*. Englewood Cliffs, N.J.: Prentice Hall, 1970.

Taviani, Paolo Emilio. *Cristoforo Colombo: La genesi della scoperta*. Novara, Italy: Istituto Geografico de Agostini, 1982.

Thompson, William. *On Global War: Historical-Structural Approches to World Politics*. Columbia: University of South Carolina Press, 1989.

Tilly, Charles. *Big Structures, Large Processes*. New York: Russell Sage Foundation, 1984.

Troeltsch, Ernst. *Die Soziallehren der christlichen Kirchen und Gruppen*. Tübingen, Germany: Mohr, 1923.

Vattimo, Gianni. *La fine della Modernità*. Milán: Garzanti, 1985.

Wallerstein, I. *The Politics for the World-Economy*. Cambridge: Cambridge University Press, 1984.

Wallerstein, Immanuel. *The Modern World-System*. Vols. 1 (1974)–3 (1989). New York: Academic Press, 1974.

Weber, Max. *The Protestant Ethic and the Spirit of Capitalism*, translated by Talcott Parsons. New York: Charles Scribner's Sons, 1958.

Welsch, Wolfgang. *Unseres postmoderne Moderne*. Berlin: Akademie V., 1993.

Wolf, Eric. *Europe and the People without History*. Berkeley: University of California Press, 1982.

Zunzunegi, J. "Los orígenes de las misiones en las Islas Canarias." *Revista Española de Teología*, 1 (1941): 364–70.

NOTES

This selection was translated by Eduardo Mendieta.

1. As a "substance" that is invented in Europe and that subsequently "expands" throughout the entire world. This is a metaphysical–substantialist and "diffusionist" thesis. It contains a "reductionist fallacy."

2. The English translation does not translate the expression Weber uses, "Auf dem Boden," which means "*within* its regional horizon." We want to establish that when we say *in Europe*, what we really mean is the development in Modernity of Europe as the "center" of a "global system," and not as an *independent* system, as if it were "only-from-within itself" and as fruit of a solely *internal* development, as Eurocentrism pretends.

3. This "we" is precisely the Eurocentric Europeans.

4. Max Weber, *The Protestant Ethic and the Spirit of Capitalism*, trans. Talcott Parsons (New York: Charles Scribner's Sons, 1958), 13 (emphasis added). Later on

Weber asks: "Why did not the scientific, the artistic, the political, or the economic development there [China, and India] enter upon that path of *rationalization* which is peculiar to the Occident?" (Weber, *The Protestant Ethic*, 25). In order to argue this, Weber juxtaposes the Babylonians, who did not mathematize astronomy, with the Greeks, who did (but Weber does not know that the Greeks learned it from the Egyptians). He also argues that science emerged in the West, and not in India or China; but he forgets to mention the Muslim world, from whom the Latin West learned Aristotelian "experiential," empirical exactitude (such as the Oxford Franciscans or the Marcilios de Padua, etc.). Every Hellenistic, or Eurocentric argument, such as Weber's, can be falsified if we take 1492 as the ultimate date of comparison between the supposed superiority of the West and other cultures.

5. Hegel, *The Philosophy of History*.

6. Following Hegel *(The Philosophy of History)*, Habermas, *Der philosophische*, 27.

7. The "world-system," or planetary system of the fourth stage of the same interregional system of the Asiatic-African-Mediterranean continent, but now (correcting Frank's conceptualization) factically "planetary." See Frank, 1990. On the "world-system" problematic see: Abu-Lughod, *Before European Hegemony*; Brenner, "Das Weltsystem"; Hodgson, *The Venture of Islam*; Kennedy, *The Rise and Fall*; McNeill, *The Rise of the West*; Modelski, *Long Cycles in World Politics*; Mann, *The Sources of Social Power*; Stavarianos, *The World to 1500*; Thompson, *On Global War*; Tilly, *Big Structures, Large Processes*; Wallerstein, *The Modern World-System* and *The Politics for the World-Economy*.

8. On this point, as I already mentioned, I am not in agreement with Frank on calling "world-system" the prior moments of the system, which I therefore call them "interregional systems."

9. Wallerstein, *The Modern World-System*, vol. 1, chap. 6.

10. Wallerstein, *The Modern World-System*, vol. 2, chaps. 4–5.

11. Wallerstein, *The Modern World-System*, vol. 3, chap. 3.

12. See Lattimore, *Inner Asian Frontiers of China*; Rossabi, *China among Equals*. For a description of the situation of the world in 1400, see Wolf, *Europe and the People without History*, 24 ff.

13. I have been to Masamba, and I have seen in the museum of this city, which is a port of Kenya, Chinese porcelain, as well as luxurious watches and other objects of similar origin.

14. There are other reasons for this nonexternal expansion: the existence of "space" in the neighboring territories to the empire, which took all its power in order to "conquer the South" through the cultivation of rice and its defense from the barbarian "North." See Wallerstein, *The Modern World-System*, vol. 1, 80 ff., which has many good arguments against Weber's Eurocentrisms.

15. For example, Joseph Needham, "The Chinese Contributions" and "Commentary on Lynn White." All of these with respect to the control of ships, which the Chinese already dominated since the first century after Christ. The Chinese use of the compass, paper, gunpowder, and other discoveries is well known.

16. Perhaps the only disadvantage was the Portugese caravel (invented in 1441), used to navigate the Atlantic (it was not needed in the Indian sea), and the cannon. This last one, although spectacular, outside naval wars never had any real effect in Asia until the nineteenth century.

17. The first bureacracy (as the Weberian high stage of political rationalization) is the state Mandarin structure of political exercise. The Mandarin are not nobles, nor warriors, nor aristocratic or commercial plutocracy; they are *strictly* a bureacratic elite whose exams are *exclusively* based in the dominion of culture and the laws of the Chinese empire.

18. William de Bary indicates that the individualism of Wang Yang-Ming, in the fifteenth century, which expressed the ideology of the bureacratic class, was as advanced as that of the Renaissance (Bary, *Self and Society in Ming Thought*).

19. Through many examples, Thomas Kuhn (Kuhn, *The Structure of Scientific Revolutions*) situates the modern scientific revolution—that is, the fruit of the expression of the new paradigm—practically with Newton (seventeenth century). He does not study with care the impact that events such as the discovery of America, the roundness of the earth (empirically proved since 1520), and so on, could have had on the science, the "scientific community," of the sixteenth century, since the structuration of the first "world-system."

20. Needham, "Commentary on Lynn White," 139.

21. A. R. Hall places the scientific revolution beginning with the 1500s (see Hall, *The Scientific Revolution*).

22. Pierre Chaunu. *Séville et l'Atlantique*, vol. 8, part 1, 50.

23. *Factically*, Colon will be the first Modern, but not *existentially* since his *interpretation of the world* remained always that of a Renaissance Genoese: a member of a peripheral Italy of the third "interregional system." See Taviani, *Cristoforo Colombo*; O'Gorman, *La invención de América*.

24. See Zunzunegui, "Los orígenes de las misiones."

25. Russia was not yet integrated as "periphery" in the third stage of the interregional system nor was it in the modern "world-system," except until the eighteenth century with Peter the Great and the founding of St. Petersburg on the Baltic.

26. Portugal, already in 1095, has the rank of empire. In Algarve, 1249, the reconquest concludes with this empire. Enrique the Navigator (1394–1460), as patron, gathers the sciences of cartography, astronomy, and the techniques of navigation and construction of ships, which originated in the Muslim world (since he had contact with the Moroccans) and the Italian Renaissance (via Genoa).

27. Wallerstein, *The Modern World-System*, vol. 1, 49–50.

28. See Chaudhuri, *Trade and Civilisation*.

29. My argument would seem to be the same as Blaut's *(The Debate on Colonialism)*, 28 ff., but in fact, it is different. It is not that Spain was "geographically" closer to Amerindia. No. It is not a question of distances. It is that and much more. It is a matter that Spain had to go through Amerindia not only because it was closer—which in fact took place, especially with respect to Asiatic cultures, although this was not the case with the Turque–Musulman empire that had arrived at Morocco—but because this was the demanded path to the "center" of the "system," a question that is not dealt with by Blaut. Furthermore, it is just the same difference to that of André Gunder Frank (Blaut, *The Debate on Colonialism*, 65–80), because for him, the year 1492 is only a secondary internal change of the same "world system." However, if it is understood that the "interregional system," in its stage prior to 1492, is the "same" system but not yet as a "world" system, then 1492 assumes a greater importance than Frank grants it. Even if the system *is the same*, there exists

a qualitative jump, which, under other aspects, is the original capitalism proper, to which Frank denies importance because of his prior denial of relevance to concepts such as "value," and "surplus value"; therefore, he attributes "capital" to the "wealth" (i.e., use-value, with a virtual possibility of transforming itself into exchange-value, but not capital) accumulated in the first through third stages of the interregional system. This is a grave theoretical question.

30. Dussel, 1993.

31. See Dussel, *1492: El encubrimiento del Otro*, appendix 4, where the map of the fourth Asiatic peninsula is reproduced (after the Arabian, Indian, and Malacan), certainly product of Genoese navigations, where South America is a peninsula attached to the south of China. This explains why the Genovese Colon would hold the opinion that Asia would not be so far from Europe (i.e., South America equals the fourth peninsula of China).

32. This is what I called, philosophically, the "invention" of Amerindia seen as India, in all of its details. Colon, existentially, neither "discovered" nor reached Amerindia. He "invented" something that was nonexistent: India in the place of Amerindia, which prevented him from "discovering" what he had before his own eyes. See Dussel, *1492: El encubrimiento del Otro*, chap. 2.

33. This is the meaning of the title of chapter 2 of my already cited work: "From the *Invention* to the *Discovery* of America."

34. See Amin, *L'accumulation à l'échelle mondiale;* however, this work is not yet developed on the "world-system" hypothesis. It would appear as though the colonial world were a *rear or subsequent* and *outside* space to European Medieval capitalism, which is transformed "in" Europe as modern. My hypothesis is more radical: the fact of the discovery of Amerindia, of its integration as "periphery," is a *simultaneous* and *co-constitutive* fact of the restructuration of Europe *from within* as "center" of the only new "world-system"—that is, only now and *not before*, capitalism (first mercantile and later industrial).

35. We have spoken of "Amerindia" and not of America, because it is a question, during the entire sixteenth century, of a continent inhabited by "Indians." It is wrongly called because of the mirage that the "interregional system" of the third stage still produced in the still being born "world-system." They were called Indians because of India, "center" of the interregional system that was begining to fade. Anglo-Saxon North-America will be born slowly in the seventeenth century, but it will be an event "internal" to a growing Modernity in Amerindia. This is the *originating* "periphery" of Modernity, constitutive of its first definition. It is the "other face" of the very same phenomenon of Modernity.

36. Unified with the marriage of the Catholic King and Queen in 1474, founding inmediately the inquisition (first ideological apparatus of the State for the creation of consensus), with a bureacracy, whose functioning is attested to in the archives of the Indies (Sevilla), where everything was declared, contracted, certified, archived; with a grammar of the Spanish language (the first of a national language in Europe) written by Nebrija, in whose prologue he warns the Catholic kings of the importance for the empire of *only one language*; Cisneros's edition of the Complutensian polyglot Bible (in seven languages), which was superior to Erasmus's because of its scientific care, the number of its languages, and the qual-

ity of the imprint, began in 1502 and published in 1522; with military power that allows it to recuperate Granada in 1492; with the economic wealth of the Jews, Andalucian Muslims, Christians of the reconquest, and the Catalans with their colonies in the Mediterranean, and the Genovese; with the artisans from the antique caliphate of Cordoba . . . and so on. Spain is far from being in the fifteenth century the semiperipheral country that it will become in the second part of the seventeenth century—the only picture of Spain with which the Europe of the center remembers it, like Hegel or Habermas do, for example.

37. The struggle between France and the Spain of Carlos V, which exhausted both monarchies and resulted in the economic collapse of 1557, was played out above all in Italy. Carlos V possesed about three-fourths of the Peninsula. In this way, Spain transferred through Italy to its own soil the links with the "system." This was one of the reasons for all the wars with France: The wealth and the experience of centuries were essential for whoever intended to exercise new hegemony in the "system," especially if it were to be the first "planetary" hegemony.

38. This event produced an unprecedented increase of prices in Europe, which was convergent with an inflation of 1,000 percent during the sixteenth century. Externally, this will liquidate the wealth accumulated in the Turkish Muslim world, and it will even transform India and China internally. Furthermore, the arrival of Amerindian gold produced a complete continental hecatomb of Bantu Africa because of the collapse of the kingdoms of the sub-Saharan savannah (Ghana, Togo, Dahomey, Nigeria, etc.), which exported gold to the Mediterranean. In order to survive, these kingdoms increased the selling of slaves to the new European powers of the Atlantic, thus producing American slavery (Véase Bertaux, 1972: "La trata de esclavos"; Godinho, "Création et dynamisme économique"; Chaunu, *Séville et l'Atlantique*, vol. 8, chap. 1, 57; Braudel, "Monnaies et civilisation"). The whole ancient third "interregional system" is absorbed slowly by the modern "world-system."

39. All of the subsequent hegemonic power will remain until the present on their shores: Spain, Holland, England (and France partly) until 1945; and the United States in the present. Thanks to Japan, China, and California of the United States, the Pacific appears for the first time as a counterweight. This is perhaps a novelty of the next century, the twenty-first.

40. Wallerstein, *The Modern World-System*, vol. 1, 45.

41. This is the entrance to the mine.

42. This text has for the last thirty years warned me to the phenomenon of the fetishism of gold, of "money," and of "capital" (see Dussel, "General").

43. *Archivo General de Indias* (Sevilla), Charcas 313.

44. Wallerstein, *The Modern World-System*, vol.1, 165 ff: "From Seville to Amsterdam: The Failure of Empire."

45. It should be remembered that Spinoza (Espinosa), who lived in Amsterdam (1632–1677), descended from a "azquenazí" family from the Muslim world of Granada, was expelled from Spain, and then was exiled in the Spanish colony of Flanders.

46. See Wallerstein, *The Modern World-System*, vol. 1, 214.

47. See Wallerstein, *The Modern World-System*, vol. 2, chap. 2: "Dutch Hegemony in the World-Economy." Writes Wallerstein: "It follows that there is probably only

a short moment in time when a given core power can manifest *simultaneously* productive, commercial and financial superiority *over all other core powers*. This momentary summit is what we call hegemony. In the case of Holland, or the United Providences, that moment was probably between 1625–1675" (*The Modern World-System*, 39). Not only Descartes, but also Spinoza, as we already indicated, are the philosophical presence of Amsterdam, world "center" of the system—and why not? The self-consciousness of humanity *in its "center"* is not the same as a mere *European* self-consciousness.

48. See Wallerstein, *The Modern World-System*, vol. 2, chap. 6. After this date, British Hegemony will be uninterrupted, except in the Napoleanic period, until 1945, when it loses before the United States.

49. See Chaunu, *Conquête et exploitation*, 119–76.

50. Europe had approximately fifty-six million inhabitants in 1500, and eighty-two million in 1600 (see Cardoso, *Historia económica de América Latina*, vol. 1, 114).

51. Wallerstein, *The Modern World-System*, vol. 1, 103.

52. See Amin, *El desarrollo desigual*, 309 ff.

53. Amin, *El desarrollo desigual*, 312.

54. The colonial process ends for the most part at the beginning of the nineteenth century.

55. The colonial process of these formations ends, for the most part, after the so-called World War II (1945), given that the North American superpower requires neither military occupation, nor political-bureacratic domination (proper only to the old European powers, such as France and England), but rather the management of the dominion of economic-financial dependence in its transnational stage.

56. See Dussel, "General," vol. 1, chap. 1, 223–41.

57. "Muslim" means here the most "cultured" and civilized of the fifteenth century.

58. I think that, exactly, to *manage* the new "world-system" according to old practices had to fail because it operated with a variable that made it unmanageable. Modernity *had began*, but it had not given itself the new way to "manage" the system.

59. Later on, it will also have to "manage" the system of the English Island. Both nations had very exiguous territories, with little population at their beginning, without any other capacity than their creative "bourgeois attitude" before its existence. Because of their weakness, they had to perform a great reform of "management" of the planetary metropolitan enterprise.

60. The technical "factibility" will become a criterion of truth, of possibility, of existence; Vico's "verum et *factum* conventuntur."

61. Spain, and also Portugal with Brazil, undertook as state (World-Empire; with military, bureacratic, and ecclessiastical resources) the conquest, evangelization, and colonization of Amerindia. Holland, instead, founded the "Company of the Eastern Indies" (1602), and later that of the "Western Indies." These "companies" (as well as the subsequent British and Danish) are capitalist "enterprises," secularized and private, which function according the "rationalization" of mercantilism (and later of industrial capitalism). This indicates the different rational "management" of the Iberian companies and the different management of the "second Modernity" ("world-system" not managed by a "world-empire").

62. In every system, complexity is accompanied by a process of "selection" of elements that allow, in the face of increase in such complexity, for the conservation of the "unity" of the system with respect to its surroundings. This necessity of selection-simplification is always a "risk" (see Luhmann, *Soziale Systeme*, 47 ff).

63. See Dussel, *1492: El encubrimiento del Otro*, chap. 5: "Critique of the Myth of Modernity." During the sixteenth century, there were three theoretical positions before the fact of the constitution of the "world-system": (1) that of Ginés de Sepúlveda, the *modern* renaissance and humanist scholar, who rereads Aristotle and demonstrates the natural slavery of the Amerindian, and thus concludes on the legitimacy of the conquest; (2) that of the Franciscans, such as Mendieta, who attempts an utopian Amerindian Christianity (a "republic of Indians" under the hegemony of Catholic religion), proper to the third Christian–Muslim interregional system; and (3) Bartolomé de las Casas's position, *the beginning of a critical "counter-discourse" in the interior of Modernity*, which in his work of 1536, a century before *Le Discours de la Méthode*, he titles *De unico modo* (The only way) and shows that "argumentation" is the rational means through which to attract the Amerindian to the new civilization. Habermas, as we will see later on, speaks of "counter-discourse" and suggests that said counter discourse is only two centuries old (beginning with Kant). Liberation Philosophy suggests, instead, that this counter-discourse begins in the sixteenth century (in 1511, in Santo Domingo with Antón de Montesinos?!), decidedly with Bartolomé de las Casas in 1514 (see Dussel, "General," vol. 1, chap. 1, 17–27).

64. Bartolomé de las Casas, *The Devatation of the Indies: A Brief Account*, trans. by Herma Briffault (Baltimore and London: The Johns Hopkins University Press, 1992), 31. I have placed this text at the begining of volume 1 of my work *Para una ética de la liberación latinoamericana* (Dussel, *Para una de-strucción*), since it synthesizes the general hypothesis of the ethics of liberation.

65. Frequently, in the contemporary histories of philosophy and, of course, of ethics, a "jump" is made from the Greeks (from Plato and Aristotle) to Descartes (1596–1650), who takes up residence in Amsterdam in 1629 and writes *Le Discours de la Méthode*, as we indicated earlier. In other words, there is a jump from Greece to Amsterdam. In the interim, twenty-one centuries have gone by without any other content of importance. Studies are begun with Bacon (1561–1626), Kepler (1571–1630), Galileo (1571–1630), and Newton (1643–1727). Campanella writes *Civitas Solis* in 1602. Everything would seem to be situated at the beginning of the seventeenth century, the moment I have called the second moment of Modernity.

66. See Sombart, *Der moderne Kapitalismus* and *Der Bourgeois*.

67. See Troeltsch, *Die Soziallehren der christlichen*.

68. See Habermas, *Der philosophische*, vols. 1–2. Habermas insists on the Weberian discovery of "rationalization," but he forgets to ask after its cause. I believe that my hypothesis goes deeper and further back: Weberian rationalization (accepted by Habermas, Apel, Lyotard, etc.) is the apparently necessary mediation of a deforming simplification (by instrumental reason) of practical reality, in order to transform it into something "manageable," governable, given the complexity of the inmense "world-system." It is not only the internal "manageability" of Europe, but also, and above all, *planetary* (center-periphery) "management." Habermas's attempt to sublate instrumental reason into communicative reason is not sufficient

because the moments of his diagnosis on the *origin itself of the process of rationalization* are not sufficient.

69. The Postmoderns, as Eurocentric, concur, more or less, with the Weberian diagnosis of Modernity. Rather, they underscore certain rationalizing aspects or mediums (means of communication, etc.) of Modernity, some they reject wrathfully as metaphysical dogmatisms, but others they accept as inevitable phenomena and frequently as positive transformations.

70. René Descartes, *The Philosophical Works of Descartes*, vol. 1, "Discourse on the Method," part IV, 127.

71. See Dussel, *El dualismo en la antropología* (at the end) and *Método para una Filosofía*, chap. 2, par. 4. Contemporary theories of the functions of the brain put in question definitively this dualistic mechanism.

72. Kant, *Träume eines Geistersehers* (1766), A 36; in Kant, *Kant Werke*, vol. 2, 940.

73. Stillman Drake, *Discoveries and Opinions of Galileo* (New York: Doubleday, Anchor Books, 1957), 237–38.

74. See Dussel, *Para una de-strucción*.

75. Martin Heidegger, *What Is a Thing?* trans. by W. B. Barton et. al (Chicago: Henry Regnery Company, 1967), 73.

76. See Martin Bernal, *Black Athena*, vol. 1, chap. 5, 224ss.

77. Amerindia and Europe have a premodern history, just as Africa and Asia do. Only the hybrid world, the syncretic culture, the Latin-American *mestiza* race that was born in the fifteenth century (the child of Malinche and Hernán Cortés can be considered as its symbol; see Octavio Paz, *El laberinto de la soledad*) has five hundred years.

78. See among others: Lyotard, *La condition postmoderne*; Rorty, *Philosophy and the Mirror of Nature*; Derrida, *L'Ecriture et la Différence, De la Grammatologie*; Marquart, *Abschied vom Prinzipiellen*; Vattimo, *La fine della Modernità*; Welsch, *Unseres postmoderne Moderne*.

79. This Spanish word *(desarrollismo)*, which does not exist in other languages, points to the "fallacy" that pretends the same "development" (the word *Entwicklung* has a strictly Hegelian philosophical origin) for the "center" as for the "periphery," not taking note that the "periphery" is not *backward* (see Hinkelammert, *Dialéctica del desarrollo desigual* and *Crítica a la razón utópica*). In other words, it is not a temporal *prius* that awaits a development similar to that of Europe or the United States (like the child/adult) but that instead it is the asymmetrical position of the dominated, the *simultaneous* position of the exploited (like the free lord/slave). The "immature" (child) could follow the path of the "mature" (adult) and get to "develop" herself, while the "exploited" (slave) no matter how much she works will never be "free" (lord), because her own dominated subjectivity includes her "relationship" with the dominator. The "modernizers" of the "periphery" are developmentalists because they do not realize that the "relationship" of planetary domination has to be overcome as prerequisite for *"national* development." Globalization has not extinguished, not by the least, the "national" question.

80. See Habermas, *Theorie des kommunikativen Handelns*, t.I, I, 2, from sec. [B] to sec. [D], and especially the debate with P. Winch and A. MacIntyre.

81. We will see that Levinas, "father of French postmodernism" (from Derrida on), is neither postmodern nor does he negate reason. Instead, he is a critic of the

totalization of reason (instrumental, strategic, cynical, ontological, etc.). Liberation Philosophy, since the end of the 1960s, studied Levinas because of his radical critique of domination. In the preface to my work, *Philosophy of Liberation*, I indicated that the philosophy of liberation is a "postmodern" philosophy, one that departed from the "second Heidegger," but also from the critique of *"totalized* reason" carried out by Marcuse and Levinas. It would seem as though we were "postmoderns" *avant la lettre*. In fact, however, we were critics of ontology and Modernity from *(desde)* the periphery, which meant (and which still *means*) something entirely different, as we intend to explain.

82. Up to now, the postmoderns remain Eurocentric. The dialogue with "different" cultures is, for now, an unfullfilled promised. They think that mass culture, the *media* (television, movies, etc.) will affect peripheral urban cultures to the extent that they will annihilate their "differences," in such a way that what Vattimo sees in Torino, or Lyotard in Paris, will be shortly the same in New Delhi and Nairobi; they do not take the time to analyze the *hard* irreductibility of the hybrid cultural horizon that receives those information impacts. Such a horizon is not *absolutely* an exteriority, but it is one that will not be during centuries a univocal interiority to the globalized system.

83. See Jameson's work, *Posmodernism*, on the "cultural logic of late capitalism as postmodernism."

84. Noam Chomsky, *Year 501*.

85. In Stalinist real socialism, the criteria was the "increase in the rate of production"—measured, in any event, by an approximate market value of commodities. It is a question of the same time of fetishism. See Hinkelammert, *Crítica a la razón utópica*, chap. 4: "Marco categorial del pensamiento soviético" (123 ff).

86. Karl Marx, *Grundrisse*, trans. Martin Nicolaus (New York: Penguin Books, 1973), 410.

87. Marx, *Grundrisse*, 410.

88. Pure necessity without money is no market; it is only misery, growing and unavoidable misery.

89. Marx, *Capital*, vol. 1, 799. Here we must remember once more that *Human Development Report 1992* already demonstrated in an incontrovertible manner that the richer 20 percent of the planet consumes today (as never before in global history) the 82.7 percent of goods (incomes) of the planet, while the remaining 80 percent of humanity only consumes the 17.3 percent of said goods. Such concentration is product of the "world-system" we have been delineating.

90. Hebert Marcuse, "Liberation from the Affluent Society" in *To Free a Generation: The Dialectics of Liberation*, ed. David Cooper (New York: Collier Books, 1967), 181.

II

LIBERATING THEOLOGY

4

The Kingdom of God and the Poor

But the more harshly they were treated, the more their numbers increased beyond all bounds, until the Egyptians came to loathe the sight of them. So they treated their Israelite slaves with ruthless severity, and made life bitter for them with cruel *servitude*, setting them *to work* on clay and brick-making, and all sorts *of work* in the fields.

(Exodus 1:12–14, NEB)

Shall they not rue it,
all evildoers who devour *my people*
as men devour bread,
and never call upon the Lord?

(Psalm 14 (13): 4, NEB)

The dialectical relationship between the Kingdom of God and the poor is one of the central themes of Christian faith and praxis today, and therefore of theological thinking and of church policy decisions.

The Kingdom of God is an "already" which has been inaugurated among men; it is God's free gift, in the redemptive reality of Christ, through his liberating lordship and his Church. But it is equally a "not yet" which is coming, which directs hope to the *parousia* and which is coming towards us as future. The Kingdom as the "already" now present

---

Enrique Dussel, "The Kingdom of God and the Poor," *International Review of Mission* 220 (1979): 115–30. This paper was originally presented at the World Council of Churches, Bossey, Switzerland, 10–13 October 1978.

and as the "not yet" in the future, as history "already" transformed by the incarnation of the poor and crucified Christ and as the "beyond" of history, as true History, this Kingdom is the dialectical unity of an action that is real yet is also in the process of fulfilling itself without end.

To remove the present aspect of the Kingdom is to accept history simply as a "vale of sorrow" without further meaning. To remove the future aspect of the Kingdom is to make a fetish of the present and so to fall into idolatry. There is an essential link between accepting the tension of the "already" and the "not yet" and the material reality of the poor. For as the oppressed, the product of injustice, the poor reveal in their very misery the necessity of the coming of that infinite fulfillment of all the insufficiencies of history that is the Kingdom. The reality of the poor makes us discover the reality of the Kingdom's "not yet;" at the same time it prevents any fetishization of the Kingdom's "already" and thus gives the Kingdom the necessary dialectical flexibility for making both faith and hope still possible.

If there were no poor, then either we would be "already" in a Kingdom without any "not yet" or else we would be in an idolatrous Kingdom of this world—in which case the fact would be not that there are no poor but that they have been hidden, exported or liquidated.

Any historical claim to be "a society without poverty" is an idolatrous claim to be the Kingdom of God on earth. This question is central to the reality of capitalism, for capitalism tends to think that it has done away with poverty in Europe and the United States—because the system produces its poor away from the centre in the underdeveloped periphery. Thus the dialectic of "already" and "not yet" allows us to secularize any idolatrous vision of the present stage of capitalism and to give a place in history to the liberation goals of the oppressed peoples and classes.

It must also be understood that the definition of the poor has to do with Christology, with struggles in this world, and with the definition that the Church gives of itself amidst those struggles.

1. *The notion of the poor has been progressively defined in the story of the people of God in the Old and New Testaments and in the history of the Church.*

Every system in history tends to close in on itself, sacralizing itself as a divine whole. It claims to be the Kingdom of God on earth. In its long history, the Jewish-Christian tradition has known many different systems and has, within each of them, fulfilled the function assigned to it by God in world history. In each successive sacralized system, God has made himself known in the poor; for their sake he was the God of Moses, of the Judges and Prophets, of Jesus and the Christians. God reveals himself in the poor because they cannot live in the divinity of the system that is oppressing them. In the very pain of their oppression is revealed to them the non-divinity of that oppressive system.

In Egypt God makes himself known to slaves. Yahweh is the God of the slaves who liberated themselves from Pharaoh and his "cruel servitude." There is no doubt that God's chosen people are poor in the quite material sense. Their poverty is evident and inevitable. And those who are materially poor are the poor in spirit.

In Israel the people want to create a monarchy based on a system of taxes. Prophets rise up on behalf of the poor against this new system. The chosen people remain a people of poverty.

The exiles in Babylon are poor. From their imprisonment in oppression they discover the meaning of Israel's sin, and give themselves to the task of editing much of the Bible. Poverty as oppression and material shortage of goods is the condition of the People of God.

The Jews scattered in the Diaspora continue for centuries this tradition of poverty, living in want and oppression, without either state or army to defend them: a people of the poor among the poor.

Under Hellenistic rule, still suffering oppression, the poor of Yahweh rise up against the oppressors. The Maccabees are an example of this revolt, of the struggle of the poor against the oppressors, the masters of their land, their taxes and the State.

In the Roman Empire both Jews and Christians are of the poor classes themselves and have no really rich people in their ranks. There are, at most, a few rather better off, yet they possess no power of any sort, political, military, economic or cultural. That is impossible because of their religious origins.

It is only from the fourth century on, thanks to the patient evangelizing work of the poor Christian communities throughout the Mediterranean world, that the Empire first gives freedom to Christians and then sees Christians become emperors. From a religion of the poor, Christianity becomes the official religion of the Empire, first in face of the Persians to the East and later over against the Muslim Arabs to the South. Christians, for the first time, face a new problem for faith: Are the rich poor? Are the rich not perhaps "poor in spirit"? The Fathers of the Church speak out again and again against a wrong answer to this question. Monks flee the new, corrupt "Christian City" for the desert, scandalized by the monstrousness of it all.

The age of confusion begins, for there is the beginning of the metamorphosis of the notion of the poor, as part of the metamorphosis of the City of God. For Augustine no earthly city could be the City of God because "Cain built his city but Abel never built one." The City of God can never

be built on earth. So those Christians who claimed to be building the City
of God in the face of Persians and Muslims were in reality only sacralizing one more historical system. The oppressors, the "rich" of Christendom (whether the Byzantine, the Latin, the Europeans or the colonial
Latin American), had to justify themselves to their own consciences as
"poor in spirit." The term "spirit" now comes to mean "intention," "in the
mind," not in material fact. Thus those who are poor "in intention" can
still be saved despite being rich (feudal lords, slave-masters, serf-holders
and the like). Critics of the state of society, of the system, are handed over
to the secular arm and killed as heretics or schismatics.

In medieval Christian Europe the poor were the serfs of feudalism, yet
at the same time there appeared others yet poorer who have lived since
the ninth century in the towns. The rising class of burghers, or bourgeois,
had to struggle for some eight centuries until its triumph under Cromwell
in England and with the French Revolution. The poor of the Middle Ages
thus became the rich, the bourgeois, the powerful masters of the capitalist system. The poor, in this particular case, were those without wages—
they were not the only ones to be poor but were those made poor according to the essential logic of this newly established system.

At the same time and as basic cause of the wealth of the rising bourgeois, other poor peoples appeared on the horizons of European colonial
expansion—black African slaves, American Indians, and Asians. From the
sixteenth century onwards "cruel servitude" was forced on all the inhabitants of the Third World, that marginal and underdeveloped world
whose labour would bring huge profits to the capitalist world that was
born, grew and enjoyed its triumph from the eighteenth century onwards.

Leadership in the capitalist world at the centre passed from country to
country—first Spain and Portugal, then Holland at the beginning of the
seventeenth century, then England at its end, until in 1945 it appeared finally, unmistakable and triumphant, in the United States.

Christianity, once again, as in the rule of the very Catholic Charlemagne,
or that of the Catholic kings of Spain, legitimizes the exercise of power ruling over the world's poor. In face of the disaster of Vietnam and the corrup-
tion of Watergate, a fervent Baptist preacher, Bible in hand, emerges as candidate for the presidency of the United States. The Trilateral Commission,
basing itself on Christian values, justifies a new period of expansion and
domination by North American capitalism over much of the world, especially the nations of the periphery. Still more disconcerting, these oppressors
think of themselves as "poor in spirit" because they consider themselves free
from the taint of their wealth. Whereas the poor—the poor classes, the poor
nations—since they envy the wealth of the rich (who know that wealth is
evil), and since they lay claim to that wealth, have fallen into "spiritual

riches" or pride. The rich have now become the poor, and the poor the rich in the religious sense. What might appear to be a laughable trick is, however, the topic for earnest theological propositions in our theological faculties, in church documents and in the everyday understanding of lower middle class Christians, in the countries of the centre as much as in those of the margin.

2. *The poor, those who are oppressed and exploited and so reduced to misery, can be open and spiritually available to God.*

The spiritual meaning of poverty (in its biblical sense, "according to the Spirit," not in its modern inversion, "in the mind," or "according to one's intention") took on a precise, eschatological significance at the end of the Babylonian exile.[1] Since we speak here theologically, let us look further into the relevant exegetical studies.

The praxis of domination, sin, as I have said elsewhere,[2] is the characteristic action of the "Prince of this world," of those who possess power and exercise it, whether in economics, politics or ideology. The oppressors' action is exercised on another person, on the oppressed. The most appropriate passage on which to base our thinking is, therefore, the christological text in Philippians 2:6–8.

> For the divine nature was his from the first; yet he did not think to snatch at equality with God, but made himself nothing, assuming the nature of a slave. Bearing the human likeness, revealed in human shape, he humbled himself, and in obedience accepted even death—death on a cross.

The righteous man, the slave in a slave-owning society, does not commit sin but suffers the logic of sin. The sinner is the oppressor; the non-sinner is not the oppressor but the oppressed, for in practice there is no third party. Neutrality, the refusal to choose, is simply not possible.

The slave (*doulos* in Greek and *'ebed* in Hebrew) is the one who is forced to work (*habodah* in Hebrew) for the oppressor. The poor are thus those who have no possessions, those who lack goods. This lack of goods is deprivation of the fruits of their work, is the result of oppression. We are speaking of course of *real* oppression, i.e., economic, political and ideological.

Poverty is a dialectical concept, embracing several terms which mutually define each other. Just as there is no father without a child, and the child is defined by its father, so the poor are defined by the rich and vice versa. Poverty is in no way a pure case of someone lacking something. There is no scarcity without someone having taken the something away from the other, oppressed person. The matter is more complex than some claim, and their efforts at simplification allow them to turn the materially rich into the spiritually poor and the materially poor into those whose envy brands them as the rich.

The oppressor belongs to the very substance of the concept of being poor. There are no poor people without the corresponding rich. Nor is there any absolute poverty in face of God (understood as absolute spiritual availability). There are real poor people in God's sight, since there are real oppressors confronting God, who make the poor what they are: oppressed and lacking their proper possibilities in life, deprived of the product of their work. To take the poor out of their dialectical and constitutive relation with the rich, the oppressors, in an ideological (i.e., theological) trick played by the rich so as to be able to define themselves as the "spiritually poor," thus rejecting the meaning of the concept. Poverty is the result of sin. To define poverty as a virtue or as an absolute stance towards God, as an openness that resembles humility, is to dissolve it in order to be able to use it as a justification of wealth. When the reality of poverty is dissolved it loses all substance as a critical biblical tool and is transformed into an ideology of oppression.

Attempts are often made to universalize poverty—"we are all poor!"—or to relativize or explain it away—"the poor aren't so very poor and they would soon become rich if they would just work like we do!"

Let us look at some examples: In one text, whose origin need not be given, we find this:

> In its immediate meaning, to be *poor* is to be affected by situations of genuine want and deprivation. Yet it is convenient to give the term a wider meaning. In economics it describes a person who lacks material goods; yet in widening this meaning it can describe whoever is unable to share in the services of society. In other words, the *poor* are the weak, those who lack economic, social, political power or simply the power necessary for living.

Notice how poverty is sheer scarcity, a "lack of," without cause or anyone to blame. The poor are poor because they "do not have," not because they have been robbed and oppressed.

Still more serious, in this type of abstract, absolute and fetishized description of poverty, oppression or material want is not yet understood as religious poverty. Indeed, real, material poverty is seen as totally distinct from "religious" poverty:

> The deeper, spiritual or specifically Christian poverty refers to the spiritual attitude of the man who, recognizing himself as weak and powerless, is open to hope in God's salvation.

By not defining poverty as an aspect of oppression, as the fruit of sin, and by not revealing the religious meaning which can be found even in the economic, political and ideological aspects of poverty, a double error is committed. On the one hand, it denies the religious nature of all oppression of many by man in its devilish, idolatrous and carnal sense (the biblical concept of "flesh"—*basar* in Hebrew, *sarx* in Greek—is more adequate than that of "matter," *hyle* in Greek). On the other hand, it banishes "religious" poverty to some ethereal, mental, unreal, and irrelevant sphere. The two errors go together; there is no awareness that the essence of poverty, in the biblical view, is not material want but being the object of oppression and sin. The condition of want has been confused with the condition of oppression.

This ideological–theological trick of dissolving, dis-carnating poverty, which seems so "religious," has both consequences and hidden origins. For it is a trick that has been working since the fourth century, since the Constantinian takeover, and which, by allowing the rich to become the "religiously poor-in-spirit" undermines the Gospel. It is the first step towards the sacralization of the existing material order; indeed, and worst of all, a Christian sacralization of the system.

Or, to take another example. In the Trilateral Commission paper by Cooper, Kaiser and Kowaka, "Towards a Renovated International System," which is something like a manifesto of the Carter, or rather the Rockefeller-Brzezinski team, we read that "disparities in conditions between political entities are natural" (p. 21), and holding fast to the moral values of Western Christian civilization, "we believe that the trilateral countries should substantially increase the flow of resources addressed to alleviating world poverty" (p. 44). For the ideologists of North American capitalism, poverty is a reality without history, something absolutely *natural*. It need not be explained by domination or exploitation but simply by the size of the surface area of the countries in question, their population, their natural resources, etc. (p. 21). There need be no blame or guilt of any sort. Poverty can be "mitigated" and "alleviated" with alms, with aid, with various projects. Those who give alms and create projects can have quiet consciences; they are, even better, admirable Christians who "love their neighbour."

These "trilateralists" overlook the unequal terms of trade, the exaggerated profits of their investments and loans, the military presence of their armies, the exercise of dictatorship by heads of state trained in their colleges and universities, for which reasons the countries concerned are in extreme poverty. Poverty for them is sheer lack of goods, not a dialectical reality. This North American capitalist concept of poverty—which is equally prevalent in European and Japanese capitalism—is also seen in those politicians in the marginal countries whom we in Latin America term "developmentalists," i.e., those who believe they can develop their countries through outside technology and capital, into a capitalism dependent on the United States. "Economic development will result in the abolition of poverty," Kubitschek, President of Brazil, wrote in the *Diretrizes Gerais do Plano Nacional*.[3] North American capitalism, the developmentalism of the marginal countries, and the theology organic to the interests of both, all conspire to deny it.

To sum up: the poor are the oppressed, and inasmuch as they suffer really and *materially* from oppression, they are religiously open to God and to his Kingdom. From out of their hunger, nakedness and suffering, their availability to the Kingdom is genuine and genuinely spiritual—according to the Spirit of God, not just in the mind. This is what Israel suffered in Egypt and in Babylon; it is what every person, every Christian, suffers when he is oppressed, whether because of his class originals or what results from his commitment to the interests of the oppressed. Moses was taken as a son of Pharaoh, but by opting for the interests of the slaves he came to be persecuted with them and eventually had to flee to the desert—as a matter of fact, and also a matter of spiritual obedience.

3. *Inorganically, the poor are "the multitude" in misery. Yet organically they are "the people" and in this positive sense the active subjects and carriers of the Kingdom of God.*

The domination of sin so structures our historical systems that some become the oppressors, the dominators, and others the oppressed, the dominated. The dialectic between dominator and dominated is strictly evangelical, is of the essence of Christianity as the critique of sin.

> Rulers lord it over their subjects, and their great men make them feel the weight of authority; but it shall not be so with you. Among you, whoever wants to be great must be your servant (*diákonos*), and whoever wants to be first must be the willing slave (*doûlos*) of all—like the Son of Man; he did not come to be served but to serve and to give up his life as a ransom for many. (Matt. 20:25–28, NEB)

Every individual ineluctably, whether he wishes it or not, whether he knows it or not, is part of a class, either the dominators or the dominated. The domination of sin thus shapes the domination of some classes over others and furthers the tension between them. Passive resistance, when oppression is simply tolerated, and active resistance or struggle are both the fruit of the domination of sin. The poor, whether an oppressed person or class, whether a dependent nation or an alienated sex, are structurally poor. Any active steps they take against the established "order," within which they are the oppressed class, are actions against the "law," i.e., against the legality, the structure, the organic power of the system.

In one sense (the negative, the passive, the inorganic) the poor function in history as "the multitude" (*ochlos* in Greek, *rabim* in Hebrew, among its other meanings).[4] They are the oppressed, those deprived of possessions, without knowledge, without history, having internalized the system into their own daily existence. It is of these poor as "the multitude" that the Gospel tells us:

When he came ashore, he saw a great crowd; his heart went out to them and
he cured those of them who were sick. (Matt. 14:14, NEB)

The Kingdom of God can never be identified with the prevailing system.
Any passive acceptance of the powers that be, of the order of oppression, is
a denial of the Kingdom inasmuch as it is a "not yet." If the poor accept
things as they are with resignation, then in that very acceptance they reject
their real share in the future Kingdom, and in such a case "the multitude" is
no more an active member of the Kingdom than it is of the present system.

For the active subject of the system is the "rulers who lord it over their
subjects." In the capitalist system this great man is the owner. For Hegel,
at the beginning of his *Rechtsphilosophie* (paragraph 34 ff.) the subject as
"free will" is an abstract and empty subject until it has been determined
by something: the subject takes on reality by the possession (*Besitz*) of
goods as his private property, exclusive and excluding. The entire capitalist system shapes its subjects as owners. The poor, then, being non-owners,
do not figure as constituent parts of the system. In such an idolatrous system there is no place for the poor. The absolute, creative subject of the system is Capital, and capitalists/owners are the subjects and carriers of partial capital. The absolute law of the system is profit. The distribution of
Profit—the sanctifying grace of the Idol—is not done in virtue of the real,
human necessities of the poor but in function of the degree of participation in the power of Capital. The poor, as non-being (for they are the
"nothing" in the system from which a new order will arise—*ex nihilo omnia fit*), are sacrificed to the idol Money, Moloch:

> Money appears as a being endowed with subjectivity—as the economist the-
> ologian tells us. Yet in contrast to the subjectivity of trade, where there is no
> hierarchy, Money is a superior being, king of the world of trade. It is not one
> commerce among others, but a quite distinct order, even if any commerce can
> be transfigured into Money. . . . "They hold a Council and give their power
> and authority to the Beast. Nothing can be bought or sold except that which
> has the sign or name of the Beast, or the number of its Name" (Revelation of
> St. John). Money now appears as the Beast, for whose sake man has forfeited
> his freedom.[5]

The capitalist system with Capital as its basis has been sacralized. The
system defines itself as kingdom, as a kingdom which is "already" universal and eternal. In its name persons, oppressed classes and dependent
nations alike can be put to destruction.

All that rises up against he Idol is the Other, the Enemy. The poor who
aspire to a different and juster order cannot but be totally opposed to the
system. This Enemy can appear at any level: at the global or international

level as an oppressed nation, at the national level as an oppressed class in struggle, and at the personal level as a poor man pleading for something to eat, as a woman demanding justice between the sexes or a child asking for truth in education.

At the national level, to take that for the moment, the possibility of militancy, of an active class struggle arising from the oppressed is discounted. Any such struggle is considered anti-Christian, opposed to love. As if it were the poor who started the struggle! For centuries they have suffered from it, and when they raise their voice they are told they are succumbing to hate, that they are not Christians. These theologians of oppression turn the meaning of evangelical love upside down and use it against the poor! When the poor are bold enough to say "I am hungry" and to hold out a hand (later, in desperation it will be the fist that is held out) to satisfy that hunger, the oppressor will shout "Class struggle!" Whereas, in fact, this is nothing more than the poor man's attempt to obtain the goods which the system by its nature denies him, yet which he needs by *natural* and *divine* right—by far superior to the *positive* right on which the ownership of the capitalist is based. The praxis of the poor, interpreted by the sacralized system as the Enemy, is the very act by which the Kingdom advances from its "already" to its "not yet" aiming at destroying whatever is oppressive, allowing history to move forward towards the *parousia*.

At the moment the mere "multitude" becomes a "people." In the moment in which the multitude, for whom Christ was filled with compassion, are organically called to transformation, as an emerging class or nation, into the *carrier-subject* of the Kingdom, they become the people (*laós* in Greek, *ham* in Hebrew).[6] God the creator and redeemer grants the Kingdom to humanity as a free gift. Humanity receives it and carries it. The multitude called for the sake of the Kingdom is, as people, the active and creating subject of Salvation History.

The task of the Servant or Worker of Yahweh is, precisely, to save the multitude and turn them into a people. "After all his pains he shall be bathed in light . . . so shall he, my servant, vindicate many" (Isaiah 53:11).[7] So also Christ, the suffering Servant, has as his mission (as has later his Church) to reconstitute the former crowd into a people by the new Covenant:

> This is my blood, the blood of the convenant, shed for many for the forgiveness of sins. (Matt. 26:28)

It remains to distinguish between "people" and "my people," between the poor who are the subject-carriers of the Kingdom, objects of the beatitude, and the Church properly speaking, i.e., the People chosen to fulfill the specific prophetic task.

For inasmuch as the poor are not subjects of the system, owners of capital and holders of power, they are both a negative factor (the pure negativity of the oppressed) and at the same time, positivity (the positively of the *exteriority*), they are the subject-carriers of the Kingdom who co-labour to build it. By being oppressed (and by that non-sinners, thus righteous) and active liberators (as members of the people), the poor are the subjects of the Kingdom:

> How blest are you who are in need;
> the Kingdom of God is yours. (Luke 6:20)

The one who is not member or subject of the kingdom of this world, of the system, is member and subject of God's Kingdom. Since the poor person is "the Other" to the system, we can here properly use Sartre's definition: "L'enfer c'est les Autres."[8] For the system the poor is hell, the Evil one, the totally opposed; for the kingdom of this world with its chiefs and princes, the Kingdom of God and its members are the Enemy, their hell. Heaven is hell for the system and vice versa—what is hell for the system is the site of the Kingdom of God.

> How blest are you who now go hungry; your hunger shall be satisfied.
> How blest are you who weep now; you shall laugh.
> How blest are you when men hate you . . .
> Alas for you who are rich; you have had your time of happiness.
> Alas for you who are well-fed now; you shall go hungry.
> Alas for you who laugh now; you shall mourn and weep . . .
> (Luke 6:21–25, NEB)

These sayings are not paradoxical; they do go against the grain of the system (*para-doxa* = against opinion). In Asia, Africa and Latin America the "many" are beginning to emerge, to be aware of themselves, to shape themselves into a force in history. "People" are being born, determined on their liberation. Jesus' priority for the poor, the "many," in his spirituality and his mercy, calls them to take part in the struggle. The struggle in the world is a contributive factor in the Kingdom of God. The struggle of the poor is the praxis of liberation; it is the activity of the Kingdom in history, raised up by Christ by his spirit, in the intimacy of the hearts of the poor, the carriers of the Kingdom.

This is why in Latin America today the dictators fulminate against the poor in revolt, not without help from Christians of "the centre," i.e., of Europe and the United States.

4. *The Kingdom of Heaven demands an adequate integration of the historical project of popular liberation with the eschatological dimension. Antiutopian Christianity criticizes this historical project of liberation as irrational and obscurantist.*

The fact of the poor can be denied by a "universalisation" (Thesis 2) by which everyone is seen as poor and the Kingdom is identified with the prevailing system. Their subjecthood can also be denied (Thesis 3), and their liberating praxis vilified by the ideological system which claims identity with the Kingdom. Thirdly, the poor can be denied their objective or project (Thesis 4) where this is not seen, in its opposition to the project of the system, as belonging to the eschatological Kingdom. In other words, hope in the Kingdom that is not mediated through a historical hope in a more just system in the future becomes twisted into a contribution to the ideologization of the system and into the possibility of yet further exploitation of the poor. Let us take this question in stages.

In Stoic or Epicurean cosmopolitanism, the Roman Empire was seen in some way as the City of the Gods: The prevailing system was by nature divine, eternal, unchanging. For Christianity, however, no system could claim to be naturally divine or eternal. Hope in the final Kingdom undermines any claim by a system in history to be fixed and unchanging. Yet any theology of hope that fails to set this out clearly will in time become idolatrous. For between the present system and the eschatological Kingdom there is always a third dimension—the project and the hope it generates of a positive and historical utopia. In Latin America, for instance, between the present situation of oppression and dependence on North American capitalism and the final Kingdom beyond history is to be found the vision of a new system in history—e.g., the socialist one. The historical goal of socialist liberation is opposed to the ruling capitalist system and can—indeed must—be expounded in relation to the eschatological project of liberation in the Kingdom.

The fundamental crisis for Christians in Latin America, and perhaps throughout the world, is precisely how to set out this dimension of historical project. For some it is quite simply a matter of maintaining the status quo, since "any future is dangerous." This is a conservatism subservient to capitalism and its religion. For others, from the reformists to the social democrats, what is needed is not to change the system radically but to improve it. For others again, given the basic structures of the present movement in history and a rational analysis of capitalism, the liberation of the poor demands in Latin America a quite new system, more humane and allowing for far more solidarity, built on quite different principles. Not those of profit but of fair participation in the means of production. All Christians can be found holding one or another of the positions. Each has a certain understanding of the poor and of the function of the Kingdom in history. In fact the first and second come together to oppose the third. Their theological critique is based on the social sciences of capitalism and on the thinkers organic to it.

Thus, for example, the German group which attacks liberation theology in *Kirche and Befreiung* starts from the social thought of Popper and criticizes any non-capitalist vision of liberation as irrational and impossible.[9] In particular, Bossle speaks of "the Marxist and praxeologically obscurantist theology of liberation."[10] They all rely on Weber, who "excludes from discussion the slightest possibility of a socialist form of trading relationship and thus posits capitalism as an unbreachable limit within human history."[11] This is why Popper holds no socialist project to be viable. In face of its practical impossibility they fall into utopian irrationalism:

> It is my firm conviction that this irrational insistence on emotion and compassion (*Gefühle und Leidenschaften*) will lead in the final instance to what can only be called a crime.[12]

For the bourgeois mind and the sciences to which it gives rise, any goal of creating a non-capitalist society in the future is simply not viable; any plan to formulate it is irrational; and so in the end all responsibility, love and compassion for the poor are considered a genuine, obscurantist crime. This bourgeois anti-utopian Christianity teaches the poor that there is no possibility of a more just order; one must simply resign oneself to one's place in the present system. One text says:

> The Church fights that the poor may receive a worthy place, not just a nominal and legal but a real and effective one, in civil society.

This anti-utopianism brings the Christian to a reformist conformism. Its elimination of utopia, of any vision of liberation in history, brings the Christian to sacralizing the system.

Anti-utopian Christians also find it hard to see the structures of domination as sinful. The same Urs von Balthasar can say that "social situations may be unjust (*ungerecht*) but not sinful (*sündig*),"[13] claiming thus to correct a text of the Medellín conference, and so concludes that "a system as complex as capitalism cannot be quickly condemned as sinful."[14] Always the same point!

If capitalism by its very structures involves domination, if the poor (whether nations, classes or individuals) are the result of that system of domination, then the system in its structures is sinful. Gehlen's teaching has apparently been forgotten, namely that social structures or institutions are only functions or roles normally filled by individual persons. An economic or social structure is sinful when the agents of that system, in acting within it, are practising domination.

By not criticizing the system as sinful, by relativizing the poverty of the poor, by declaring impossible any project of a new and non-capitalist society, this view shuts out any historical release for the poor. The Kingdom of Heaven has to be hoped for within the present system, without overcoming or destroying it. The "already" of the Kingdom in the system has overcome the "not yet" of the future. Hope is ideologized. To catechize or evangelize the poor is to teach them resignation. As one document says:

> In evangelizing them the Church lets the poor share in a supreme hope (sic), based on the Lord's promises. Even when they are deprived of all things (sic), it is a matter of their possessing the riches of God, who being rich made himself poor (2 Cor. 8:9), and of faith—as the word which nourishes—allowing them to live with fortitude and with that joy in the Kingdom (sic) which is already in bud and which no human sorrow can suppress.

5. *If the essence of sin is oppression of the poor and alienation of the fruits of their work, then the essence of religion is "service" of the poor as liberation and as restitution of the fruits of their work. To evangelize is to turn the multitude into a people who can free themselves and be transformed into the People of God and subjects of his Kingdom.*

Herman Cohen said, in his *Religion und Vernunft*, that the essence of prophecy consisted in the discovering of who and where the poor were in any system, and from that making a diagnosis of the pathology of that State. In their visible, material and undisguisable poverty the poor show clearly where the system cannot adequately distribute its goods, i.e., who are suffering from domination by others, and are evidence of the sin of the system. The poor are the sign, the bleeding wound, of the deep, structural sickness of the system. *The presence of the poor is the measure of the absence of God's Kingdom in a society.*

The poor, moreover, by having no part in the system, by being oppressed, marginal, non-subject of rights and property, are outside the system. By being outside the system they are inside the Kingdom. In other words, the marginality of the poor in respect of the kingdom of this world is a measure of their participation in the eschatological Kingdom of God. Non-possession and marginality in the system are possession and participation in the Kingdom.

The princes of this world are already ensconced in their kingdoms. They have nothing more to hope for except the final consecration of the kingdom they possess. Against that, the poor *in* this world are not *of* this world. They are all hoping for "the new," especially for the end, the destruction of the system that oppresses them and names them poor. Hope in the Kingdom has its starting point in hunger, thirst and want. The hope of having enough to eat and drink, as Feuerbach said in his *Essence of Christianity*, is a religious act. It is an eschatological hope—as is also the eating and drinking of the Eucharist.

The poor, like exteriority of the system, are "already" in the Kingdom. It may well be that they have no knowledge of this; it may well be that no explicit mention of Christ and his Gospel has come to their ears. Yet anything they do in order to eat and drink, in order to achieve a juster order, is a being "already" in the Kingdom. This point deserves to be made at greater length, but I must not take the space to do so here.[15]

Though it would not please Bultmann, I believe that Christianity is a religion and that the heart of religion is worship. In Christianity the essence of worship is "service" (as productive work or gift) of the poor as prayer to God. In the current liturgy we say:

> We offer you, Lord, this bread, fruit of the work of man.

In the Old Testament doves were offered, fragments of bread, wine. Worship is *praxis* (i.e., a personal relationship in action—he who offers worship and the God who receives it) shown forth in the gift, the offering, the fruit of work (the relation of man to nature). The "bread" of sacrifice is the technical product, offered without return to God, destroyed in his presence. This is an economic-theological relationship. Someone offers something to someone, just like someone selling something to someone else. Thus for the scholastics *religio* as a virtue was dependent on *justitia*.[16]

Under Thesis 2, we have looked at the fact that the poor have been dispossessed of the fruit of their work by the oppressors. This want is an injustice that cries to God. For its sake the prophets and Jesus fiercely denounced all false worship; this has not yet been sufficiently understood:

> I tell you, there is something greater than the temple here. If you had known what that text means, "I require mercy, not sacrifice," you would not have condemned the innocent. For the Son of Man is sovereign over the Sabbath. (Matt. 12:6–8, NEB)

Christ is the poor man; the poor man is more than the temple; he who gives bread to the starving (Matt. 25:40) gives food to Christ and offers worship to God. This closes off the vicious circle of sin and opens the way to the Kingdom. Where sin is oppression of the poor and the denial to them of the fruit of their work, the Kingdom is being built by the liberation of the poor and the restoration of the fruit of their work as worship of God. This is why worship is, at the end of the day, the same as economics, divine economics, since Christ made himself a slave, as we have said from the outset of this study. Yet there is more. For on the whole the

capitalist mind has lost sight of the essential relationship between political economics and liturgy, between work and religion.

We read in Ecclesiastes:

> To offer a sacrifice from the possessions of the poor is like killing a son
> before his father's eyes.
> Bread is life to the destitute,
> and it is murder to deprive them of it. (34:20–21)

No greater clarity could be needed! To rob the poor of the fruit of their
work (in unjust international relationships, in the low pay of the capitalist systems, etc.) and to offer that product (bread and wine) on God's altar is like killing a son (the poor, the oppressed classes, the dependent nations) in the sight of God himself. It is to offer worship not to God but to
the Beast, the Idol, Satan.

Worship, the heart of religion, has much to do with work and with political economy. Sin has much to do with dispossession and want among
the poor. For the Hebrews, to work (*habodah*) the ground in agriculture was
expressed by the same term as that which designated the act of worship in
the temple or divine "service" (*habodah*). *Habodah* is the action/work of the
"Servant" (from the same root: *hebed*). Work (= service, in Greek *diakonia*),
i.e., economic and material help for the poor, and worship of God have the
same basic structure of meaning. Worship, the heart of religion, i.e., of the
underlying religion, is fulfilled in the *praxis* of service and liberation of
one's poor brethren, of the stranger, the widow and the orphan. This is
why Hosea exclaims in the name of God, as he attacks priestly liturgical legalism and all "spiritualizing" (= dematerializing, de-economizing, ideol-
ogizing): "I desire mercy and not sacrifice" (6:6).

Within religion, in its full meaning, worship has an economic significance
(understanding by "economic" the relationship of man with nature, with the
fruit of work, and with other men). Giving food to the hungry, helping an
oppressed nation or class to free itself, is thus to render service to the poor as
worship of God. "Mercy" to the poor is the "sacrifice" God desires. The new
economic, political and ideological order in history, built as a home for a people newly liberated—if always no more than partially so within history—is
the fruit of an act of worship: it is the innovating production of goods for
those who today are outside, the poor. To love others as indeed other, as outside, as citizens of the coming Kingdom still beyond us (i.e., *agape*), is the dynamic power of his underlying infrastructure. Thus religion is not some ideological superstructure which justifies the prevailing system; religion is
rather the infrastructural undermining of the sinful status quo and the construction of a new order in history as an offering or sacrifice to God, a sharing in that building of his Kingdom which is God's own gift.

The revolutionary who is a believer will not see his religious position as a matter of accident or of little importance. His religion is a radical openness, an enabling condition of greater political and economic creativity in his work, his service of the poor. This service, "already" in the Kingdom since mediation of the act of worship of the Infinite. In being an epiphany of the crucified God appealing for help, the poor are also the necessary path of salvation. The poor are the *origin* of the calling (vocation to their service) and *mediation* of salvation, for it is through service to the poor that worship is offered to God.

All actual, material and thus religious service of the poor is in itself worship of God and the building of his Kingdom.

To deny poverty is to deny the absence of the Kingdom in the present system. It is to affirm the existing system as the Kingdom of this world. To affirm the poor, on the other hand, and to serve their eventual liberation, in the structures and in history, is to witness to the presence of the Kingdom in the satisfying of the poor and to the absence of the Kingdom in the imperfection of society. *The poor are the epiphany of the Kingdom or of the infinite exteriority of God.*

It remains to distinguish between the inorganic multitude and the people as the emerging subject of history (Gen. 41:40), and the People of God as Church (Acts 15:14) called to a special role in history:

Come out of her (Babylon), my people, lest you take part in her sins. (Revelation 18:4)

The Church, God's remnant among the peoples of earth, has evangelism for its calling. To evangelize is to bring good news to the poor, to turn the many into a people and to make that people aware of the destiny that God has prepared for them: the Kingdom. Not just aware, but active, now that there is a real possibility of conquering sin, of restoring their wealth to the poor and of building a new order in which there will be neither rich nor poor, neither oppressors nor oppressed, neither nations of the centre nor nations of the periphery, neither ruling classes nor those that suffer the rule of others. . . .

NOTES

1. Cf. Jorge Pixley, "El Reino de Dios: Buenas Nuevas para los pobres de América latina?" in *Servir* (Mexico) 73 (1978), pp. 7–46; and Alvaro Barreiro, "Comunidades Eclesiales de Base y evangelización de los pobres," in *Servir* 69–70, 1977, pp. 279–346.

2. See my article "Domination—Liberation: A New Approach," para. 5, in *Concilium* 96, 1974 English edition, pp. 40–42.

3. Quoted in Miriam Limoeiro Cardoso, *La ideologia dominante* (Mexico: Siglo XXI, 1975) p. 94.

4. Cf. TWNT (Kittel), vol. V, pp. 582–90.

5. Franz Hinkelammert: *Las armas ideológicas de la muerte*, EDUCA, San José (Costa Rica), 1977, pp. 25–26.

6. Cf. TWNT, vol. IV, pp. 29–59.

7. See my article "Universalismo y misión en los poemas del Siervo de Yahveh" in *El humanismo semita* (Buenos Aires: EUDEBA, 1969), pp. 127–70.

8. Jean-Paul Sartre, *Huis Clos* (Paris, 1944).

9. Cf. Hengsbach, Vekemans, Lope Trujillo, Bossle, and others in *Christlicher Glaube und gesellschaftliche Praxis* (Pattloch, Aschaffenburg 1978), the publication of an "encuentro" held in Rome from March 2 to 7, 1976.

10. Ibid. p. 253.

11. Hinkelammert, op. cit. p. 74.

12. *The Open Society and its Enemies.* Munich: Francke, 1977, German edition, vol. II, p. 287.

13. "Heilgeschichtliche Ueberlegungen zur Befreiungstheologie" in *Theologie der Befreiung*, ed. Krl Lehman, Einsiedeln, 1977, p. 169.

14. Ibid., p. 170.

15. See my *Religión como supra- o infraestructura* (Edicol, Mexico), 1977.

16. Aquinas, *Summa Theologiae*, II–II, p. 81.

5

"Populus Dei" in Populo Pauperum: From Vatican II to Medellín and Puebla

The question of the "popular church" (*iglesia popular*) as a theological issue in need of clarification is immensely complex and cannot be given a quick explanation, as many critics have tried to do. I have to point out right from the beginning that part of the difficulty derives from the ambiguity, not just of the multi-faceted category "people" (*pueblo*) but also of its various uses. "People" may refer to the first people (Israel) or the new people (the Church); it may refer to the Gentiles (non-Christian) or a "Christian people" (as in the Christian tradition of Latin America or Poland). John XXIII's expression "the church *of the poor*," taken up in *Laborem Exercens* 8, may be an exact synonym of "the popular church" if by "popular" is meant the "poor" of a Christian people. If, on the other hand, as we shall see, "people" is taken as *gentes* (Gentiles), and it is said that "The church is born *solely* of the people," the result is sort of Pelagianism. Obviously to say, as has been said, that "The church is born solely of the Holy Spirit," is in turn a sort of monophytism.

On the other hand, if by "church" are meant those Christians, part of the one official and institutional Church, who are being renewed, and evangelised, who make a choice for the poor, the oppressed and live among them, then this renewed "church" (not a *new* church) can "be born of the people" (from among the poor and oppressed, who in Latin America are already Christian, baptised and believers) through the action of the

Enrique Dussel, "'Populus Dei' in Populo Pauperum: From Vatican II to Medellín and Puebla," *Concilium* 176 (1984): 35–44.

Holy Spirit (which the theology of liberation has never denied). This is what is meant by Medellín, by Puebla, by the Christians who "make the option" and live among the poor. It is absurd to say that the theology of liberation is the inspiration behind the popular church (in the sense indicated). The situation is precisely the opposite.

1. "POPULUS DEI" AT VATICAN II (1962–1965)

If we take a historical perspective, no-one would have thought in 1965 that Chapter II of the constitution _De Ecclesia_ would be the one we would be discussing, but Chapter III, on the bishops, which then appeared to be the central issue to put the definitions of Vatican I into their proper context.

The first schema "De Ecclesia," presented on 1 December 1962, had a first chapter on "the militant nature of the church" and a second on "members of the church."[1] Cardinal Liénart, in a speech which became famous, rejected the schema because only the juridical aspect was discussed (_mere iuridico appareat_),[2] and not the Church as mystery, the "mystical" aspect (_in natura sua mystica_),[3] and ended with the ringing declaration, "I love Plato, but I love truth more." No less a person than Cardinal Koenig argued that the attribute of "_indefectibilitas fidei_" belonged to the "believing people as a whole" (_populo credentium_),[4] since the faithful not only received doctrine, but also, "as a community of believers" (_communitas fidelium_), had a positive influence on the _magisterium_. Mgr. Devoto of Goya, Argentine, said that there was "also a need for a clear and explicit restatement of the idea of the whole people of God . . . as the beginning of the whole constitution _De Ecclesia_." Cardinal Hengsbach too favoured the rejection of the schema for its "clericalism and legalism" (_clericalismi et iuridismi_).[6] In the end the schema was rejected.

A theological commission worked to prepare the new schema, which was presented in Congregation 37 (30 November 1963). Fr. Chenu tells how a Polish cardinal pressed for the doctrine of the "societas perfecta," but the commission preferred the more biblical and spiritual idea of the "people of God."[7]

The question of the "people of God" had already made its appearance in other conciliar schemas, as had that of the poor, the "hungry multitudes"[8] who "demand social justice."[9] In the event, in the new schema "The mystery of the Church"[10] was followed by the question of the episcopate and only in Chapter III that of "The People of God and in particular about the laity."[11] Immediately an important debate began. Does "the people of God" mean the laity or the whole Church? If it is the whole Church, it should come in Chapter II and the bishops in Chapter III. Cardinal Frings, for the Germans, proposed that Chapter II be devoted to the question "Of the people of God."[12] There was a change of meaning: from being only the laity, "people of God" was transformed into a synonym for the Church. Some Latin Americans even then connected the issue of the "people of God" with "a greater apostolic dedication to the evangelisation *of the poor.*"[13] In Congregation 54, on 23 October, Mgr. Manuel Larrain spoke about the *Populus Dei*, emphasising its role of prophecy and martyrdom (witness), not "passive acceptance," but active participation.[14]

Finally, in Congregation 80, on 15 November 1964, the "corrected text" of Chapter II, "De populo Dei," was presented.[15] With minor changes, this was to be the final text of *Lumen Gentium*. The opening statement "Christ is the light of all nations," (LG 1), brings us right to the issue: *Gentium* is not the same as *populorum*. But the terms used all refer to groups, communities, societies:

> It has pleased God, however, to make men holy and save them, not merely as individuals without any mutual bonds, but by making them into a single *people*. . . . He therefore chose the race of Israel as a *people* unto himself . . . [called together] the new *people* of God (LG 9).

This sets up a dialectic between a *first or old* people and a *new or second people* ("the new covenant").

A fundamental question, which will be central to the rest of this discussion, is the following: Does God call or summon individuals separately from their Gentile community or from the people of Israel, or does he call them communally? The Council is clear: he does not call them "as individuals without any mutual bonds." But, it could be objected, he forms the *new* people from the *old* people of Israel, but not from the Gentiles *as peoples*. It is true that the people of God are "among all the nations of the earth" (LG 13), but there is no reference to "Gentile peoples." Nevertheless it would seem that we can say that the new people have been born from the old, from the "remnant" of Israel (as Jesus was from Mary), by the work of the Holy Spirit.[16] Jesus was part of the old people, Mary was, the apostles were. The *new* people were born by the Holy Spirit of the old (the *flesh*): "I will pour out my Spirit upon all flesh, and your sons and your daughters shall prophesy, and your young men shall see visions" (Acts 2:17). Israel is the flesh, as "the Word became flesh" in Mary: it is the incarnation. Without *flesh* there would be no Christ; there would be only one nature (it would be Monophysitism). Without a *people* there would be no *new* people, but a collection of individuals "without mutual bonds" (LG 9). Obviously the idea that the old people could have produced the new people by its own *potentia* (δυνάμει) is a negation of the incarnation of Christ, which is the fruit and the work of the Holy Spirit himself; this is an absurd proposition which no Latin American theologian has even thought of putting forward.

Schema 5.1.   The Origin of the Church

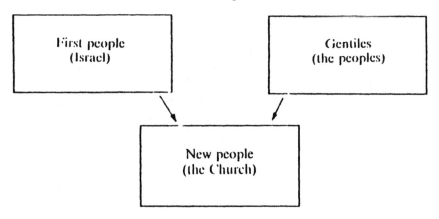

The important point is that, having *subsumed* in the Holy Spirit, with Christ as head, by the will of the Father, the old people of Israel and the Gentiles ("Jew and Gentile, making them one, . . . to be the new people of God" LG 9), the *new* people, the Church, has been born, like Christ, in human history, into a specific people, into a real race, language and tradition, with *real* struggles and heroes. To take (on or up—*aufheben*) a historical people (Israel and the Gentiles) is to take the *flesh*, the history, the richness of the *previous* history of humanity. The history of peoples ("Israel according to the *flesh* wandered . . . in the desert," of history, we may add) as communities, is "made holy and saved" in the *new* people of God, and not just the ego-centered life of each individual who is called. It is a dialectic between the old "people," and the new "people," and not between an "individual" (Christ) exclusively calling abstract "individuals," without community, history, memories, struggles or martyrs.

At Vatican II the fact that the subject of the episcopate (Chap. III) was preceded by that of "the people of God" *in genere* (Chap. II) was an explicit indication that the papacy, the episcopate, the ministerial priesthood, etc., are parts or elements *within* the "people of God."

2. THE "PEOPLE OF GOD" AND "POPULAR" PASTORAL WORK AT MEDELLÍN (1968)

At Medellín the double meaning of "people" was taken over from Vatican II:

> Just as Israel of old, the first People, felt the saving presence of God when he saved them from the oppression of Egypt, so we also, the new People of God, cannot but feel his saving passage (Introduction 6); . . . the hope that all the People of God, encouraged by the Holy Spirit, commit themselves to its complete fulfillment (i.e., of the work of the conference, ibid. end).

However, we immediately find a difference from Vatican II, not a contradiction, but an added detailed, elucidation, a Latin American touch:

> Among the *great mass* of the baptised in Latin America, the conditions of Christian faith, beliefs, and practices . . . (6, I, I, "Pastoral Care of the Masses"). In evaluating popular religion, we cannot start from a Western cultural interpretation (6, I, 4). Faith, and therefore the Church too, is planted and grows in the different cultural forms taken by religion among different *peoples* (6, II, 5). Far from being satisfied with the idea that *the people* as a whole already possesses the faith, far from contenting herself with the task of preserving the faith of *the people* . . . proposes . . . a serious re-evangelisation, . . . a reconversion . . . of our people, . . . which will push *the believing* people toward the twofold dimension of personal and community fulfillment . . . (since) according to God's will human beings are to be made holy and saved, not individually but as members of a community (6, II, 8–9).

And immediately afterwards we find:

> All manifestations of *popular* religion, such as pilgrimages, processions, and devotional practices, should be imbued by the word of the Gospel (6, III, 12.).

These texts make it quite clear that by this time "people" no longer has the same meaning as "people of God" in *Lumen Gentium*. There are two reasons for this. The first is that "the great mass of the baptised" in Latin America already form *a people*. "People" means on the one hand the historical and cultural community and, on the other, the community of believers (the Church). In other words, in Latin America, because of the continent's ambiguous status as a "Christian continent" (a Christian culture or civilisation), there is a confusion between "people" in the sense of a social group in civil society and the "people of God," the Church. On the other hand, even the people understood as a social group is not any longer a community of Gentiles, but, a "Christian people." This is why there can be a dialectic between a people already Christian but not sufficiently evangelised or converted and a people (Church) which is re-evangelised, re-converted. In this strict sense (the Christian people not sufficiently evangelised, the Christian people re-evangelised), we may find references to a *renewed, communitarian* "Church," and so on.

These adjectives described the church and groups within it, bishops, priests, religious, laity. They do not imply that those so described are a *different* church, one that is new, parallel, in opposition to the "official" one, etc.

The second reason is that terms such as *"popular* religion" refer to the *real* poor, oppressed groups, classes ethnic groups, etc.: a social group consisting of the dominated. This is not the whole community, but a part:

> the material needs of those who are deprived of the minimum living conditions, and the moral needs of those who are mutilated by selfishness, . . . the oppressive structures that come from the abuse of ownership and power and from exploitation of workers or from unjust transactions (Introduction, 6).

"Popular" in this use means specific sectors of society, not the whole Christian people of Latin America. In this second sense the "popular church" means that part of the "people of God" (in the Vatican II sense) which is part of, or which has made a special commitment to re-evangelise, reconvert, the oppressed, the real poor, the exploited, the victims of repression and torture, etc. The adjective "popular" comes to mean almost the same as what John XXIII meant by "the church *of the poor*"—or at least one of its possible legitimate meanings:

> A deafening cry issues from millions of human beings, asking their pastors for a liberation which reaches them from nowhere else (14, I, 2, "Poverty of the Church"). In the context of poverty and even utter deprivation in which the majority of the Latin American people live, we bishops, priests. . . . (14, I, 3). In this context a *poor* church denounces the unjust lack of this world's goods. . . . (14, II, 5, italics added). With the help of all the people of God we hope to overcome the system of fees (14, III, 13). For all the people of God they will be a continual call to evangelical poverty (14, III, 16).

Of course, not everyone responds to these appeals for objective poverty, the poverty for which Francis of Assisi fought. Those who make a *real* response and commit themselves in their everyday lives to the *real* poor, the oppressed and exploited, are one part of the one institutional, official church. This part may be given the label "popular church" because its members live among the real poor people, speak like them, suffer with them and fight for them: "re-evangelise," "reconvert" (as Medellín says).

Some people, not without an express awareness of engaging in falsification, pronounce this church "parallel," in opposition to the "official" church, a "different" church. Liberation theology has never sponsored these naïve and simplistic terms, though that is not to say that a judge taking a phrase out of its context might not come across some expressions which might imply this deviant meaning.

Thus, on 6 May 1973, the bishops of the North-East of Brazil published a memorable document of the official, institutional Church, the one Church:

> Confronted by the suffering of our people, their oppression and humiliation for so many centuries of our country's history, we have called on you [*convocar*, an

ecclesial act *par excellence*] through the word of God to take up a position. We call on you to take up *a position alongside the people*, a position, more precisely, with all those who, *with the people*, commit themselves to work for their true liberation. . . . We are servants, ministers, of liberation. . . . As ministers of liberation, our first task is to be converted in order to serve better. We must accept this demand of the people of the North-East, who are crying out for this ministry of liberation, begging to share their "hunger and thirst for justice."[17]

We could produce hundreds of other witnesses, but it is not necessary. The *popular* church (that is, those Christians who, as part of the one *official* church, make an effective commitment to the real poor) has been called "the church born of the people." This phrase provoked storms, mainly from those who had not opted for the real poor, the people of the oppressed and unjustly despoiled:

> We are persecuted because we are *with the people*, defending their rights. The prelature of São Felix [said Mgr. Casaldáliga] is a *persecuted church* because it has refused to be involved with the power of politics and money. And we shall be persecuted more and more because, by the power of God, we shall continue *at the side of the oppressed and poor.*[18]

Being with and among poor people is what it means to be a *popular* church. These people are a Christian people, and that is why the renewed,

Schema 5.2. The Renewed (Part of the) Church Which is Born or Proceeds from the Church as the (Whole) "Christian People"

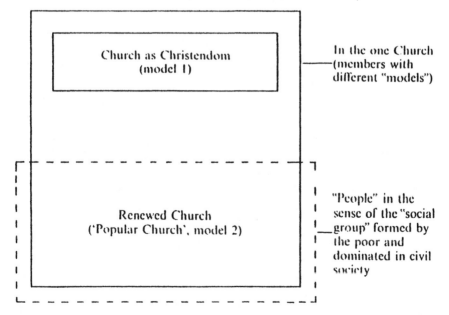

re-evangelised, reconverted church is born of the people, who are part of
the same church (because they are the great believing, Christian mass of
the baptised) through the Holy Spirit of renewal of life. In no sense is this
"people" the "Gentiles" of *Lumen Gentium*, and consequently there is no
reason—as we shall shortly see—to fear a desire that the (non-Christian,
Gentile) people may, exclusively from itself, produce the people of God,
the Church.

3. "PEOPLE OF GOD" AND "BASIC ECCLESIAL COMMUNITIES" AT PUEBLA (1979)

The preparations for Puebla took place in an atmosphere of confusion,
sometimes deliberately created. Take this commentary, for example:

> Without admitting the simplistic identification of the *people* (*pueblo*) with the
> *poor* (*el pobre*) and taking the expression People of God in the sense proposed
> by the Second Vatican Council . . . it would be also perfectly correct to say that
> the People of God is the bearer of the Gospel, the subject of the Church. . . .[19]

Many levels are muddled here. "People" (*pueblo*) in the first lie is something
like a sociological concept (like the "social group" formed by the oppressed),
and the author opposes its identification with the "poor" (an identification
which is, *sociologically*, quite possible, but has no theological implication one
way or the other). It is obvious that to attempt to identify the sociological category "people" with the "people of God" of *Lumen Gentium* is an oversim-
plification which no theologian could make (not, that is, in the real meaning
of a text, as opposed to a phrase taken out of context). But it can also be
maintained that those who opt for or live in the situation of the people,
among the real poor, as Christians ("the people of God" who make an option for the poor and share their lives, if we accept the phrase, which is not
a tautology—the *popular* "people of God"), are also, though not exclusively,
bearers of the gospel and the subject of the Church. This sense—which is
what those they attack intend and what their texts say—never occurs to the
critics of the "popular church," who are trying to find a *sect* in what is a legitimate *part* of the church, the one, official, institutional Church.

At Puebla the word "people" was used in all the senses we have indicated, but there is often no clear realisation of the move from one sense to
another. Let us look at some examples.

> CELAM created an environment among the Catholic *people* in which it could
> open itself with a degree of case to a Church which also presented itself as a
> "*people*" (*pueblos*) a universal *People* which permeates other *peoples* (*pueblos*)

(Puebla, 233). Our Latin American *people* (*pueblo*) spontaneously call a church "God's house," . . . expressing the deepest and primary reality of the people of God (238).

It can be seen here that in *one case* the reference is to Latin American civil society, in *another* to society as a whole but as already Christian, and in other cases it is to the Church. It was in these not very well defined terms that the issue of the popular church was raised:

> The problem of the popular church, the church born of the people (*Iglesia popular, que nace del pueblo*) has several aspects. The first obstacle is surmounted if it is understood as a Church trying to become incarnate in the *popular* environments (*medios populares*) of our continent and so arising out of the response in faith of these groups to the Lord (263).

This sense, obviously, is the true meaning of the concept of the "popular church," a part of the one Church, the people of God, which has made a commitment to the people in the sense of the *real* poor, oppressed, those who suffer, etc. In this sense the Church "has been born" ("*Ecclesia orta sit* . . ." a council father said) *through* the work of the Holy Spirit, *of* the flesh, *of* the historical people of Latin America, but as an Israel *already* chosen (because *already* in the Church, although its evangelisation has not finished): it has been "reborn." The popular church is the part of the Church (from cardinals, through bishops, priests, lay people, etc.), which has opted for or shares the lives of the *real* poor. It is not a "parallel" church set against an "official" Church. This Manichean excision is the product of a falsifying interpretation, which is still being put forward, but it is based on a wish to destroy the legitimacy of a legitimate part of the *one* Church.

At the same time there is an accusation of a sort of Pelagianism: the Church is born of the people (in the sense of the "Gentiles"). From this we get to a contrary position, one which is certainly outside the concilior tradition on the Church:

> This is the only way of being the church; *it is not born of the people*, but makes the people of God in that it is a call, . . . but it is not "popular" in that it originates in the people as such.[20]

The attempt to deny legitimacy to a Pelagian position (the Church as "people of God" is born totally of the people, in the sense of "Gentiles") falls into a Monophysite position: the Church is born exclusively of God; no value is given to the flesh, the community which is called together. The call "*makes* the people;" in other words, each man or woman is made holy and saved "individually and in isolation"—in contradiction of *Lumen Gentium*. There is no sense that the Church—as Puebla teaches in many texts—calls and takes to itself a "people," a human "community," and in so doing also enriches itself with all the historical fruits of those peoples. The "people of God," the *new* people, is not born *solely* or *exclusively* either from the *first* people, nor solely of the Spirit, *excluding* the flesh. Without Mary there is no Christ, and equally without flesh there is no incarnation. Without a *people* which has been called there is no "people of God."

This, in any case, is not the issue in the discussion about the popular church, since it is not about the origin of the Church in the beginning (the *new* people, the Church, born of the *first* people, Israel, by the work of the holy Spirit and with Jesus as its head), but about the renewal, re-evangelisation, reconversion of an *existing* Church, one which is the Christian people but can still reach the full development of its faith. In other words, the *"renewed* church," which has been transformed by its option and by being poor with the poor, is born from the "one, official Church," but it is born of the poor of that Church, of the oppressed people. This "renewal" of the Church is born of the Christian people itself. There is, in addition, an organisational element, but not one in opposition to the official church, since it includes *part* of the whole official Church, from lay people and religious to bishops and cardinals:

> in a basic ecclesial community . . . developing their union with Christ, they are searching for a more evangelical life in the midst of the *people*. . . . "The basic ecclesial communities are an expression of the Church's preferential love for the simple *people*" (Puebla, 641–43).

There can be no doubt that the basic ecclesial communities are, as it were, the natural habitat of Christians who belong to the oppressed people and the "people of God," belong to the poor and belong to the Church. Not all the members of the Church opt for the poor or are poor. The basic community is also the appropriate place for the participation of the poor, the poor as a people, in the Church, the "people of God," and for those who opt for them. The poor and those who opt for them, both being members of the "people of God," can perfectly well be called the "popular church." *Church* is the noun, denoting the "people of God" according to *Lumen Gentium*; *popular* is the adjective, implying a commitment to the poor and oppressed, the historical people, the social group consisting of the oppressed. In this sense, the "popular church" means those Christians, *within the one official and institutional church*, who have a different "model" (meaning vision and practice) of the type of evangelisation the Church should be carrying out in the world and among the poor, and so a different "model" of the church to which they belong wholly and legitimately.

4. CONCLUSIONS

The "popular church" or the Church committed to the poor, in solidarity with them, in the sense indicated, has been defined for us in general terms by John Paul II:

> The Church is passionately committed to this cause (of the workers) because she regards it as her mission, her service, as a proof of her fidelity to Christ, in order to be genuinely the Church of the poor. The poor are to be found in many forms: they appear in different places and at different times—in many cases we find them to be the product of the violation of the dignity of human work (*Laborem Exercens*, 8).

The Polish theologian Jozef Tischner, in his "Ethics of Solidarity," has enabled us to see the importance to his local church of the concepts of "country," "nation," and "freedom":

> The problem of the country faces us daily . . . and arising from it is the question of the preservation of the country. . . . This consciousness guides the whole nation. . . . Freedom is, as it were, a space in which we can move with security.[21]

In Latin America we have a different view of things. The "people," rather than the country or the nation, is the chief protagonist of our current history, and this "people" aspires, not so much to "freedom" as to "justice." It is not a matter of being able to eat in freedom, but of having something to eat at all. Consequently, where some may talk of the *"national* church" or the church which embodies the *national* identity, in Latin America we feel that our "identity" is embodied in a *popular* church. Devotion to Mary, for example, is "popular": It was with the Virgin of Guadalupe on his banner that the priest Hidalgo fought against the Spanish in the nineteenth century to liberate Mexico, and the peasant Emiliano Zapata occupied Cuernavaca, also using as his banner a picture of our Lady of Guadalupe (taken from a church). And, "as John Paul II has pointed out, [this devotion] is part of the innermost *identity of these peoples*" (Puebla, 283). "Mary was also the voice which urged us to unity as human beings and Latin American *peoples*" (282).

There are people, even within the Church, with a clear desire to create confusion. In any situation, however, it is necessary to understand the experience of a particular church, such as that of Latin America, in order not to judge it simplistically in terms of different parameters, different cultures, nations or peoples. Our "believing people" (*pueblo creyente*) deserves the respect of being listened to, of being incorporated into the "people of God" as a historical people, with a memory, language and culture, with heroes, martyrs and saints. Archbishop Oscar Romero died for this "people" with an *explicit* sense of being part of the *"popular* church."

If someone asks us, for valid reasons, to give up a word, "popular," it can go. But the underlying meaning was clearly stated by Pope John XXIII, and I may say that I had a deep personal experience of it with Paul Gauthier in Nazareth from 1959 to 1962, when we talked about "Jesus, the Church and the poor" while working as carpenters in the Arab *shikum* in the village where Jesus said, "The Spirit of the Lord has anointed me *to evangelise the poor*." It is "the church *of the poor*."

NOTES

This selection was translated by Francis McDonagh.

1. See *Acta Synodalia S. Conc. Oec. Vaticani Secundi*, I/1 (Vatican 1970); I/4 (Vatican 1971), Congregation 21.
2. Ibid. I/4, p. 127.
3. Ibid. p. 126.
4. Ibid. p. 133.
5. Ibid. p. 250.
6. Ibid. p. 254.
7. *Le Monde*, Paris (May 1983).
8. In Congregation 3, in the message to all human beings, the Council says, "Caritas Christi urget nos . . . super turbam fame, miseria, ignorantia laborantem" (Ibid., I/I, p. 225).
9. Ibid. p. 256. Mgr. Enrique Rau remarked, referring to the "language of the liturgy," that "the Latin American view is that the mass is *for the people*, and how can they take part if they cannot understand?" (Ibid., pp. 4800).
10. Ibid. II/I, p. 216.
11. Ibid. pp. 256ff.
12. Ibid. p. 334.
13. Ibid. p. 798.
14. Ibid. II/2, pp. 236-26. Cardinal de Barros Camar also spoke on "De Populo Dei in genere" (Congregation 51, 18 Oct. 1963, pp. 55ff.
15. Ibid. III/I (1973) pp. 181ff.
16. "The new Israel . . . is also called the church of Christ. For He has bought it for Himself with His blood, has filled it with His Spirit, and provided it with those means which befit it as a viable and social unity" (LG 9).
17. *SPES* (Lima) 4.21 (1973) 5ff. *Los obispos latinoamericanos entre Medellín y Puebla* (San Salvador 1978) pp. 40–63. See E. Dussel, *De Medellín a Puebla* (Mexico 1979) pp. 229ff.
18. See *Mensaje* (Santiago de Chile) 226 (1974) 52.
19. B. Kloppenburg. *Informé sobre la Iglesia popular* (Mexico 1978) p. 58.
20. J. Lozano Barrangan. *La Iglesia del Pueblo* (Mexico 1983) p. 106.
21. Italian translation, Bologna 1981, p. 137.

6

Exodus as a Paradigm
in Liberation Theology

The re-reading of Exodus runs through the history of the Latin American church. In the middle of the sixteenth century, shortly after the conquest, the holy bishop of Popayan, Juan del Valle, said that the primitive inhabitants of the region were "treated worse than the slaves in Egypt."[1] The valiant revolutionary, the Inca Tupac Amaru, in the decree by which he summoned hundreds of thousands of indigenous people to rise against Spain in Peru on 14 November 1780, wrote:

> The Catholic zeal of a son of the Church, as a professed Christian in most holy baptism . . . hoping that many others will shake off the yoke of this Pharaoh, the magistrates, I have set forth to speak for and defend the whole kingdom. . . . The purposes of my sound intention are [to win] for my nation complete freedom from all forms of oppression.[2]

When we reach our own century we find the expression "land flowing with milk and honey" at the end of the Sandinista anthem in Nicaragua. Or we have Fidel Castro's reference, in his defense, *History Will Forgive Me*, to

> the 100,000 small farmers who live [in 1956] and die working a land that is not theirs, contemplating it sadly as Moses did the promised land. . . .[3]

That is why, as part of this tradition of the Latin American people, liberation theology from its very beginning understood the paradigm of the Ex-

---

Enrique Dussel, "Exodus as a Paradigm in Liberation Theology," *Concilium* 189 (1987): 83–92.

odus as its fundamental schema. So strong is this sense that it is even criticised for this continual return to a re-reading of Exodus.

1. THE RELEVANCE OF THE EXODUS
PARADIGM FOR THE THIRD WORLD TODAY

The Exodus appears as a central point in *African liberation theology*, [4] and we should not forget that the setting for the Exodus story was actual North Africa. The same can be said of *Asian liberation theology*, [5] where, perhaps even to a greater extent than in Latin America, the oppression of the poor is a blatant fact, beyond concealing. In *Latin America*, from the beginning, we have always come back to Exodus. I recall that as early as 1967 I used to begin my courses at IPLA (CELAM's Instituto Pastoral Latinoamericano in Quito) with exegesis of Exodus, [6] there one could find, spelt out, the main categories of liberation theology. In the same way, at different times, liberation theologians have always had to refer to the basic texts of Exodus. [7]

According to Rubem Alves in 1970,

> The Exodus was the experience which created the consciousness of the people of Israel. The people formed in the structuring centre which determined its way of organising time and space. Note that I am not saying simply that the Exodus is part of the contents of the consciousness of the people of Israel. If that were the case, the Exodus would be one item of information among others. More than an item of information, it is *its structuring centre*, in that it determines the integrating logic, the principles of organisation and interpretation of historical experience. That is why the Exodus does not persist as a secondary experience. . . . It has come to be *the paradigm* for the interpretation of *all space and all time*. [8]

Sixteen years ago the great Brazilian Protestant theologian pointed explicitly (even in his use of the term "paradigm") to the topic which concerns us. We shall examine it in stages.

By "paradigm" we mean the generative matrix or "schema" (in something like the Kantian sense), the *structure* which, from fundamental *categories*, originates a fixed number of *relations* which become generative, not only of a theology, but also of the everyday hermeneutic of the Christian people's faith.

There are essentially six of these categories: (1) Egypt and the Pharaonic class (Ph, the dominators, the sinners (Exod. 1:8); (2) the slaves (S), the exploited, the just (Exod. 1:11); (3) the prophet, Moses (M) (Exod. 2:1 ff.); (4) God (G), who listens and converts (Exod. 3:1 ff.); (5) the passage (P) through the desert, the passover, the trials, the ambiguity—such a contemporary theme—of the priest Aaron (Exod. 12:37 ff.); (6) the promised land (L) (Exod. 3:8).

There are eight *relations* which, arising from the *categories*, make up the *structure* of the paradigm: (a) domination or sin (Exod. 1:1–22); (b) the cry of the people (Exod. 3:7); (c) conversion, the call of the word to the prophet (Exod. 2:11–4:17); (d) challenge to the dominator, the sinner (Exod. 4:18–6:1); (e) challenge to the people of God (Exod. 6:2–27); (f) departure, liberation (Exod. 7:8 ff.); (g) critical prophetic action, even against the priest Aaron (prophet-priest dialectic, continuing throughout the passage through the desert); (h) entry, the building of the new system (Josh. 3:16 ff.); (i) salvation, the kingdom, the community of life, which may be another Egypt (1 Sam. 8:10–18) and so splits: the historical promised land (always liable to be surpassed) and the kingdom of God (the absolute, only fully realised after history).

However, as Alves indicates, there are three space-time areas which organise the discourse, praxis: (1) Egypt as the past, the "first land;" (2) the

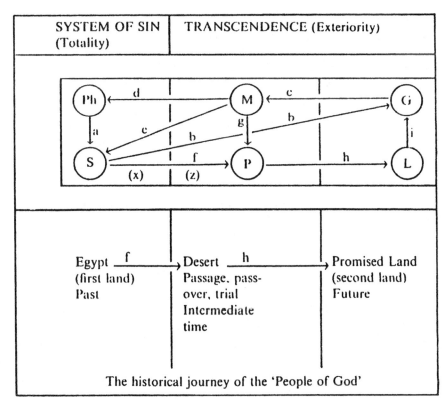

Figure 6.1. The Exodus "Paradigm"

desert as the "intermediate time" and space of passage; (3) the promised land as the utopian term, the future, the "second land."

The totality of the discourse, of historical praxis, of the paradigm, has a *subject*, "the children of Israel,"[9] the people of the oppressed liberating themselves from the slavery of exploitation, of sin, in an alliance with their God:

> I will go down with you to Egypt, and I will also bring you up again (Gen. 46:4).

The paradigm can be seen, theologically, in the re-reading which the Bible performs of itself:

> By faith Moses, when he was grown up, refused to be called the son of Pharaoh's daughter, choosing rather to share ill-treatment with the people of God than to enjoy the fleeting pleasures of sin. . . . By faith he left Egypt. . . . By faith he kept the Passover and sprinkled the blood. . . . By faith the people crossed the Red Sea as if on dry land. . . . By faith the walls of Jericho fell down (Heb. 11:24–30).

For us Latin Americans, certainly, the text of Exodus makes a powerful call on our attention. The reason is clear:

> The liberation of Israel is a political action. It is the breaking away from a situation of despoliation and misery and the beginning of the construction of a just and fraternal society. It is the suppression of disorder and the creation of a new order. The initial chapters of Exodus describe the oppression in which the Jewish people lived in Egypt, in that "land of slavery" (13:3; 20:2; Deut. 5:6): repression (1:10–11), alienated work (5:6–14), humiliations (1:13–14), enforced birth control policy (1:15–22). Yahweh then awakens the vocation of a liberator: Moses.[10]

Let us now see how, historically and in practice, liberation theology has moved in and across the Exodus paradigm.

2. DIACHRONIC UNFOLDING OF THE PARADIGM

It should not be thought that everything was present from the beginning, or that everything has already taken place. There has been a *history* (a "diachrony" of the "synchronous" moments of the paradigm) which still has to be written. What follows are introductory notes for that history.

In my view, the liberation theologians, as a "school of prophets"—not as individuals of genius, since they are a community phenomenon in Latin America—have *gradually been "taking consciousness" of the categories and relations indicated.* They have been semantically deepening their content and, as a result, starting from the "consciousness of the Christian people" of Latin America themselves, the theology has been growing alongside, starting from and following the historical praxis of that people. Everything could not be expressed in the sixties because the Christian people had not lived through fundamental historical spiritual experiences. History determined the explicit gaining of consciousness of the moments of the Exodus paradigm in liberation theology. No theologians from one Latin American country alone could perform this task; it was the communal achievement of the "school of prophets" stimulating each other, and based on the experience of the Christian people of various countries. Underplaying some theologians in liberation theology, or exaggerating the importance of some countries, impoverishes an ecclesial and continental phenomenon which is already a "historical fact" which in a short time has gone round the small world of theology, and indeed of the Church.

On at least five levels there has been a *diachronic maturation* in the gaining of theological consciousness of the structures of the paradigm. First, there has been a move from "personal" (abstract individual) and "subjective" experience of *poverty (as a virtue) to poverty as a requirement for the whole Church.* The "Church of the poor," it is now seen, must be a poor church (the pope, the Vatican, bishops, priests, activists, with a spirit of poverty, without any triumphalism, giving away unnecessary wealth, land, etc.). Secondly, there has been a move from this "subjective" poverty, as a virtue or "spiritual infancy," to the objective fact of "the poor," *other people.* It is no longer Moses poor in the desert, but Moses discovering the poor man being ill-treated by the official (Exod. 2:11–12). Thirdly, there has been a move from the poor discovered in the spiritual experience of the Gospel to the definition of these poor (thanks to the hermeneutical mediation of the social sciences) as a "class"—first in specific countries—and subsequently as a *"people"* in other Latin American countries. The move has been from "subjectivity" (poverty-virtue) to "objectivity" (poor-class-people).

Fourthly, there has been a movement from these poor, the class, the people, as object of an "option-for" (I, subject, opt-for another), to the affirmation of these poor, this class, this people, as the *"subject" of the Church and history* (a move from the people as "object" to the people as "subject"). Only at this point do we have the emergence of the "Church of the poor," not the "poor" Church of the Vatican II period with the emphasis on the poverty of bishops, priests, etc., but the Church which has as its "privileged subject" the historical Christian people, made up of the real poor, flesh, bone, blood and oppression, whom the hierarchical structures (pope, Vatican, bishops) have to serve and keep as a point of reference. (A necessary stage here was the "popular Church," though this has now been superseded.)

And, finally, the fifth aspect is that the diachrony is perhaps more in accord with Exodus. In other words, the Christian people are re-reading scripture in terms of their *actual historical situation*. Oppression, dictatorships, exploitation without hope, form a *Latin American Egypt* (S): today in Chile, but in 1976 in Brazil, Argentina, Nicaragua, etc. Pre-revolutionary situations are the Egyptian "plagues" (today Guatemala, for example— point x on arrow f, the beginning of liberation). Revolutionary situations in the strict sense as in El Salvador are the going out into the desert (point z on arrow f). The wandering in the desert, the violent persecution by Pharaoh's armies, could be compared with the "contras" in Nicaragua (this was the interpretations of the basic ecclesial communities in Esteli), Aaron's treason (then the priest, now the bishop?), the prophet's rage (Miguel D'Escoto?), etc. Finally there is the building of a new order (before the First Cuban National Ecclesial Encounter, ENEC, in February 1986 we seemed to catch sight already of a new order, which, however, is never the final kingdom). We shall look at these elements in turn in summary form, more as suggestions than a finished analysis.

3. THE FIRST SEMANTIC SHIFT: FROM THE "INDIVIDUAL" TO THE "POOR" CHURCH

In what was still the prehistory of liberation theology, in the 1950s, many people went through the spiritual experience of a *radical demand for poverty*. Examples are Charles de Foucauld, a Franciscan renewal in various areas of the Church, the presence of French worker priests in the refugee camps during the Second World War. I myself was with Paul Gauthier in Nazareth between 1959 and 1961.[11] Our rule of life there was the text: "The Spirit of the Lord has anointed me to evangelise the poor" (See Isa. 61:1; Luke 4:18). Working in the Arab *Sikkun* of Nazareth (as a carpenter) or as fishermen on Tiberias (in the Ginnosar Kibbutz), we discovered the poor Jesus and Jesus the poor worker. At the beginning of the Second Vatican Council Mgr Hakim, the bishop of Nazareth, Mgr Hammer of Tournai and others, including Helder Camara, launched through the Nazareth team the idea of the "Church of the poor," which Pope John XXIII took up personally. It was a personal, individual requirement of poverty, accepted by people from the pope and cardinals down to bishops, priests, religious and lay activists. The archbishop of Medellin left his Episcopal palace and went to live in a poor district. Mgr. Manuel Larrain distributed his diocese's land for the sake of poverty, bishops began to sell their gold pectoral crosses and replaced them with crosses without precious metal. It was a shift from personal poverty, from the "spiritual childhood" of Teresa of Lisieux, which made such a great impact on us in our adolescence, to community and ecclesial poverty on the part of the universal institution. The goal was a non-triumphalist Church, humble, a servant, poor. This took place in many parts of Latin America from 1952 to 1965, and it later had repercussions in the first works of liberation theology.

4. SECOND SHIFT:
FROM "POVERTY" TO "THE POOR"

"Subjective" poverty (on the part of the Christian or of the church) was still something of a preparatory stage (*M* in the schema or paradigm). It was the "Put off your shoes from your feet" (Exod. 3:5), a demand and conversion, an anticipatory spiritual experience, and as such the origin of the liberation theology which was to come. But now the prophet (*M*) in the desert, converted, can begin a discourse. At the beginning the theme was "faith and politics," the possibility of political commitment, on the part of university students (YCS) and worker activists (YCW). The Cuban revolution (in 1959, the same time as John XXIII launched the idea of a council) had encouraged many young people to go beyond a subjectivist spirituality; it was the time for action—remember Camilo Torres: faith and charity combined with effectiveness. The "objectivity" of the demand for commitment led to the use of the social sciences, of even Marxist analysis if necessary (remember the Brazilian Acao Popular of the early sixties).

I believe that it was only when a revolutionary political idea was able to combine synthetically with the spiritual experience of subjective poverty that something fundamental took place. The idea was "the poor."[12] I recall Assmann's very sensible criticism of the ambiguity of the category "poor." By that time it had not been assimilated by liberation theology outside Argentina. The El Escorial meeting (1972) broached the idea explicitly: it was the first time that so many liberation theologians had come together. There the *idea of "the poor" exploded as a category and a reality.*

It was now possible to talk, not of a "poor" Church (a subjective and hierarchical approach), but of an "option *for the poor*" (an objective approach). Note, however, that if the Church, the prophet (*M*), opts for the slave (*S* and arrow *e* on figure 6.1), that means that it is not yet poor by birth. It is a moment of maturation, but in no sense the end of the process or of the objective conversion of the Church.

5. THIRD SHIFT: FROM
"THE POOR" TO "CLASS" AND "PEOPLE"

Who are the poor? The abstract poor or real people? Very soon, following El Escorial, where the idea was raised, the answer was given: *the poor are also a social "class."* But they can also be *"the people."* The term "poor," even in Marxist thought, cannot be identified with a social "class," but has been used ambiguously to take advantage of its social and Gospel relevance. A Chilean and Peruvian strand, at the height of the Popular Unity government, placed more stress on class analysis. The southern cone, Argentine, line (with the experience of the return of Peronism) tended toward the category "people," "Classism" had a partial aspect, as did "populism." What is certain is that both currents merged in their best aspects, around 1973. "I have heard the cry of my people" (see the Exodus expression), the document of the bishops of the Brazilian North-East, marks, approximately, the beginning of the spiritual experience of a "popular Church." The Argentine element combined with the "class" line but, at the same time, the category "poor," previously absent, now became central.

In reality there was a twofold maturation (of *S*). On the one hand, as we have noted, the "poor" Church (subjective) opted for "the poor" (objective), but "the poor"—thanks to the mediation of the social sciences and the political commitments of Christians—were now seen as a "class," and even more, "the people." The idea of "the poor" had been filled out, made historical, identifiable. It was now real, Latin American: *"the Latin American Christian people."*

In addition, the Church, from being subjectively poor, now discovered itself as "the people of God," as the (objectively) popular Church. This is no longer an option (options are made by the prophet of the prophetic Church, *M*), but an affirmation of itself, the people has become the subject (the *S* of figure 6.1 is now the subject, "the children of Israel"). In other words, the poor, the class, the people, for whom the objective option is made, *now became subjects.* This is a subjectivisation of the process, but not now focused on virtue, the individual virtue of poverty, as in the 1950s, but the subjectivisation of the poor themselves, who now have the "consciousness" of being the people of God, the most hidden part of the Church, the necessary reference for evangelisation. The poor, who were evangelised (the "basic ecclesial communities," etc.) *now become the evangelisers.*[13]

This last step, after the Nicaraguan revolution (1979), brings a realisation that it is no longer necessary to speak of a popular Church, and there is a return to John XXIII's description "the Church of the poor." Now,

however, "of the poor" does not mean just that the Church is poor, but—
and this is fundamental that the real, historical poor are the privileged
"subject" of the Church itself. The implication is that the slaves (S) are
"subjects" of a possible process of liberation (arrow *f*).

The "praxis of liberation" then also started to change direction, from the
liberating praxis of prophets and heroes to the praxis of the people themselves in their liberation. It would be easy to demonstrate his "semantic
shift" in all the liberation theologians. Liberation theology, as a humble
expression of this praxis, can also fulfill a critical prophetic function
which enables this praxis to be reproduced (arrow *g*).

NOTES

This selection was translated by Francis McDonagh.

1. See E. Dussel *El episcopado latinamericano y la liberación de los pobres* (CRT, Mexico 1979).
2. Quoted in B. Lewis *La rebelión de Tupac Amaru* (SELA Buenos Aires 1967) pp. 452–53. See E. Dussel, "Introducción general" *Historia General de la Iglesia en América Latina* (Sigueme, Salamanca 1983) pp. 268–80.
3. Fidel Castro *la revolución cubana 1953–1962* (Era, Mexico 1976) p. 39.
4. See Jean-Marc Ela "Une lecture africaine de l'Exode" in *Le Cri de l'homme africain* (L'Harmattan, Paris 1980) pp. 40–51.
5. Tissa Balasuriya *Planetary Theology* (Orbis Books, New York 1984) p. 184; Cyris Hee Suk Moon *Minjung Theology* (Orbis Books, New York 1986) p. 120. Also Emerito Nacpitl "A Gospel for the New Filipino" in *Asian Voices in Theology* (Orbis Books, New York 1976) p. 129.
6. See E. Dussel *History and Theology of Liberation* (Orbis Books, New York 1976) pp. 155ff.
7. See Hugo Assmann *Teologia desde la praxis de la liberación* (Sigueme, Salamanca 1973) pp. 54, 55: "Opresión en Egito, Exodo"; Samuel Silva Gotay *El pensamiento cristiano revolucionario en America Latina* (Sigueme, Salamanca 1981) pp. 141–47: "La liberación del éxodo centro estructurante de la fe"; H. Bojorge "Exodo y liberación" *Vispera* 19–20 (1970) 33ff; Andres Lanson *Liberar a los oprimidos* (Kaitas, Buenos Aires 1967); Pedro Negre "Biblia y liberación in *Cristianismo y sociedad*" 24–25 (1970) pp. 49ff; see the references to the Exodus in the meeting on liberation theology (at the beginning on development) in November 1969 in Mexico: *Inf. Cath. Internat.* 351 (1970) pp. 12ff; Jorge Pixley *Exodo. Una lectura evangélica y popular* (CUPSA, Mexico 1983); "El Nuevo Testamento y el socialismo" *El apostol* 3/1 (1973) 14ff; R. Sartor "Exodo-liberación: tema de actualidad para una reflexión teológica" *Revista Biblica* 139/32 (1971) 73–77; Luis Rivera "La liberación en el éxodo" *Revista Biblica* 139/32 (1971) pp. 13–26. The list could be endless, since reference to the Exodus in liberation theology is continual. Even the second Instruction of the Congregation for the Doctrine of the Faith ("Instruction on Christian Freedom and Lib-

eration," 22 Mar 1986) deals with it in its para. 44: "The exodus and Yahweh's liberating acts." Nor can we forget Porfirio Miranda *Marx and the Bible* (Orbis Books, New York 1974: SCM, London 1977 pp. 78–88 ff: "The God of the Exodus"); Elsa Tamez *La Biblia de los oprimidos* (DEI, San Jose 1979); Segundo Galilea "La liberación como encuentro de la politica y la contemplación" *Espiritualidad y Liberación* (DEI, San Jose 1982) pp. 45ff; Ignacio Ellacuria *Freedom Made Flesh* (Orbis Books, New York 1976) p. 16; for the position of Ernesto Cardenal, see Phillip Berryman *The Religious Roots of Rebellion* (Orbis Books, New York 1984) pp. 20, 23, etc.; S. Croato "Liberacion y libertad. Reflexiones hermencuticas en torno al Antiguo Testamento" *Revista Biblica* 32 (1981) 3–7; *Liberacion y liberatad* (Mundo Nuevo, Buenos Aires 1973).

8. In "Puebolo de Dios y la liberación del hombre" *Fichas ISAL* 3/26 (1979) p. 9.

9. See J. Pixley *Exodo*, p. 19.

10. Gustavo Guiterrez. *A Theology of Liberation* (Orbis Books, New York 1973 and SCM Press, London 1974) pp. 155, 56. See also the texts on pp. 155, 60 and 287ff.

11. See Methol Ferre "La Iglesia latinoamericana de Rio a Puebla (1955–1979)" *Historia de la Iglesia* ed. Fliche-Martin (EDICEP, Valencia 1981) suppl. Vol. I pp. 697–725; Gustavo Gutierrez "Teología de la Liberación y ciencias sociales," duplicated text. See Paul Gauthier *Les Pauvres, Jésus et l'Eglise* (Ed. Universitaires, Paris 1963) pp. 101ff: "De Nazaret vers Rome." I remember the little community of Paul, Andrés and myself—which I left in 1961 to start my theological studies in France. The community's rule of life contains the following statement at the beginning: "Its aim is to live the Gospel in the light of that text from Luke 4 in which Jesus, quoting Isaiah 61, reveals his messianic anointing and his mission to evangelise *the poor*" (Gauthier p. 113).

12. This was made possible by the convergence of the Nazareth experience (1959–1961) and a reading of E. Levinas (1969): the "poor" (Isa. 61:1; Luke 4:18), the Latin American poor, the poor as real people and as a theological category (see E. Dussel *Para una ética de la liberación latinoamericana* (1970) (Buenos Aires 1973) I, Chap. 3.

13. See Jon Sobrino *Resurreción de la verdadera Iglesia. Los pobres, lugar teológico de la ecclesiologia* (Santander 1981).

III

ETHICS AND ECONOMICS

7

Racism: A Report on the Situation in Latin America

I propose to deal here with racism as discrimination against the African slaves, not against the native Indians.[1] A brief remark first about some of the postulates used. There is a school of "economicism" which would see class economic domination as the sole cause of racism (assessment *a* in Figure 7.1). On the other hand, there exists a "subjectivist psychologism" which denies any possibility of considering the problem if one has not first suffered humiliation "in one's own skin" (assessment *b*). Then there is the classic "biological racism" which seeks to define the cause of racism as the natural or physical differences between individuals of different races, with the supposition that one race is genetically superior to another (assessment *c*). Finally, there are those who adopt a "cultural" viewpoint and see everything being played out on the level of symbols, in cultural traditions, dance and song (assessment *d*). In fact the problem of racist domination operates on all these levels, once one understands that its chief characteristic is a part of *ideological* development.

The struggle against racist domination therefore needs to take account of all these levels. A theology of liberation of the Black population of Latin America should also take account of all the different assessments if it is not to be left working from a partial standpoint.

Enrique Dussel, "Racism: A Report on the Situation in Latin America," *Concilium* 151 (1982): 54–60.

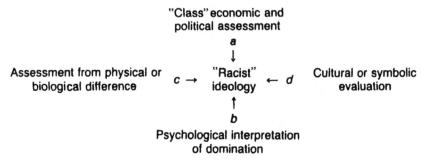

Figure 7.1.   The "Practical Circle" of Racist Ideology

1. HISTORICAL CLASS ASSESSMENT[2]

The Portuguese discovery of the route to India in the fifteenth century and the conquest of America by the Spaniards and Portuguese led to the decline of the Arab commercial world (since that route was no longer the only one open to world trade), and to a crisis in all the kingdoms of the Savannah countries (as a result of Arab decline), mainly because Europe now sought its gold in America.[3] This explains why communities such as the Soninke, Sosso, Mandingas, Sourhay, Haoussa, Bornu, etc., which were divided into ruling and ruled classes, began to engage in the *sale* of their African brothers on the West Coast of Africa, in order to produce a continuing level of commercial profit. The Portuguese, the English, the Dutch, and the French all became involved in the dreadful slave trade from Africa to tropical Latin America, which led to agriculture on the "plantations dedicated to the growing of cash crops for export: sugar, cocoa, cotton, etc. And in Latin America a "slave-based patriarchal Catholicism" appeared.[4]

Although the Spanish crown had banned Jews, Moors, "new Christians," and *negroes* from going to the West Indies, the latter were already common in Santo Domingo by 1505. The "sugar cycle," lasting till 1520, started there, and the sugar mills were populated with African slaves. "All work linked to the land was carried out by African slaves. The slave population of Melchor de Torres reached 900. By 1548 the number of mills and mines had reached thirty-five."[5]

E. Genovese has proved that the production systems operative in the plantations were not anti-capitalist, though it must be recognised that the English and Dutch slave-owning bourgeoisie in the Caribbean developed a more modern and truly capitalist system than the Spanish—even than the most developed of the Spanish societies, the slave-owning middle-classes in Cuba. "Slavery should be seen primarily as a *class* question, and only secondarily as a racial question."[6] Nicolás Sánchez Albornoz points to the same conclusion: "Negroes were first and foremost capital goods, and their importation was governed by the rules of commerce and the stimulus of trade."[7] Of course the system was not the same in the case of the patriarchal paternalism of the mill owner of North-East Brazil as in that of the English capitalist who lived in London and owned "plantations" in Jamaica, Trinidad or Guyana. But the fact is that Latin America had a slave population.

As early as 1513 the Spanish king gave the first license to charge two ducats for each African slave sold. By 1578 this had risen to thirty ducats. The Africans were treated monstrously, not only by the human hunt in Africa and the inhuman passage across the Atlantic—during which up to 30 percent died—but equally by the "palming" (measuring height and therefore price) and branding (with a hot iron on the back, chest or thigh, to show that the tax had been paid) to which they were subjected once they arrived at the ports of Cartagena, Vera Cruz, Bahía, Río, Pernambuco, etc.

Besides the Caribbean and Brazil, the whole of northern South America (Venezuela and Colombia) and the Pacific coast down to Guayaquil had a Black majority. In Mexico, Central America, Peru and the River Plate district, Black slaves were used as domestic servants or *Majordomos* in charge of Indians. Whatever use they were put to, the basic reason for their presence in Latin America was mercantile capitalism.

2. THE ABOLITION OF SLAVERY IN LATIN AMERICA

One factor was the work *Instauranda Aethiopum Salute* written by Alonso de Sandóval, SJ, at the end of the seventeenth century. (He taught St. Peter Claver, the apostle of the slaves, in Cartagena.) Another was the formation of slave and negro confraternities in the colonial period. Another the endless revolts by Africans—in Haïti alone in 1522, 1679, and 1691; in Santo Domingo in 1523, 1537, 1548, etc.; in the British Antilles in 1647, 1674, 1702, 1733, and 1759; few as impressive as the establishment of a real State in the "shanty-town" of Los Palmares in Brazil, in which the hero Zumbi Gangozuma was killed in 1695. A major factor was the way the Black leader and liberator of Haïti, Toussaint Louverture, showed the world that negroes could be political leaders and rulers. But as a matter of historical fact, the abolition of slavery was chiefly due to the growth of industrial capitalism. While mercantile capitalism needed slaves in order to export tropical products, industrial capitalism needed *free* workers whose labour it could buy for wages. This does not mean that a class-based racism did not carry on in the capitalist system, but industrial capitalism was incompatible with the slavery of the plantations.

So, "the abolition of the slave trade was declared by the Supreme Court of Caracas in 1810, by Hidalgo in Mexico in the same year, by the Chilean Parliament in 1811 and by the Government in Buenos Aires in 1812."[8]

Table 7.1.   Total Importation of Slaves to America from the Fifteenth to the
Nineteenth Centuries (from Curtin, p. 178). Figures in thousands

Region or nation	1451-1600	1601-1700	1701-1800	1811-1870
United States	—	—	348·0	51·0
Latin America	75·0	292·5	578·6	606·0
British Caribbean	—	263·7	1,401·3	—
Jamaica	—	85·1	662·4	—
Barbados	—	134·5	252·5	—
Leeward Islands, St Lucia, Tobago, etc.	—	44·1	371·9	—
Trinidad	—	—	22·4	—
Grenada	—	—	67·0	—
Other British West Indies	—	—	25·0	—
French Caribbean	—	155·8	1,348·4	96·0
Haïti	—	74·6	789·7	—
Martinique	—	66·5	258·3	41·0
Gaudelupe	—	12·7	237·1	41·0
Louisiana	—	—	28·3	—
French Guyana	—	2·0	35·0	14·0
Dutch Caribbean	—	40·0	460·0	—
Danish Caribbean	—	4·0	24·0	—
Brazil	50·0	560·0	1,891·4	1,145·4
Rest of the World	149·9	25·1	—	—
Europe	48·8	1·2	—	—
São Tomé	76·1	23·9	—	—
Atlantic Isles	25·0	—	—	—
TOTAL	274·9	1,341·1	6,051·7	1,898·4
Annual quota	1·8	13·4	55·0	31·6

For the same reasons that led to the victory of the northern states over
the "old South" of the plantations based on patriarchal slave-owning in
the American Civil War, the São Paulo coffee magnates in Brazil
(1870–1880) destroyed the aristocratic slave owners of the North-East of
the country with the law *Lei aurea* of 13 May 1888, which signaled the abolition of slavery and the triumph of the capitalism (though dependent) of
the South.

While slavery disappeared from Latin America in the nineteenth century, "racism" as a *class ideology* discriminating against the manual
labourer, the worker, the marginalised Blacks, did not. In Latin American
countries with a large Black population, racism is still a living, active, real
social injustice.

3. THE BLACK PRESENCE IN LATIN AMERICA

The importance of this question can be seen from the fact that by the end of
this century Brazil alone will have a Black and mulatto population of 80 mil-

lion, making it perhaps the country with the largest negro population in the world. The survival of African customs and religions is everywhere obvious—Bantu, Fanti-ashanti, Black Islam, Calabar, and Yoruba with its famous *Orishas*.[9] The most relevant forms of creative expression are the Voodoo of Haïti and the *candomblé* of north-eastern Brazil, with their own spirits, gods, saints, cosmologies, liturgies and dances, ecstasies, ways of life, and popular communities. Piling one form of syncretism on another, they show traits of African religions, Catholicism, and even Protestantism, together with spiritualism and magic. Arthur Ramos defines *macumba*—another African cult in Brazil—as a mixture of *gégé* (Fon), *nago* (Yoruba), *musulmi* (Black Islam), Bantu, *camboclé* (Indian), spiritualism, and Catholicism.

All such cults derive from three main traditions: genuine African (survivals such as the Bantu "sacred dances"); negro folklore originating in the plantations of America (through a process of "creole-ising," like the stories of "Papa John" who deceives his master, through which the slaves affirmed their own personalities and laughed at their masters); and finally, the whole sphere of the infiltration of Black culture into the dominant White culture, through symbols, music, or effective participation by Blacks in the White way of life.

In recent decades a new political situation for the Blacks in Latin America has begun to emerge. This has happened mainly in the Caribbean, with revolutionary leaders; in the Mosquitia region of Nicaragua, and even through the presence of Cuban negro soldiers in wars of liberation in Africa itself. Could the Africans who left those shores as slaves in the

Table 7.2. The Negro and Mulatto Population of Latin America in 1940 (with percentage of the total population of each country)

Country	Negroes	%	Mulattoes	%
Brazil	5,789,924	14·0	8,276,321	20·01
Antilles	5,500,000	39·29	3,000,000	21·43
British Guyana	100,000	29·30	80,000	23·44
Dutch Guyana	17,000	9·55	20,000	11·23
French Guyana	1,000	0·25	1,000	0·25
Belize	15,000	25·55	20,000	34·03
Colombia	405,076	4·5	2,205,382	24·32
Venezuela	100,000	2·79	1,000,000	27·93
Nicaragua	90,000	6·52	40,000	2·88
Honduras	55,272	4·99	10,000	0·90
El Salvador	100	0·0001	100	0·0001
Costa Rica	26,900	4·09	20,000	3·14
Guatemala	4,011	0·12	2,000	0·06
Mexico	80,000	0·41	40,000	2·04
Ecuador	50,000	2·0	150,000	6·0
Peru	29,054	0·41	80,000	0·71
Bolivia	7,800	0·26	5,000	0·15
Paraguay	5,000	0·52	5,000	0·52
Uruguay	10,000	0·46	50,000	2·30
Argentina	5,000	0·038	10,000	0·076
Chile	1,000	0·02	3,000	0·06

past produce today the liberators of their brothers in their continent of origin? History has long and mysterious ways which must be explored and deciphered.

As can be seen, the negro population is concentrated in tropical produce regions, the old "plantations": the Brazilian coastal region, the Caribbean, and the Pacific coast from southern Paraguay to Ecuador.

4. RACISM AND LIBERATION THEOLOGY IN LATIN AMERICA

The question of racism poses a challenge to liberation theology in its growth process. Domination of one *nation* by another (understood through the theory of dependence), of one *class* by another (where sociological considerations and those of political economy are at stake), of one *sex* by another (where Freudian categories must be taken into account), is not of the same order as domination of one *race* by another, which involves a multi-level complex of economic, political, psychological, cultural and symbolic, ideological, and other factors. Theology has to deal with liberation from all these dominations epistemologically, taking account of the differences between each. The erotic-subjective factor is one thing, the economic-objective another, the symbolic-cultural yet another. Ideology cannot be set aside, either, but needs to be situated on the level of its relative autonomy and so assessed in relation to the other factors.

I have said that industrial capitalism was the basic cause of the freeing of the slaves in the plantation system. Yet German national capitalism (the Krupps and Thyssens, who are never mentioned nowadays but who were responsible for Hitler) has in our century been the economic and political starting-point for anti-Jewish racist ideology. So capitalism is at one time anti-slavery and at another anti-Jewish racist (in order to eliminate international Jewish capital from Germany). In relation to the negroes, capitalism uses colour difference as an ideological tool in the domination of the middle class over the working class—the urban proletariat, since in Latin America the negroes are rarely peasants.

The theological *sin* of racism takes on connotations of economic and political domination, psychological domination (the sadistic aggressiveness of the dominator, the masochistic passivity of the dominated), symbolic domination (the devil is Black, like sin), and ideological domination as such (the negro race is inferior). This is why Boesak's "the courage to be"[10] is immensely important. Not only as negation of the negation involved in oppression, but also as affirmation of Black, African actuality, the dignity of being a *historic people* with its own traditions, heroes, art, and religion.

All this has to be linked *explicitly* to the question of the *oppressed class* in Latin America's system of dependent capitalism. The Black struggle for liberation is a struggle for the affirmation of *negritude* within a national project of liberation, together with other oppressed races, and aiming at a socialist system for Latin America. Without this strategic socio-political focus, liberation of the race can become an absolute, a "reformism," leading in the end to a dissolution of its efforts and an attack on the wrong enemies. These are not "whites" as such but the whites who dominate the capitalist system. To regard any white as an enemy for the simple fact of being white is to fail to distinguish which whites use racism for their own advantage, and, at the same time to alienate white allies who are also *oppressed* by those who dominate both white and black. Theology cannot bypass such questions: if it does, it could become populist or reformist and cease to be liberation theology properly so-called.[11]

NOTES

This selection was translated by Paul Burns.

1. I have given a partial treatment of this question in "Modern Christianity in the face of 'the other'" in *Concilium* 130 (10/1979) 49.

2. The following is a classified bibliography of the question:

(i) *Latin America in general*

J. Saco *Historia de la esclavitud de la raza negra en el Nuevo Mundo* (Havana 1938); E. Vila Vilar *Hispanoamérica y el comercio de esclavos* (Seville 1977); R. Mellafe *Breve historia de la esclavitud negra en América Latina* (Mexico 1973); L. Rout *The African Experience in Spanish America: 1502 to the Present* (Cambridge 1976); F. Knight *The African Dimension in Latin American Societies* (New York 1974); L. Foner *Slavery in the New World* (Englewood Cliffs 1969); J. Gratus "The Great White Lie: slavery, emancipation and changing racial attitudes" in *Monthly Review* (New York 1973).

(ii) *Particular areas*

(a) Brazil:

F. Cardoso *Capitalismo e escravidão no Brasil meridional* (São Paulo 1977); R. Conrad *The Destruction of Brazilian Slavery* (Berkeley 1972); P. Verger *Flux et reflux de la traite des nègres entre le golfe de Bénin et Bahía de Todos os Santos* (Paris 1968).

(b) The Caribbean:

J Handler *The Unappropriated People: Freedmen in the Slave Society of Barbados* (Baltimore 1974); H. Aimes *A History of Slavery in Cuba: 1511–1968* (New York 1970); V. J. Baptiste *Haïti: sa lutte pour l'émancipation* (Paris 1957); O. Patterson *The Sociology of Slavery in Jamaica* (Jamaica 1973); L. Díaz Soler *La esclavitud negra en Puerto Rico* (San Juan 1957); G. Martin *Histoire de l'esclavage dans les colonies françaises* (Paris 1948); J. Fouchard *Les Marrons de la liberté* (Paris 1972).

(c) Mexico:

G. Aguirre *La población negra de México 1519–1910* (Mexico 1946); R. Brady *The Emergence of a Negro Class in Mexico 1524–1640* (Iowa 1965).

(*d*) Central America:

W. Sherman *Forced Native Labor in XVI-century Central America* (London 1979); S. Zavala *Contribución a la historia de las instituciones coloniales de Guatemala* (Guatemala 1953); L. Diez Castillo *Los cimarrones y la esclavitud en Panamá* (Panama 1968).

(*e*) Colombia and Venezuela:

A. Escalante *El negro en Colombia* (Bogotá 1968); J. Palacios *La trata de negros por Cartagena 1650–1750* (Tunja 1973); M. Acosta *Vida de los esclavos negros en Venezuela* (Caracas 1966); E. Tronconis *Documentos para el estudio de los esclavos negros en Venezuela* (Caracas 1969).

(*f*) The Southern Tip:

R. E. Chace *The African Impact on Colonial Argentina* (Santa Barbara 1969); C. Sempat *El tráfico de esclavos en Córdoba 1588–1610* (Córdoba 1965); E. Scheuss de Studer *La trata de negros en el Río de la Plata en el siglo XVIII* (Buenos Aires 1958); G Cruz *La abolición de la esclavitud en Chile* (Santiago 1942); C. Rama *Los agro-uruguayos* (Montevideo 1967).

(*g*) Peru:

F. Bower *The African Slave in Colonial Peru 1524–1650* (Stamford 1974).

3. See F. Braudel "De l'or du Soudan à l'argent d'amérique" in *Annales E.S.C.* (Paris[1] 1946) 1–22.

4. See G. Freyre *Casa grande e senzala* (Rio[18] 1979).

5. F. Moya Pons *Historia Colonial de Santo Domingo* (Santo Domingo 1974) p. 71ff.

6. See E. Genovese *Esclavitud y capitalismo* (Barcelona 1971).

7. *La problación en América latina* (Madrid 1973) p. 93; see P. Curtin *The Atlantic Slave Trade* (Madison 1975).

8. R. Mellafe in the work cited in note 2, pp. 141ff; see E. E. Williams *Capitalism and Slavery* (New York 1944).

9. See R. Bastide *Las Américas negras* (Madrid 1967) pp. 121–207.

10. See A. Boesak *Farewell to Innocence* (New York 1977).

11. These questions were discussed at a seminar held in Kingston, Jamaica in December 1979.

8

An Ethics of Liberation: Fundamental Hypotheses

I f it required an effort on the part of Paul Tillich to explain in the United States the different function of the Church in Europe, how much greater will be the effort required of a theologian from Latin America, from the peripheral world, to explain the critical function of ethics in situations in need of profound social change?[1]

1. MORALITIES INSIDE THE SYSTEMS

In the last 50 years there has taken place in the United States and Europe a shift from criticism of the system as a totality to merely reformist criticism of the social order. One significant date is 13 April 1931, when the name of Tillich[2] appeared on the list which Hitler's national-capitalist government had drawn up of intellectuals who were "critical" of the system.[3] Tillich himself was to write later that "the fact that National Socialism crushed the religious Socialist movement and drove it underground or into exile, as it did the many creative movements of the twenties, could not prevent the spread of these ideas in churches and cultures beyond the borders of Germany and Europe."[4]

In 1932 Reinhold Niebuhr published his *Moral Man and Immoral Society*,[5] and Emil Brunner *The Divine Imperative*.[6]

Enrique Dussel, "An Ethics of Liberation: Fundamental Hypotheses," *Concilium* 172 (1984): 54–63.

The crisis of 1929—the crisis of capitalism and the growing repression of the working class of the "centre"—the victory of the Russian revolution and the rise of Stalin produced an upheaval in theology. The "early" Tillich, the "early" Niebuhr (and a little earlier the "early" Barth) talk to us about moving from a critique of the system to a prudent reformist morality. "Christian realism": "The illusion is dangerous because it encourages terrible fanaticism," was the ending of Niebuhr's book,[7] and Tillich, who had written *The Socialist Decision*,[8] was subsequently to move much more toward a theology of culture. Another movement of great importance finally died in these years, the "social gospel."[9] Richard Ely's *French and German Socialism* (New York, 1883) or Washington Gladden's *Tools and the Man, Property and Industry under the Christian Law* remain impressive today, particularly chapter 10 of Gladden's book, "Christian Socialism,"[10] where he explains, "In the latest books on socialism we always find a chapter entitled "Christian Socialism." Has this phrase any meaning? Is Christianity in some sense socialist, or perhaps socialism is Christian?[11] What is important today is not the explanations—nor even Gladden's criticisms of Marx (which are excellent, because he knew Marx);[12] what is important is the Christian attitude of criticism of the capitalist system as a whole. Walter Rauschenbusch forcefully criticised "our semi-Christian social order," which he described as "under the Law of Profit."[13] These Christians, who were linked with the social struggles of the period from the end of the nineteenth century to 1929, were buried by the violence of European and North American capitalism between the two wars (1914–1945) for the leadership of that capitalism from which the United States emerged victorious (and the Commonwealth, like Germany and Japan, defeated).

The postwar moral theologies could not break out of the reformist mould. They accept the system as it is; they suggest *partial* reforms. This is the inescapable conclusion of an examination of the main moral treatises.[14]

It is interesting to consider Brunner's book of 1932. While it is far superior in its treatment of the Catholic treatises of the period, it manages first to criticise capitalism ("Capitalism is a form of economic anarchy; the Christian is therefore obliged to fight against it and for a true social order"),[15] but subsequently also criticises actual socialism.[16] In the same way Helmut Thielicke, in his *Theologische Ethik*,[17] clearly shows his reformism in the section on "revolution as a last resort."[18] As in the works previously mentioned, and in those to be mentioned later, there is of course no reference to the oppression of the peripheral countries, even though it has been clearly posed theologically as long ago as the sixteenth century by Bartolomé de las Casas.

We find a movement from criticism of capitalism to a critical acceptance of it, leading finally, in the present crisis, to a moral justification of it. The whole of the North American neo-conservative movement (and the European conservative movement)[19] could assent to the conclusions of Robert Benne, in his book *The Ethic of Democratic Capitalism, A Moral Reassessment.*[20] In his chapter 7, "The Virtues of Democratic Capitalism," he writes, "Democratic capitalism has been an undervalued social system, especially by the liberal intellectual community, both religious and secular. We have attempted to challenge that underassessment by emphasising the values and achievements that are often overlooked."[21]

For these moralities which remain within the system, radical criticism of the system is anarchy, fanaticism; it is the irrationality of "historicism" apparently refuted by Popper, translated into economic terms by Milton Friedman in the neo-capitalism of the "self-regulating equilibrium of the free market." Within this framework moral theologies have to consider "norms" (laws), values, virtues, good and evil, the problem of language, of technology, and even of peace, without ever questioning the "system" as such. Analytic thought is fundamentally hostile to any dialectical proposition.

2. THE ETHICS OF LIBERATION

In contrast, for the Christians of the countries which are peripheral to capitalism and the oppressed classes of those countries, the irreversible crisis came after the second war for the leadership of capitalism. Ten years after the end of the war the expansion of North American capitalism destroyed the endeavours of peripheral national capitalism. (In 1954 Vargas committed suicide in Brazil, in 1955 Perón fell in Argentina. Rojas Pinilla fell in Colombia in 1957. Nasser in Egypt and Sukarno in Indonesia are parallel cases in Africa and Asia. In the countries of the periphery "populism" was the last effort of a non-dependent, autonomous *national capital*, under the leadership of a national bourgeoisie, such as the Congress Party in India.) The crisis of the model of "dependent capitalism" in Latin America between 1955 and 1965 (from Kubitschek to Goulard in Brazil or from Frondizi to Ilia in Argentina, and eventually to Onganía's coup of 1966) shows the invariability of peripheral capitalism. The pretence of aid in "capital" and "technology" (confronting the "capital" and "technology" of poor and backward national capitalism) did not produce "development," but implanted the "transnational corporations" which increased the extraction of wealth (in economic terms "profit" in theological terms the "life" and "blood" of the peoples and workers of the periphery).[22]

The ethics of liberation originated historically as a theoretical attempt (in theology and philosophy) to clarify a praxis which originated in the failure of "developmentalism."[23] Consequently, just as Karl Barth said of theology in general, "The relation between such a God and such a man, and the relation between such a man and such a God, is for me the theme of the Bible and the essence of philosophy."[24] To indicate the actual and existential nature of the relationship, for the ethics of liberation (and so for fundamental theology, as we shall see), the premise would be: The relationship of the *living* God with this *poor* person, and of this *poor* person with the *living* God, is what the Bible and theology are about. In this way we connect with, and continue on new foundations (no longer European and North American, but worldwide), the leading ideas of the "early" Barth, Tillich, Niebuhr, and so many others. But the theoretical connection is possible because there is a practical and historical connection. The Christians of the twenties and thirties opposed capitalism in crisis (and were buried by fascist capitalism in Europe and the United States). We too are opposing capitalism, but a capitalism in a crisis which is structural and much deeper, because autonomous national capitalism is now impossible at the periphery. The production of wealth in the underdeveloped countries of the periphery and its distribution to the vast impoverished majorities is impossible for capitalism. The ethics of liberation comes into being as theory preceded and required by a praxis which opposes the system as a totality. Reformist "developmentalism" puts forward without success alternative models (the varieties of "developmentalism" represented by the UN Commission for Latin America, "National Security," "neo-populism," "Christian democracy," and so on), but accepts the system as a whole. It is once more a moral system with "norms," "virtues," and "values" as a basis. In contrast, the first task of the ethics of liberation is to de-base (to destroy the basis of) the system in order to arrive at another basis which transcends the present system. Analytic thought gives way to dialectical thought, and negative dialectics to the "analectic" approach (affirmation as the origin of negation, as we shall see).

see Badiou, "The Affirmative Dialectics"

(a) "Flesh" (Totality)

Reformist moral systems ask themselves, "How is it possible to be good *in* Egypt?" Their answers are in terms of norms, virtues, etc., but they accept Egypt as the system in force. Moses, on the other hand, asked himself, "How is it possible to get *out of* Egypt?" But in order to get out,[25] I have to be aware that there is a totality within which I am and an "outside" to which I can move. In other words, the *ethics* of liberation (in contrast to the "intra-systemic" moral systems)[26] starts by describing the system within which the subject always starts, whether the practical subject (oppressor or oppressed) or the theoretical subject (the theologian himself). In the Bible the system as a totality is "this world,"[27] or the "flesh" (*basár* in Hebrew and *sarx* in Greek), which is not to be confused with "body" (*sóma* in Greek), though the two are sometimes confused in the Septuagint and Paul. The "sin of the flesh" or the "sin of Adam" is, precisely, idolatry, fetishism; it is treating the "totality" as the ultimate, absolute totality and by so doing denying the existence of the other (Abel) and so of God (the absolute Other). The absolutisation of the totality is the sin of the flesh because there has *already* been a denial of the other in practice: "Cain rose up against his brother Abel and killed him" (Gen. 4:8).

Today in Latin America, without making invalid connections, we can say that "the system" is Anglo-Saxon capitalism in society, machismo in sexual attitudes, ideological domination in education: idolatry on every level. The idea has the inexhaustible profundity of reality, and in it is revealed the infinite human capacity to create "systems" which may set themselves in opposition to God as idols.

(b) The "Other" (Analectical Exteriority)

Ethics, before dealing ontically with the range of moral problems, has to clarify the fact and the reality of the continued presence of the other "beyond" any totality. *Totalité et Infini* has demonstrated this in phenomenological terms,[28] but not in terms of political economy.[29] Contrary to the charges of its critics, the ethics of liberation is not in the Nietzschean echo a "Marxism for the people," but has firm roots in metaphysics (Xavier Zubiri rightly maintains in *Sobre la esencia* that reality transcends being), in an ethics as a first philosophy. This is a favourite remark of Levinas, and, as we shall see, a theological ethics is a fundamental theology in its primary essence. "Beyond" (*jenseits*), transcendental (ontologically transcendental), on the horizon of the system (of the flesh, of totality), "the other" appears (as an "epiphany" and not a mere "phenomenon"), as a person who "provokes" (calles—*vocare* in Latin—from in front—*pro* in Latin) and demands justice. The "other" ("the widow, the orphan, the foreigner," in the prophets' formulation, or under the universal name of "the poor person") confronting the system is the metaphysical *reality* beyond the ontological *being* of the system. As a result he or she is "exteriority,"[30] what is most alien to the system as a totality, "internal transcendence," in F. Hinkelammert's phrase;[31] he or she is the "locus" of God's epiphany, the poor person. *In* the system the only possible *locus* of God's epiphany is those who are non-system, what is other than the system, the poor. Jesus' identification with the poor (Matt. 25) is not a metaphor; *it is a logic*. God, the other absolute, is revealed in the flesh (the system) by what is other than the system, the poor. The metaphysical (and eschatological) exteriority of the poor, which is both

theological and economic, in the sense of a "theological economy,"[32] situates
them as the key (historical) reality and (epistemological) category of the
whole ethics of liberation (or of fundamental theology as such).

(c) Alienation, Sin, Oppression

In the system (the first element of the method and the first concept) the
other (the second element, but the "key," more radical than the first) *is alienated* (the third element and category). The "alienation" of the "other" (making it "other" than itself) is, metaphysically making it "the same," a mere
functional part within the system. The human being, the living and free
subject of creative labour, sells his labour and *becomes* a "wage-earner," an
intrinsic, optic element of capitalism, dependent on the *being* of capital. The
"other" (who is free) becomes other than himself or herself, a thing. Just as
Christ "became other than himself and took the form of a servant,"[33] so the
"other" becomes oppressed, "poor" as a complex category (as exteriority
and interiority dominated in the *flesh*). The "poor person," as the one who
does not enjoy the fruit of his or her labour, is the manifestation of sin *in the
system*. Sin, which is simply domination-of-the-other, is revealed when
someone is poor. The poor are the others stripped of their exteriority, of
their dignity, of their rights, of their freedom, and transformed into instruments for the ends of the dominator, the Lord, the Idol, the Fetish.
   It is clear that the whole of this description is applicable to the social
reality of exploited classes, oppressed countries, the sex which is vio-
lated, and so on, but this "application" destroys the very foundations of
the moral theologies current in Europe and North America. It starts by
posing problems which cannot be "conveniently" relegated to an appendix of ethico-social theology. Rather, since what is at issue is the very
construction, the very a priori of the subjectivity which does theology—
as a theory—and of Christian subjectivity in practice, they are the *primary* questions of all theology (as fundamental theology). The question,
"Is it possible to believe?" is preceded by the question, "What are the
practical and historical conditions of this question itself?" If I ask this
question from the point of view of the "Pharaonic class" in Egypt, it is
not the same as if I ask it from the point of view of "the slaves." *From
what position* am I now asking my first question in fundamental theology? This "From what position?" in historical and social terms is the
first chapter of *all theology*, and not an additional question in the section
on "alms": "aid to under-developed countries." We know that our col-
leagues of the "centre" do not agree about this. The next few decades
will tell us who is right.

(d) Liberation, Salvation, "Going Out"

Only in this "fourth" (methodological and real) element is it possible to understand the question of redemption (Christology), as salvation (eschatology), and liberation. Each of these concepts says the same thing, but in relation to different terms. "Liberation" implies a relation with a previous term (*ex quo*), from where? from prison. The "prison" is at the same time (because *it is the same thing*) the system of oppression and sin. The concept (and the reality) of liberation includes two terms and one actuality (like the concept of movement): departure *from* somewhere, *to* somewhere, and the journey itself. Theologically, metaphorically, and historically these terms are: from Egypt, to the promised land and the journey through the desert. The concept of "freedom"—as in Häring's moral theology—does not have the same dialectical density or the historical complexity or the practical clarity of the category (and praxis) of liberation. The fact that Abraham, Moses, and so many others "depart" from the "land" of Chaldea or Egypt for another "land" "which I shall show you,"[44] sets up a dialectic between *two* terms. Because the current moral theologies (those mentioned before) do not radically question the first "land" (the "old man;" in Latin America the *present* system of oppression, today, is dependent capitalism), because they do not set up as the necessary horizon of *all* their discourse the utopia of the future "land" (the "new man"), everything they deal with in their treaties is reformist morality, in the land of the Chaldeans, in Egypt. They will never "go out" into the desert, nor will they receive, in the desert, the "new" law (the "new" norms of morals).

The question of norms, laws, virtues, values, and even ends must from the start be placed "within" the problematic of the two lands (totality/exteriority, current system/utopia, dependent capitalism/alternatives, etc.) Consequently the question of an ethics *of liberation* (objective genitive) is that of how to be "good" (just, saved), not in Egypt or in the monarchy under David, but in the journey of transition from an "old" order to the "new" order which is *not-yet* in force. The heroes and the saints do not guide their conduct by the "current" norms. If they had, Washington would have remained a good subject of the English monarchs, the priest Hidalgo would have obeyed the Laws of the Spanish Indies, the heroes of the "French resistance" would have submissively carried out Nazi commands in France, or Fidel Castro would have allowed Cuba to continue being a "weekend" colony of the United States. What is the ethical basis of the praxis of the heroes when they rise against laws, rules, alleged virtues and values, against the ends of an *unjust* system? This question, which for Europeans and North Americans can occupy an appendix in moral theology, is for the Christian of the periphery the first chapter of any fundamental theology, since it answers the question "What is theology *as a totality* for?" Barth, Tillich, Niebuhr, before the crisis of 1929, glimpsed these questions, but remained a long way from any possibility of dealing with them in a way adequate to the complexity of the world situation.

The ethics of liberation is a rethinking of the totality of moral problems from the point of view and the demands of "responsibility" for the poor,[35] for a historical alternative which *allows struggle* in Egypt, a journey through the desert in the time of transition, and the building of the promised land. This promised land is the historical promised land which will always be judged by the eschatological land "beyond any possibility of historical material production," the kingdom of heaven which will never be built *at all* in history, but which is already being built in the building of the lands which precede it in the same history.

3. A WORD ON METHOD

When one imagines (like Popper in *The Open Society and its Enemies*) that one has proved that any alternative social vision is a utopia, and that utopias are the root of all evil, the result in theology is an anti-utopian Christianity. It is then quite logical that the method of moral theology can only be analytic (in the tradition of Ayer, Wittgenstein, etc.),[36] more or less eclectic, taking something from sociology, from medicine, from politics, according to the branch of moral theology in question. These methods are valid, but provided they are treated as elements in a partial account of moral theology. They become ideological methods, methods which obscure reality, when they claim sole validity and when they criticise holistic methods as imprecise and unscientific.

Challenging the system as a whole is the characteristic of the dialectical method, from Plato or Aristotle,[37] via Thomas Aquinas, Kant, Hegel, and Sartre. In reality, to use the language of Heidegger, whose concept of "the world" is strictly dialectical, it is an attempt to situate ontologically every object or thing which appears to me ontically. Being ready to refer the means, the instrument, "to the hand," the object to its basis (to being) is the characteristic of the dialectical method. In these terms, Marx is simply inquiring into commodities, money, production, etc., in the light of, in relation to the basis of the being of capital (the essence of capitalism). However, the ontological method, in this case an economic ontology,[38] has insisted on "negation of the negation" or "negative dialectic" (for example Adorno or the Frankfurt School, and even Ernst Bloch may be included). The revolutionary process, of negation of the totality in force (Lukács), is a praxis which arises out of the negation of the negation: out of the negation of the oppression produced by the system among the oppressed. In a sense, the negation of the negation has the system as its horizon and can only be transcended in terms of a utopia. This may be an artistic fantasy (Marcuse, *Eros and Civilisation*) or a future alternative, but in fact it is a possibility in terms of "the same" system. The origin of the negation is either the same system or an empty horizon (pure possibility or transcendent horizon: the kingdom of freedom as absolute free time).

The ethics of liberation, in contrast, starts from the affirmation of the real, existing, historical other. We have called this trans-ontological (metaphysical) positive element of the impetus, this active starting point of the negation of the negation, *the analectic element*. The Greek prefix *ana-* is meant to indicate a "going beyond" the ontological horizon (the system, the "flesh").[39] This *logos (ana-logos)*, a discourse which has its origin in the transcending of the system, contains the originality of the Hebrew-Christian experience. If "in the beginning God created" (Gen 1:1), it is because the Other is prior to the very principle of the cosmos, the system, the "flesh." The metaphysical priority of the other (who creates, reveals himself or herself) also has historical, political and erotic elements. The poor, the oppressed class, the nation on the periphery, the woman treated as a sexual object, have reality "beyond" the limits of the system which alienates, represses, and dehumanises them. The "reality" which the people of Nicaragua embodied, "beyond" the limits of the Somoza regime and dependent capitalism, is the basis for a negation of oppression and the motivation for a practice of liberation. The oppressed contain (in the structure of their subjectivity, of their culture, of their underground economy, etc., in their analectic exteriority) the trans-systematic (eschatological) impulse which enables them to discover themselves as oppressed *in the system*. They discover themselves "as oppressed" if they make attempts to be (eschatologically) other than the system in their exteriority to it. The analectical affirmation of their dignity and freedom (which is negated in the system), of their culture, of their labour, outside the system is the source of the very mobility of the dialectic. (They affirm what is "unproductive labour" for capital, but real in its own terms, and affirm it outside the system, not because the poor have conquered the system, but frequently because the system considers them "nothing," non-being; and it is out of this [real] nothingness that new systems are built.)

The method, and historical reality, does not begin with the negation of oppression, but negation of oppression begins with the analectical affirmation of the (historical and eschatological) exteriority of the other, through whose project of liberation the negation of the negation and the building of new systems is put into effect. These new systems are not simply univocal results of the actualisation of what was present potentially in the old unjust system. The new system is an analogical realisation which includes something of the old system (*similitudo*) and something absolutely new (*distinctios*). The new system was impossible for the old one; there is creation in the bursting in of the analectical otherness of the poor in their own liberation.[40] The method of the ethics of liberation is analectic, because it is an element in the creative action of the unconditioned freedom of God and in the redemptive act of the subsumption in Christ of the flesh (the system) by the analectic irruption of the Word, the negation of sin and the building of the kingdom. There is not merely a negative dialectic, but also a positive dialectic in which the exteriority of the other (the creator, Christ, the poor person) is the positive practical condition of the very movement of the method. Consequently the poor, and their own liberating praxis, are, as an analectical priority, the fundamental and initial element. The ethics comes afterwards, affirming as its first premise the absolute priority of the poor person, this poor person in whom we encounter, as an absolute challenge and responsibility, Christ, a poor person who is God himself.

In Latin America an ethics of liberation must justify the goodness, heroism and holiness of an oppressed people's action for liberation in El Salvador, Guatemala, Argentina, or Brazil (in Egypt), of a people already journeying through the desert (as in Nicaragua) where "Aaron the priest," wanting to return to Egypt, pays homage to the golden calf (the idol), while the prophet (Moses: the ethics of liberation?) has not only to destroy the fetish, but also to offer to the people who are liberating themselves the "new" law. But the new law is born in dialectical opposition to the law in Egypt. It is not possible to begin by defining as moral theologies do the morality of an action by its transcendental relation to a norm or law. On the contrary, the absolute morality of the action indicates its transcendental relation to the building of the kingdom in the historical processes of the liberation of actual material peoples, "who are hungry." It is only subsequently, within this framework, that it becomes possible to situate all the problems of abstract moral subjectivity (with which all moral theologies start).

The publication of the encyclical *Laborem exercens* has given us a good foundation on which to build an ethics of liberation in the exploited flesh of poor workers, a Eucharistic or economic radicalism which must be developed in the future.[41]

NOTES

1. See Paul Tillich, "The Social function of the Churches in Europe and America" *Social Research* 3, 1 (New York 1936), and (in German) in *Gesammelte Werke* III (Stuttgart 1962) pp. 107ff. Tillich says: "I know that the social functions of the churches cannot be fully understood without considering their social structure

and their economic basis and examining the social order to which they belong" (translated from the German, p. 119).

2. It is impossible for the author not to remember 30th March 1975, when he was included in similar lists and expelled from the "National University of Cuyo" for similar reasons, and many other cases in Latin America.

3. Hitler's "Nazism" was a right-wing government which made German national capitalism (Krupp, Thiessen, Siemens, etc.) viable and staked a claim for the world domination of the capitalist market. The military governments of Latin America (since 1964) have been ensuring the viability of a capitalism dependent on the United States, which is much worse.

4. Prologue to vol. II of his *Gesammelte Werke, Christentum und soziale Gestaltung* (1919–19, 33), p. 11

5. New York, 1932.

6. (London 1937). Original: *Das Gebot und die Ordnungen* (Tübingen 1932).

7. See the work cited in note 5, at p. 277. The book is "a social analysis which is written, at least partially, from the perspective of a disillusioned generation" (p. XXV). "In Germany E. Bernstein . . . changed the expectations of catastrophe into hope of evolutionary progress towards equal justice" (p. 181).

8. Eng. ed. New York 1977. Original in *Gesammelte Werke* II.

9. See C. Howard Hopkins *The Rise of the Social Gospel in American Protestantism (1865–1915)* (New Haven 1940); Robert Handy *The Social Gospel in America 1870–1920* (Oxford 1966); Aaron Abell *American Catholicism and Social Action 1865–1950* (Garden City, New York 1960).

10. Boston 1893, pp. 275ff.

11. *Ibid.*, p. 275.

12. At pp. 257ff. there is a discussion on the concept of value in Marx (50 years before the publication of the 1844 manuscripts, which accounts for some naïve misrepresentations). At one point he asks, "We go part way with Marx and Robertus; then we part company with them. How far can we wisely go with them? How many of their projects may we safely adopt?" (p. 280). "Socialism, as we have seen, is simply a proposition to extend the functions of the State so that it shall include and control nearly all the interests of life (sic). Now, I take it, we are agreed that, as Christians, we have a right to make use of the power of the State, both in protecting life and property, and in promoting, to some extent, the general welfare" (p. 281). This was written in the United States in 1893. What happened afterwards? The working-class movement was brutally repressed (see James Weinstein, *The Decline of Socialism in America* 1912–1925 (Boston 1967).

13. *Christianizing the Social Order* (New York 1919), pp. 222ff.

14. See for example Bernhard Häring, *Free and Faithful in Christ. Moral Theology for Priests and Laity*, 3 vols. (Slough 1978–1981). Though much better than other Catholic moral theologians, Häring nevertheless treats as subsidiary questions of economic and political ethics (vol. III, ch. VII, pp. 244–325), and discusses "life" solely in relation to medical matters and abortion (vol. III, pp. 4–113, not with work or social life (repression of the poor, etc.).

Similarly in the *Handbuch der christlichen Ethik*, ed. A. Hertz, W. Korff, T. Rendtorff, and H. Ringeling, 3 vols. (Freiburg 1978–1982), the main problem is "modernity," and the first moral topic is "rules" (vol. I, pp. 108ff.). "Life" has to do only with medicine. Politics is defined in terms of "the principles of constitutional government" (vol. II, pp.. 215ff.). There is a little on economics, but under the title (directed at the peripheral countries) "Aid" (II, pp. 417ff.). The "new international order" is given no biblical, ontological or anthropological basis, but defended solely on sociological grounds (III, pp. 337ff.).

15. Chapters 34 ("The Nature and the Task of the Economic Order") and 35 ("The Christian in the Present Economic Order"), pp. 395ff. The quotation is from p. 426 (translated slightly amended).

16. Ibid., pp. 426ff. For the author the Christian position is a sort of social democratic "third way" (pp 431ff.).

17. (Tübingen), esp. vol. II/2 (1958). He leaves the problem of property to a separate appendix (vol. III, 1964, pp. 224ff.), showing a sort of "economic blindness." His analyses are exclusively in legal or socio-political terms. There is an abridged English edition of vols. I–II. *Theological Ethics.* 2 vols. (London and Philadelphia 1968–1969). Vol. II of the English corresponds to vol. II/2 of the German.

18. English ed., II, pp. 341–43.

19. See Jürgen Habermas "Die Kulturkritik der Neokonservativen in den USA und in der Bundesrepublik" *Praxis*, II, 4 (1983), pp. 339ff. See also Habermas's book *Theorie des kommunikativen Handelns* (Frankfurt 1981), but here he does not deal at all with the question of the peripheral countries—though it is intimately connected with that of "instrumental reason."

20. Philadelphia 1982, p. 174. Take the case of Michael Novak, who, after beginning his career as a liberal Catholic theologian with *The Open Church* (1964) and *The Men who make the Council* (1964), went on to write *Toward a Theology of the (transnational) Corporation* (1981), published by the American Enterprise Institute, and *The Spirit of Democratic Capitalism* (1982). These neo-conservative theologies are not "economically blind": "The official documents of the popes and the Protestant economical bodies are notably strong on moral vision, much less so in describing economic principles and realities. The coming generation will inherit as a task the need to create and to set forth systematically a theology of economics" (Novak 1981, p. 21).

21. At p. 174.

22. See my article "The Bread of the Eucharistic Celebration as a Sign of Justice in the Community" *Concilium* 152 (1982) 56, [In this book see chapter 2, p. 41 ff] where I demonstrate the relationship between life, blood, labour and production. A "theology of money" and of the economy must start from these metaphysical and biblical postulates (see *zao*, "life," "live," in Kittel, TDNT II, pp. 832–75 [Bultmann and Bertram].

23. The disparaging term "developmentalism" is meant to indicate the ideological and false character of the European and North American "doctrine of development" (and of "development aid") which dominates in Christian (and United Nations) circles. This is an attempt to provide a partial remedy for *effects*, aggravates the problem and does not attack the structural and global *causes* of the "crisis."

24. *The Epistle to the Romans*, 6th ed. (London, Oxford, New York 1968) p. 10.

25. The concept of "going out," "being brought out" (Gen. 21:1, Exod. 13:16, etc.) is a fundamental theological metaphor.

26. On the difference between "morality" and "ethics" see the end of this article in *Para una ética de la liberación latinoamericana*, Siglo XXI (Buenos Aires 1973), II, 20 (2nd ed., Mexico 1977, vol. II, p. 13), and "One Ethic and Many Moralities" in *Concilium* 150 (1980) 54.

27. See *Para una ética de la liberación (EL)*. II, sect. 21, pp. 22ff. On the category of "flesh" or "totality," see *EL*, chs. 1–2 (I, pp. 33ff.); *El humanismo semita* (Buenos Aires 1969); *El dualismo en la antropolgia de la cristiandad* (Buenos Aires 1974); *History and Theology of Liberation* (New York 1976) ch. 1, etc.

28. The title of a book by Emmanuel Levinas *Totalité et Infini. Essai sur l'extériorité* (The Hague 1961).

29. For my view on Levinas, see *Emmanuel Levinas y la liberación latinoamericana* (Buenos Aires 1975) prologue.

30. In *Filosofia da Libertaçào*, 2.4 (pp. 45ff.); *EL* I, ch. III, pp. 97ff.; III, ch. VII, sect. 46, pp. 97ff.; ibid., sect. 52, pp. 168ff.; IV, ch. IX, sect. 65, pp. 94ff.; V, ch. X, sect. 72, pp. 76ff.

31. *Las armas ideológicas de la muerte* (San Jose 1977) p. 61: "Praxis is directed towards a transcendence within real, material life. It is a vision of community full of this real life without its negativity."

32. See the article cited in note 22 above.

33. It is known that Luther translated the Greek of Phil. 2:7 by *äusserte sich*, "dispossessed himself," a term characteristic of "kenotic" theology, from where it came down to Hegel through his professors of Christology at Tübingen. It is a fundamental Christian concept.

34. The category "land" (*'arets*) has a strict eschatological sense in the Bible. See Kittel TWNT I, 676, art. *ge*, "earth." This sense is present in Ps. 37:11; Matt. 5:5, and Heb. 11:9. Here, however I want to show the dialectic between the two lands: " . . . from the land (*me'aretskha*) . . . to the land (*'el-ha'rets*) which I shall show you" (Gen. 12:1); "out of that land to a good and broad land, flowing with milk and honey" (Exod. 3.8). It is a going "out of Egypt" (*mi-mitsraim*, Exod. 3.10).

35. "Responsibility" for the other, for the oppressed, in the face of the actual oppressive economic system (Hans Jonas *Das Prinzip Verantwortung*, Frankfurt 1982, does not give the contextual meaning of "responsibility," which remains at an abstract level. He considers "technology," but never as an element "of capital" (*als Kapital*). He does not understand this "subsumption").

36. See *Handbuch der christlichen Ethik*, vol. I, pp. 68ff., F. Boeckle's contribution ("Der sprachanalytische Ansatz," etc.).

37. See my *Método para una filosofia de la liberación* (Salamanca 1974).

38. Marx's *Grundrisse* and, more recently, the manuscripts of 1861–1863, authorise us to reinterpret Marx in terms of an ontology in the strict sense: K. Marx *Grundrisse* (London 1973); *Zur Kritik der politischen Oekonomie* (*Manuskripte 1861–1863*), MEGA III/2, vols. I, VI (Berlin 1977, 1982: "Capital thus becomes a very mysterious creature," p. 2163, line 11)

39. See my recent article on "analectic," "Pensée analectique en philosophie de la libération," *Analogie et Dialectique* (Geneva 1982), pp. 93–120.

40. *EL* sect. 25, vol. II, pp. 58ff.; sect. 47, vol. III, pp. 109ff; sect 66, vol. IV, pp. 109ff; sect 73, vol. V, pp. 91ff.

41. Polish thinkers have rightly taken "labour" as the centre of theological reflection (see Josef Tischner *La svolta storica* (Bologna 1982), esp. "Il lavoro privo di senso," pp. 76ff). For the Poles the problem is control of the product of labour by the producer. For Latin America the problem is the consumption (why there is a hunger as a result of oppression and structural theft) of the product of labour. In Poland the workers (the nation) want to know why they are producing bread, and want control of their production. In Latin America the nation (the people) want to possess the fruits of their work, the Eucharistic bread. See John Desrochers *The Social Teaching of the Church* (Bangalore 1982), esp. pp. 637ff. It is clear that *Laborem exercens* allows the ethics of liberation to sharpen its arguments considerably.

9

Theology and Economy: The Theological Paradigm of Communicative Action and the Paradigm of the Community of Life as a Theology of Liberation

Take and eat, this is my body.

(Matt. 26: 26)

This chapter relates the theology of communicative action—described in terms of dialogue, speeches, and texts—to the community of life as the manifestation of the human being's liberation from oppression. It critiques hegemonic "communities of communication," including those in the established church, for failing to allow the people to transcend the abstract solipsism produced by the regime of capital or the destruction of a rural community experience. Living labour, value, and cost should be central to contemporary theology; worship should be regarded not merely as an act of good faith but as both an offering and a product of human labor.

INTRODUCTION

With reason the European–North American theology has begun to give importance to the "paradigm of language," to the theory of communicative action.[1] Therefore, toward the end of the decade of the 1960s, the theology of liberation had to be delimited[2] from the theology of hope that

Enrique Dussel, "Theology and Economy: The Theological Paradigm of Communicative Action and the Paradigm of the Community of Life As a Theology of Liberation," in Kenneth E. Bauzon, ed., *Development and Democratization in the Third World: Myths, Hopes, and Realities* (Washington, D.C.: Crane Russak, 1992), 119–34.

was inspired by Ernst Bloch or the political theology that arose from the critical theory of the Frankfurt school. Today we should undertake once again the task of "delimitation" with respect to that which could be called a theology of communicative action. It is a task that is all the more urgent because at the same time it signifies for the theology of liberation a consciousness raising and an in-depth examination of its own development— and as a passage of the ordinary theme of faith and politics to the most current and pertinent in Latin America of praxis and economy.

By basing itself upon the paradigm of language and rational communication, the theology of communicative action (like the philosophy that inspires it),[3] has enormous resources and advantages but, at the same time, it has its limitations. If it is true that, as J. L. Austin explains it, there are ways of "doing *things* with words"[4] still those things (e.g., contracts, promises, etc.) will never be a piece of bread, a plow, or *material* instruments produced by labor. In other words, there are things that words cannot do although material things can be produced when someone orders his serf—the oppressed—to make them, but only by means of the mediation of the labor of the serf.

In the exploited and poor capitalist nations of the periphery (e.g., Argentina or Venezuela, countries that were until recently among the richest of the Third World, not to mention India or African countries, whose impoverished masses steal food so to eat and not die of starvation), a mere theology inspired in the theory of communicative action (i.e., of the language of dialogue, of words, of speeches, of texts, of conversations) is not sufficient.

THE PARADIGM OF LANGUAGE:
THEOLOGY AND COMMUNICATION

In Latin America, thanks to a long experience of popular organization, there appeared at the end of the decade of the 1960s, first in Brazil (and from the movement of base education inspired in part by the pedagogical philosophy of Paulo Freire),[5] a so-called grass-roots movement[6] in which the simple people, some of them illiterate, can go beyond the situation of abstract solipsism produced by the regime of capital gain in the urban marginality or by the destruction of a rural community experience. This is an organization in which—thanks to dialogue, discussion, and critical reflection (using as a point of departure the biblical text, that is, an authentic, popular, and political hermeneutic)—these isolated individuals are able to constitute a community by arriving at an agreement based on their own arguments. It is a unique experience, because the members of the base communities are found outside of all of the hegemonic communities of communication in which they have not had any right to express their own voice.[7] It is in this context that the theology of liberation, since its beginning, has understood the church as a community of interpretation (to use the expression of Francis Schüssler Fiorenza), especially the base communities, as the most essential expression of the church of the poor. Thus, the entire categorical horizon of the theology of communicative action can be applied to an ecclesiology, a christology, an exegesis, and so on of a theology of Latin American liberation. The taking of the "word" of the people has been an experience in our continent by widening the horizon of argumentative critical rationality of the marginal, e.g., the working class, the rural farmer, and so on. This fact that has been called consciousness raising, or argumentative consciousness raising of the political conditions toward a possibility of organized popular action vis-à-vis the institutions and their very essence for the purpose of structural change.

As a matter of fact, what happens is that the community of communication in the base is found in a world of daily life that seeks to be colonized by the economic system and by the state in a completely different way than in late capitalism: central, developed, and repressive. For that reason, all of the analysis should be done in a different way than it is developed in the works of Jürgen Habermas.[8]

In reality, the world of daily life suffers such a type of contradiction that the semibureaucratized state has no control over the disarticulation that the economic "system" of dependency produces on this world. Besides, there is no economic compensation that could make citizens the accomplices of a veiled but bearable system of oppression. Much to the contrary, the conditions of poverty, or horrible misery (from the nondistribution of wealth), are such that exploited members of the people have their own means to raise their consciousness to avoid being colonized so absolutely or obviously. It is on that "fissure" that the base community is established as a critical community of communicative action, and a "revolutionary consciousness" (or, at least, a deep dissatisfaction in the face of a repressive regime that has no opposing party of any type) is not impossible a priori.

Modernity, on the other hand, has not been realized since 1492 in Latin America; instead it has been a "disrealization,"[9] or the other face of modernity (like the world and system that pays for the development of European modernity). All of the Habermassian categories should be reduced to an essential reconstruction of a "world system," as Immanuel Wallerstein would say, and where "late capitalism" would be part of its system, within which it fulfills a function of a developed center of exploitation of the periphery. That categorical reconstruction would essentially, not accidentally, affect the categories because they would be redefined in their real function not only in the center, but also on the planet, which is the real concrete totality.

By saying this, we wish to indicate the usefulness of such a theology of communicative action (or one that uses the Habermassian categories). However, all of them should now (and this is the first limit) be reconstructed, not only to be useful to the Third World but also to take on another meaning in the central developed world. That is, the economic system can economically compensate the salaried worker in the center, which would make the world of daily life "bearable," because the economic system is an accomplice in extracting the value of the Third World worker's salary by means of an immense exploitation of surplus value (value accumulated and stored in goods produced by human labor) and of international transference of the same. In Mexico, the so-called maquiladoras (in Santo Domingo, they are called duty free zones) pay a monthly wage of $80. Because of this, international concerns annually transfer $20 billion from the periphery to the center, and all of it coming from Mexico alone. This means that in only four years this country would pay off its foreign debt completely if this type of transference of labor could be accounted for, an impossibility in this capitalist economy.

Therefore it is difficult to affirm the following statement of Habermas for countries of the Third World:

> In the face of the pacification of class struggle carried out by the social state and the making anonymous of the structures of class, the theory of class consciousness loses its empirical references.[10] . . . Instead of anxiously pursuing the evanescent trail of a revolutionary consciousness, its objective would be to discover the conditions that would permit a reconnection of a rationalized culture with a daily communication that needs living traditions that nourish it.[11]

In the capitalism of the Third World, which is underdeveloped because of exploitation—80 percent of the world population under capitalist regimes (and from that can be diagnosed the failure of capitalism to develop in these countries)—society demands other types of analytical categories, and what in late capitalism is considered a mere juxtaposed system becomes the pertinent originating moment of human existence: the economic base (in an anthropological, ethical, and even ontological sense).

PARADIGM OF THE "LIVING CORPOREALITY": THEOLOGY AND ECONOMY

The paradigm of consciousness ("I think") was subsumed in a paradigm of language ("I speak"), which later was situated in a "community of communication" (K. O. Apel) as an a priori condition of possibility. As

Aristotle defined it, a person is a living being (*zoon*) that has the capacity of speech (*logon*). Language subsumes all rational functions of consciousness and surpasses them, because, as Paul Ricoeur has clearly demonstrated, a concept is not the same world or discourse, and even the latter has a statue that is totally different from text.[12] The philosophy of language has made immense advances in this field, and theology cannot help but assume them. From there follows the importance and pertinence of the theology of communicative action to which we have been referring all along, above all if one bears in mind that the Bible is a text and that hermeneutics is an essential constitutive part of theology.

But what we are dealing with now—the result of an exigency that is imposed upon us by the reality in Latin America (as well as in Asia and Africa)—is that a person is not only language but also essentially and above all a living being—not merely as an irrational animal, but also as a living being always human. The logic of life becomes present in every moment of a human being. His own rationality, language, spirituality, and so on are moments of his own human life. These are functions of life. For this reason, before the person is part of a community of communication (and subjected to the same communicative action), he is already a priori a member of a community of life; and because of his being a part of it, there is a community of communication serving as a function of the community of life. It is this fundamental human level that we will call "the economic base," not as a "system" in Habermassian fashion (as a *Wirtschaftswissenschaft*) but as a practical and essential constitutive relational moment of human life in which are established the primary practical "relations," the production of the objects of life, their distribution, the exchange, and consumption for human life.

The capitalist system is worldwide. The circulation of wealth throughout the world has a structure. In the analyses of the theory of communicative action, this dual aspect is not accounted for: The part (central capitalism, called "late" from an ideological point of view) is taken for the whole (the world system), which hides, first, the function of domination of the capitalist center and, secondly, the poverty and misery of Third World capitalism (*that should not be understood as exploited*), which cannot be explained in any way. It would seem to be a secondary question, but the capitalist system produces the ideological implantation of all of the categorical structure and, therefore, invalidates the meaning of what is analyzed in the center as well as in the periphery (that is, everywhere). We call this the fallacy of development, an aspect of "eurocentrism" that invalidates in part the Habermassian philosophy and the theology that uses these categories.

The first practical human relationship is person to person,[13] and it is the economic moment par excellence.[14] The economic is not only a question of market or money, but also one of corporeality, or the practical relationship of bodies (the master exploits the slave or serf, and the capitalist exploits the salaried employee) and the consumption or material reproduction of life ("lesser circulation" or *kat,exokhén* as Karl Marx said).[15] "Hunger" as necessity is the point of departure of economy with respect to the essence of the market. And in capitalism, "hunger without money is not a market, because it is not solvent." On this rests the problem: If the hungry have no money because the system does not permit them to work and therefore earn a salary, how can they be fed? And the system of Third World capitalism, because it is a system exploited by central capitalism (that is, the latter transfers value in a structural way)[16] and unable to accumulate sufficient value, has only "weak" capital. That is, it cannot absorb the totality of the population as salaried; as a consequence, it overexploits[17] by the force of labor with very low salaries that do not create a sufficient national market. The result is a capitalist economy of misery to which the Habermassian categories cannot be applied (because the world of daily life and the systems respond to a logic and to a crisis that are completely different from those of central capitalism, which is euphemistically described as "late").

The second relationship of the economic base is that of person to person nature by means of labor. In this case, living labor is subsumed in the institutionalized totality of capital.[18, 19] Only in this case can the worker work because other possibilities for exercising that right have been taken away. The process of labor is the second moment of transformation (change of form) of nature as a product (the "bread" to which we will refer later).

The economic statue of the product can be described in many ways. In the first place, living labor materializes part of its life (the objectified value) into the product, a property of capital by means of the same process of production (that equally subsumes technology and competition among capital, which determines the obsolescence of the worst technologies and allows to stand only the most productive ones and, thence, the permanent technological revolution of capitalism). In the second place, because of the competition among capital, and also among nations, a transfer of value can be produced, which, in fact, it is. This phenomenon of impoverishment of Third World national capital is of the greatest importance and can be discovered only if one takes into account the Marxist category of value, which is so essential for the underdeveloped counties. It is here that a theology of communicative action remains limited to the region known as the United States and Europe, including Eastern Europe emancipated from Stalinism (13 percent of the present world population). A theology of liberation that strives to place repression in its world context cannot be circumscribed *only* by the paradigm of communicative action or by communication in general (and in view of this, merit cannot be denied to this progressive and very important theology).

LIVING LABOR, VALUE, AND COST

Living labor, value, and cost should be a central aspect of contemporary theology. The question of the "theory of value"[20] is not only a theoretical problem, but also the necessary categorical mediation to connect the capitalist market, which has shown itself to be very efficient but not necessarily moral with human life and personal dignity. In effect, their market is the place where products are transformed into merchandise and where they acquire their cost that will be the determination of value in money for an anthropological and ethical doctrine like that of Marx.[21] Even for the marginalists (William Jevons, Karl Menger, or Leon Waldras), cost would be simply that which is valued according to how much it is desired or needed by the buyer (although this need is not that of the producer). For a theory in which a human being is the absolute (and to transform or use him as a thing or merchandise is considered a fetishistic inversion that constitutes sin from a theological point of view),[22] it is important to reconnect the market, that is, the cost of merchandise to the human subject (living labor). The only way of articulating the relationship of labor to the cost of merchandise is by the mediation of value. The value is in the product (and in the merchandise and therefore in the cost), which is the same objectified human life. The central question in the intent—and this is my interpretation—of the author of *Das Kapital* (an economist who, as we will prove in a future work, developed a negative or metaphorical theology in its strong meaning, as Ricoeur would say) was Marx being able to articulate the exchange of goods or market matters or the subjectivity of the producer (that is, the worker)[23] by basing each category or moment of method on a previous one, and all, lastly, on living labor. Not until 1872 did Marx distinguish value in general from the concept of value of exchange when he prepared the second edition of *Das Kapital*. For his concept of value, the essential distinction is not between concrete and abstract work but between living labor and objectified (dead) labor. Living work is not valuable because it is the "creative source of value from the nothingness" of capital (a creationist position of Schelling[24]). The force of labor indeed has value because it assumes the means of subsistence that the worker consumes for the reproduction of his capacity for labor. Value is then life, but *objectified* life. It is not life itself as subjectivity but as an activity that, nevertheless, is found in absolute poverty.

In an anthropological view—and beyond the humanist view—of Marx's position, it can be discovered that in reality the latter analyzed the totality of the moments of economy as an unfolding of the human being. Capital (in the anthropological and ethical view of Marx) is the fruit of accumulation, whose being is the nonbeing of the worker, whose reifying realization is human "disrealization," death, perversion, and ethical injustice (not merely moral):

> This process of realization [of capital] is at one and the same time the process of disrealization [Entwirklichungs] of labor. Labor is given objectively, but it posits this objectivity as its own Non-being or as the Being of its Non-being: capital.[25]

In 1871, Jevons published *The Theory of Political Economy*,[26] only four years after the appearance of Marx's *Das Kapital*. The former work produces the beginning of the "inversion" that is at the base of all contemporary capitalist economics—of "marginalism" and of the theologies that follow. Jevons says:

> The science of Political Economy rests upon a few notions of an apparently simple character. Utility, wealth, value, commodity, labor, land, capital are the elements of the subject. Value depends entirely upon utility. Prevailing opinions make labour rather than utility the origin of value; and there are even those who distinctly assert that labour is the cause of value.[27]

The determination of value has as its base pleasure or pain,[28] the feeling[29] of the buyer of the merchandise; for greater pleasure or feeling (or necessity but in a subjective sense and abound to the market, fashion, etc.), merchandise has a greater utility, that is, value for me, for us, here and now. If there is a variation in the feeling, then that determines a certain variation in the value (determined for its part of supply and demand and by the abundance and scarcity of merchandise). For this reason, "pleasure and pain are undoubtedly the ultimate objects of the Calculus of Economics,"[30] and "the degree of utility" determines that of value (especially the "final or ultimate degree of utility"[31]). Therefore, Jevons believes Adam Smith is wrong when he thinks that "labour was the first price, the original purchase-money that was paid for all things."[32]

Thus, a complete inversion has been produced. From living labor and the person as a point of departure, we pass now to the market or to capital as said foundation. This fetishistic inversion (theologically it is the idolatry and the atheism of the living God and his creatures: the human being as the absolute criterion of all economics) is consummated when one thinks that to still talk about value is to unnecessarily complicate things. With Marshall, Hayek, and Friedman, it is only necessary to refer to cost; the fetishization is complete. The last of the above authors says to us in the chapter entitled "The Power of the Market" in his work *Free to Choose*:

> Costs play three roles in the organization of economic activity: first, they transmit information; second, they provide stimulus to adopt more cost-efficient means of production; third, they determine who obtains the different quantities of the product—the so-called income distribution.[33]

Now the whole discourse (and also the theological discourses that depend on this type of analysis)[34] begins from its only founding principle: the market, capital. Science—which in Max Weber received absolute independence from anthropology, from the person, and from ethics[35]—begins from the horizon of capital and the market as something already given and as natural facts as we saw in Smith[36] and in Rawls. For Friedman, inequality (the most serious problem for Marx to resolve, because of the rationality of the economy, in order to determine the foundation of injustice or of unpaid labor) is now a matter of simple chance (the purely irrational and contradictory to all reason):

> Chance determines our genes. Chance determines the type of family and cultural context into which we are born, and consequently, our opportunities to develop our physical and mental capacities. Chance fixes equally other resources that we may inherit from our parents or other benefactors.[37]

As we have already expressed with respect to Rawls and equally with Friedman, it is pure chance that one person is born the son of a New York millionaire and another the child of a New Delhi beggar. Theologically, there exists an ethical exigency with respect to whether that historical initial difference should later be remedied. Chance does not justify that the differences ethically should be maintained (of course, their elimination is concomitant with new difficulties, such as duty to create new types of differences in the new social organization). At any rate, chance should not be confused with nature (nor believed to be irremovable, immutable, or untouchable, as are the pariahs of India).

THE "WORSHIP" OF THE FETISH
AND EUCHARISTIC SACRAMENTALITY

Because we have dealt with the question of the worship of the fetish and eucharistic sacramentality in other works,[38] we will not devote much space to this topic.

In reality, Hegel writes in his *Lessons on the Philosophy of Religion* that for worship to exist, it is necessary "for me to be separate from God,"[39] and this is imperfect worship. On the other hand, perfect worship is "for me to be in God and for God to be in me."[40] This concrete unity can be realized only with "the certainty of Faith and Truth,"[41] remembering that the Truth is the All and that the All is God. Faith for Hegel is an act by means of which representation—not like thinking—affirms the believed object as the absolute idea—that is, the Being of God that is only represented objectively and not speculatively. This supreme act of belief, of which representation is the idea (very superior to the act of esthetics, but inferior to absolute knowledge is perfect worship):

> Worship is an act that has a purpose in itself, and this act is the Faith that is the concrete Reality of the Divine and consciousness in itself.[42]

This perfect worship, a moment of our understanding that approaches reason, is the central moment of the Kingdom of the Son whose supreme (and Eurocentric) expression is Germanic-European culture and the Christian religion, that which is the foundation of the state as one and the same thing.[43] In this case, worship (the liturgy) is an intellectual act and faith, understanding, representations, certainty, reason, and knowledge are all moments of knowledge.

Once the market or capital has been disconnected from living labor, the science of economics concerns itself essentially with fetishized problems within the horizon of said market (or exclusively from capital). Fundamentally, economics deals with the calculation of the amount of profit (the determining of value) without any relationship whatsoever with the person, value (as an objectification of life), or ethics (as a judgment on unpaid labor). The economy having been separated from "the world of daily life" (*Lebenswelt*) comes to be set up as a system.[44] In that case, culture and religion constitute moments of said *Lebenswelt*, and it is in relationship with the latter that theology effects its reflection. At any rate, the narrow horizon of the community of communication where communicative action is fulfilled cannot be avoided.

Much to the contrary, our intent is to show that worship or liturgy demands an objective material moment, a product of work as a relationship of carnality or corporeality, the Hebrew *basar* or the Greek *sarx* that was not the mere body (*soma*) opposed to the soul whose statute is, in a precise sense, *economic*. That is, it is a practical relationship (among the celebrant community and with God) a person-to-person relationship and a productive one (person-to-nature relationship through work). The person is not only a member of a community of communication, but also previously and radically of a community of life:

They were steadfast in hearing the teaching of the apostles and in the community (*koinonía*), in the breaking of bread and in prayer. . . . The faithful lived together and they held everything in common (*koiná*); they sold their possessions and goods and divided them according to the needs of each one. . . .They broke bread in their homes and ate together (Acts 2:42–46).[45]

In this description we have all the elements of a theology of the community of life (as a subsumption of a community of communication), a community in which they ate together. Eating is neither an act of language (texts are neither lived nor eaten, as Ricoeur knows, although eating is celebrated with beautiful symbols) nor an act of communication (discourse is not eaten: Habermas cannot deny it, even though all discourse is always related to life, human life, and its reproduction). In this case, religion is not a mere moment of *Lebenswelt* (with its own intentionally), but it should be situated in an even more radical level of human life,[46] in a level appropriately called "economic" (that is, of practical relations, of work, bread, consumption, and the satisfaction in which consists of Kingdom of God).[47] Therefore, worship or the liturgy is not an interior act of good faith; it is an objective act that should count on an offering, a material of sacrifice, a product of human labor: "We offer you this bread, the fruit of labor and of the earth" says the celebrant in the offertory of the Catholic Mass. The sacramental bread—about which Feuerbach talks to us in the text cited at the beginning of this chapter—that can be eaten is material in the sense of the material of human labor.[48] Worship then requires a "pro-duct" (*Herstellt*) of labor because of a transformation (change in form) of nature. That labor objectifies human life in the product and, therefore, said bread is already sacred at the outset. Biblically, objectified life was symbolized with blood[49] (which we call value in anthropological and ethical economy).

If the injustice of a contract taken as natural (Rawls gives salary as an example) appropriates a part of the value produced (as surplus value), then said profits obtained from the life of the worker should be judged as sin. Poverty, or misery (like that which is suffered in present-day Latin America because of a transfer of the value of capital from Third World countries to industrialized countries) is a wage of sin.[50] But this sin is invisible to the one who does not possess the categories that would lay bare this social relationship of repression (a relationship of capital as such and the relationship of dependency between global national and capital of the periphery and that of the center). In this case, the worship of God is as the prophet expressed: "I want compassion and not sacrifices." To deny the denial (i.e., negation) of the poor person, who in his flesh suffers sin (in his cold, in his thirst, in his sickness . . . all of which the Latin American, African, and Asian peoples suffer under Third World capitalism), is the worship desired by God—who has an economic objective, material sacramental statue such

as bread, wine, oil, salt, water: the material of the sacraments that repro-
duce carnal and spiritual life.

On the other hand, the Devil (Satan, the Antichrist) lives off the lives of
the poor, and the economic structures control the poor the same way as
"the princes of the nations control them and the powerful oppress them"
(Matt. 20:25):

> These [the powerful] have the same purpose, and will deliver their power
> and their authority to the Beast. . . . And that no one could buy nor sell, but
> he who had the sign or the name of the Beast, or the number of his name
> (Rev. 17:13 and 13:17).[51]

By obtaining an economic perspective one is allowed to obtain a sufficient level of reality in which religion becomes sacramental, and corporeal; where practical concepts such as grace or sin determine the relationship between persons and of production with nature, and where the
liturgical bread can be the bread of life. For this reason, by placing themselves in this concrete, real level, the poor suffer persecution and death—
like Ignacio Ellacuría and his companions in November 1989 in the moment of the fall of the Berlin Wall:

> The hour is coming in which those who murder you will think to worship
> God (John 16:2).

In reality, the "worship" of Satan is consummated by the accumulation
of the blood of the poor (because the poor must sell their bodies for a
salary, and their objectified life, value, is accumulated as the profits of capital) or the blood of the martyrs who fight concretely to free them from the
(practical-productive, economic) "social relationship" that controls them.
Those "structures of sin" are historical; in them consists the essence of the
Devil, the Antichrist. But a theology of economy is necessary—in its
strong meaning—to be able to bring about a hermeneutic of this invisible
being that is not apparent in the world of merchandise, the market, or capital as seen from itself and not from living labor.

NOTES

1. See Helmut Peuckert, *Wissenschaftstheorie, Handlungstheorie, Fundamentales
Theologie* (Frankfurt: Patmos, 1976). Also see Edmund Arens, *Habermas und die
Theologie* (Düsseldorf: Patmos, 1989); especially the following pieces: H. Peuckert,
"Kommunikatives Handeln, System der Machtsgteigerung," pp. 39–64; Francis
Schlüssler Fiorenza, "Die Kirche als Interpretations—gemeinschaft," pp. 115–44;
and Matthew Lamb, "Kommunikative Praxis und Theologie," pp. 241–70.

2. This task was realized especially by Hugo Assmann in his work *Teología desde la praxis de la liberación (Theology from the Praxis of Liberation)* (Salamanca, Spain: Sígueme, 1973), particularly in his essay "Confrontaciones y similitudes" ("Confrontations and similarities"), pp. 76–89.

3. On Jürgen Habermas, we believe that the most important works for our purposes are *Erkenntnis und Interesse* (Frankfurt, Germany: Suhrkamp, 1968); *Theorie des Kommunikativen Handelns* (Frankfurt, Germany: Suhrkamp, 1981), Vols., I–II; *Moral Bewusstsein und Kommunikativen Handelns* (Frankfurt, Germany: Suhrkamp, 1983). Also see R. J. Siebert, *The Critical Theory of Religion* (New York: Mouton de Gruyter, 1985).

4. We are referring to Austin's *How To Do Things With Words* (Oxford: Oxford University Press, 1962).

5. See Dussel, *La pedagógica latinamericana* (Latin American pedagogy) (Bogota, Colombia: Nueva American, 1980).

6. See Dussel, "La base en la teología de la liberación. Perspectiv latinoamericana" ("The base in the theology of liberation: A Latin American perspective"), *Concilium* 104 (1975): 76–89.

7. As Otto Apel would call them in his *Transformation Der Philosophie* (Frankfurt, Germany: Suhrkamp, 1973), vols. I–II.

8. About his 1989 trip through Latin America, some have said that Habermas probably would have expressed confusion in the face of the reality of this continent. No wonder! His categories were thought out for "late capitalism," but not for an exploited and peripheral capitalism like ours.

9. See Dussel, "Comentario a al *Introducción* de la *Transformacion de la Filosofía*" ("Commentary on the *Introduction of the Transformation of Philosophy* of K. O. Apel from Latin America"), In *Ethik und Befreiung* (Augustinus-Buchhandlung, Aachen, 1990).

10. See Habermas, *Theorie des Kommunikativen Handelns* (Spanish ed.) (Madrid: Taurus, 1987), Vol. II, pp. 497–517ñ.

11. Habermas, *Kommunikativen*, pp. 502, 522.

12. See, for example, Ricoeur's "Qu'est-ce qu'un 157" in *Du texte a l'action. Essai d'hermeneutique* (Paris: Seuil, 1986), Vol. II, p. 137.

13. See Dussel, *Ethics and Community* (Maryknoll, N.Y.: Orbis, 1988), Chapters 1, 4, and 5.

14. For Karl Marx, capital is essentially a "social relationship," fundamental practical question forgotten by those who criticize his putative "productivist paradigm." See Dussel's *El último Marx (1863–1882) y la liberación latinoamericana* (Mexico City: Siglo XXI, 1990), Chapters 9 and 10. That is to say, "the practical" is the essential constitutive part of "the economic" (that can be relegated because of this to a mere "system" that is connected by means of "money" to the "world of daily life," as Habermas repeatedly states).

15. See Marx's *Gründrisse* (Berlin: Dietz, 1974), B. 570: "The small circulation between capital and the capacity of labor. . . . The part of capital that enters into this circulation—the means of subsistence—is circulating capital *kat,exokhén*."

16. See Dussel's *Hacia un Marx desconocido (1861–1863), Comentario a la segunda redacción de "El Capital."* (Toward an unknown Marx [1961–1963], Commentary on

the second printing of *Das Kapital*) (Mexico City: Ciglo XXI, 1988), Chapter 15 on the "Concept of Dependency" (with a copious bibliography and debate).

17. Thesis of Mauro Marina in *Dialéctica de la dependencia* (Dialectic of dependency) (Mexico City: Era, 1973).

18. There would be much to correct here in the well-expressed thesis of Martin Jay, *Marxism and Totality* (Berkeley: University of California Press, 1982).

19. The subsumption of the capital of living labor from the outside is grounded in a contract, which is established by two sides: a violent situation (the part of living labor) and repression (the part of the owner of capital). In *Theory of Justice* (Cambridge, Mass.: Harvard University Press, 1971) John Rawls takes as his point of departure a formal and abstract situation but never descends to the real level of capitalism, where essentially the two parties of the contract are in unequal positions. Marx emphasized this point even in *Das Kapital*, when he writes, "A true Eden of innate human rights. What reigned there was liberty, equality, prosperity, and Bentham. Freedom!" (1873, ed. cap. 4; MEGA II, 6, p. 191).

20. See how Habermas treats this question in *Kommunikativen Handelns*, Vol. II, pp. 477, 496. In reality, Habermas has only a "sociological" and never, properly, an economic interest. Therefore, he cannot enter into the present line of thinking we are introducing. The same will apply to the post-Marxist theology of those who follow in his steps.

21. When value and cost are disconnected, all of the scientific intent of Marx's theoretical work is destroyed. See Piero Sraffa, *Production of Commodities by Means of Commodities; Prelude to a Critique of Economic Theory* (Cambridge: Cambridge University Press, 1960). See also Ian Steedman, *Marx After Sraffa* (London: Verso, 1981). The polemic of Ian Steedman, Paul Sweezy, Anwar Shaikh, and others, *The Value Controversy* (London: Verso, 1981), attempts to adequately show this disconnection. Franz Hinckelammert answers in his unpublished *La coherencia lógica de la construcción de una mercancía patrón* (The logical coherence of the construction of a merchandise pattern) (San José, Costa Rica: 1988), especially Chapter 12, "Las posiciones ideológicas de Sraffa" ("The ideological positions of Sraffa"). In addition, see Roy Bhaskar, *Scientific Realism and Human Emancipation* (London: Verso, 1986), especially Chapter 3, "The Positivistic Illusion, Sketch of a Philosophical Ideology of Work," pp. 224ff: George McCarthy, *Marx's Critique of Science and Positivism* (Boston: Kluner Academic Publishing, 1987), or Paul Rojas, "Das Unvollendete Projekt. Zur Entstehungsgeschichte von Marx 'Kapital'," *Argument* (Hamburg) (1989), where the value and cost transformation problem is studied (pp. 208ff).

22. See Dussel, *Ética comunitaria*, Chapters, 2, 3, and especially 12 on capital as a structural, institutional, and historical "social relationship" of sin.

23. On this topic, see Dussel, *El Marx definitivo*, Chapter 10, pp. 2–4.

24. Defining living labor as a creative source rather than as a foundation of value created from nothing is a position of the definitive Schelling of the *Philosophie der Offenbarung* of 1841—a matter that I believe would have given Habermas another completely different interpretation of Marx.

25. Marx, *Gründrisse*, pp. 345–58, 411.

26. We will cite from the fifth edition (New York: Kelly and Millman, 1957).

27. Jevons, *Political Economy*, p. 1.

28. Jevons, *Political Economy*, p. 28.

29. Jevons, *Political Economy*, p. 29.

30. Jevons, *Political Economy*, p. 37.

31. This "final degree of utility" (Jevons, *Political Economy*, p. 52) is the point of departure of the future "marginalisms."

32. Jevons, *Political Economy*, p. 167, cites Smith in *The Wealth of Nations*, Book I, Chapter 5. Evidently, Marx does not accept Smith's definition either because "cost" determines "value," and the latter is that which determines "cost." This criticism is found repeatedly in Marx (see Dussel, *Marx desconocido*, Chapters 1, 2, and 6), who writes: "A. Smith [. . .] confuses at times and at others displaces the determining of the value of merchandise for the quantity of necessary labor and he confuses it [. . .] with the quantity of living labor." [See his *Theories of Surplus Value*, Spanish ed. (Mexico City: FACE, 1980), Vol. 1; Mega II, 3, 2, pp. 365–65]. The value produced in the "necessary time" is part of the value of the merchandise (because it would be necessary to add to it the surplus value); the "quantity of merchandise" that is bought with a salary (value of the capacity of labor) includes surplus value that now the worker pays for with his salary. That is, the value that is produced in the "necessary time" is less than the value of merchandise; the money that is obtained by a salary is equal to the cost-value of the merchandise. (In other words, the worker can buy less value with his salary than the value he produced to obtain his salary.) In this lies the theological question par excellence. If a human being is not the substance (effecting cause) of the foundation of the determination of value, then all economics become fetishized, that is, they are founded on capital and not on the human being.

33. Milton Friedman and Rose Friedman, *Free to Choose* (New York: Avon Books, 1979), p. 6. See also Friedman's *Capitalism and Freedom* (Chicago: University of Chicago Press, 1982) or his teacher Friedrich Hayek's *The Road to Serfdom* (Chicago: University of Chicago Press, 1976).

34. See, for example, the work of Michael Novak, *The Spirit of Democratic Capitalism* (New York: American Enterprise Institute, 1982), especially Chapter 2: "Theologically speaking, the free market and the liberal polity follow from liberty of conscience. . . . In this sense, a defense of the free market is, first, a defense of efficiency, productivity, inventiveness and prosperity. It is also a defense of the free conscience" (p. 112). See the work of Hugo Assmann and Franz Hinckelammert, *Teología y economía* (Theology and economy) (Petrópolis, Brazil: Vozes, 1989).

35. See the excellent critique of the thoughts of Max Weber in Franz Hinckelammert, *Las armas ideológicas de la muerte* (The ideological weapons of death) (San José, Costa Rica: DEI, 1977), pp. 64ff (English ed. Maryknoll, N.Y.: Orbis, 1987) This is all the more important because Weber certainly is under the analyses of Habermas (and therefore the theology that is constructed on his thought). In Weber's *Economía y sociedad* (Mexico City: FACE, 1984), we read: "we purport to speak here of economy in another sense. . . . We have, on the one hand, a necessity or groups of necessities and, on the other, according to the subject's evaluation, a scant supply of means. . . . It is necessary that the specific attitude of economic come into play: scarcity of means in relation with *what is desired*" (pp. 273–74). The coincidence with Jevons can be seen: The economic part is the relationship of merchandise with

pleasure, feeling the "necessity" of the buyer in the market (it is not the "necessity" of the worker or producer, who was at the origin of the "producing" that which, because of not existing, came into existence by means of labor).

36. Smith says to us naively: "In that early and rude state of society which precedes both the accumulation of stock [capital] and the appropriation of land, the proportion between the *quantities of labour* necessary for acquiring different objects seem to be *the only* circumstances which can afford any role for exchanging them for one another. . . . *As soon as stock* [capital] has accumulated in the lands of particular persons, some of them [why?] will naturally employ it in setting to work industrious people . . . in order to make a profit . . . by what their labour *adds* [from where?] to the value of the materials" [*The Wealth of Nations*, I, 6 (New York: Penguin, 1985), pp. 150–51]. The only question that should be put to Smith would be: That "as soon as stock . . .," is it a state of *nature* or is it a moment and product of a historical institution? And if it is a historical institution, the problem of a priori "effect" that has no "cause" should be studied; said "effect" should not simply be accepted as an a posterori fact of natural reason. On this rests the entire problem of a "critical" economy—that of the Theology of Liberation—because this "historical" fact is a historical and originating "structural sin." (See Dussel, *Ética comunitaria*, Chapters 2.2–2.6 and 12.4–12.10.) I think that this is the essential problem of all contemporary theology.

37. Friedman, *Free to Choose*, p. 13. "Chance" is the concept that replaces the "rationality" to which Marx aspired.

38. See Dussel, *Ética comunitaria*, Chapters 1.6–1.8, 6.3–6.7, 11, and 12; Dussel, *Herrschaft und Befreiung* (Freiburg, Switzerland: Exodus, 1985); and especially Dussel, "Christian Art of the Repressed in Latin America," *Concilium*, 15(2) (1980); 215–31; and Dussel, "Le pain de la célébration: signe communautaire de justice," *Concilium*, 17(2) (1982): 89–101. This is a theme dealt with at length in the Introduction to Dussel, *Historia general de la Iglesia en América Latina* (General history of the Church in Latin America) (Salamanca, Spain: Sígueme, 1983), Vol. I, pp. 6ff, starting with the theme of the "conversion" of Bartomé de las Casas. Also, in Dussel, *Para uma ética da Libertacâo Latino-americana* (Toward an ethic of Latin American liberation) (São Paulo, Brazil: Loyola, 1984), Vol. 5, "Archeological Economy," pp. 87–99; or in Dussel, *Filosofia de la liberación* (The philosophy of liberation), Chapter 3.4.8, "Critical Materialism and Worship as Economy" (an idea that was equally inspired by Emmanuel Levinas and Karl Marx and, of course, by the New Testament), English ed. (Maryknoll, N.Y.: Orbis Books, 1985).

39. Hegel, *Religionsphilosophie*, in Werke (Frankfurt, Germany: Suhrkamp, 1970), Vol. 16, p. 202.

40. Hegel, *Religionsphilosophie*, p. 202.

41. Hegel, *Religionsphilosophie*, p. 203.

42. Hegel, *Religionsphilosophie*, p. 218.

43. Hegel, *Religionsphilosophie*, p. 2236.

44. For Habermas, the economic, like "money" or like "power" on another level, colonizes the *Lebenswelt*. (See the *Theorie des Kommunikativen Handelns*, Vol. II, "Entkoppelung von System and Lebenswelt," pp. 229–94, and "Marx und Die These der Inneren Kolonisierung," pp. 489–547, in Spanish ed., Vol. II, pp. 215–80 and 485–501).

45. See the way in which we treated this text in Dussel, *Ética comunitaria*, Chapter 1, pp. 10–11. Equally, for what follows, keep in mind the work cited in note 9, especially point 4: *"The community of life* and the *interpolation of the poor. Liberating praxis"* (and even 4.3 of "the community of communication of *language* to the community of communication of life"), where we confront the position of K. O. Apel with that of Marx—reinterpreting the latter in light of his four unknown editions of *Das Kapital*.

46. Years ago, this question was raised in Dussel, *Religión* (Mexico City: Edicol, 1977), where we spoke of "religion as infrastructure." By not being able to attribute to Marx himself that type of categories (as "supra-" and "infrastructure")—or at least, they were not fundamental categories of his thought as we have proved in our commentary on the "four versions" of *Das Kapital*—we should put the problem better at a purely "economic" level (but as *Oekonomie*, anthropological, ethical ontological, and not only as *Wirtscharfswissenschaft*).

47. See the concept of the Kingdom of God as "satisfaction" (in its carnal and spiritual sense, at one and the same time) in Dussel, *Ética comunitaria*, Chapter 1.7–1.10.

48. Marx has a productive meaning of "matter" (the theologian would call it sacramental) That is, the "cosmic" matter of a putative "dialectical materialism" (to which Marx never referred) is not what is important, but a constructing of nature as a matter of labor. [See Dussel, *La producción teorética de Marx* (The theoretical production Marx) (Mexico City: Siglo XXI, 1985), pp. 37ff]. "This nature prior to human history is not the nature that lives in Feuerbach, but a nature that, might be of one of the Australian coral reefs of recent formation, does not exist now today anywhere nor does it exist either, therefore, for Feuerbach" [Marx, *La ideología alemana*] (German ideology) (Barcelona: Grijalbo, 1970), p. 48: MEW 3, p. 44). Marx is not interested in the "A priority of external nature" (Dussel, *Ideología alemana*, p. 48). He says to us: "This is the matter [material] in which his [man's] work is realized, in which he works, with which and by which he produces." (*Manuscript* I 44; MEW EB 1, p. 512).

49. "He who does not pay a just salary sheds blood." BenSira, Eccles.

50. See Dussel, *Ética comunitaria*, Chapter 2.7–2.8 on "the poor" and "death."

51. It is well known that Marx quotes this text of the Apocalypse in Chapter 2 of Vol. I of *Das Kapital* (Spanish ed.), (Mexico City: Siglo XXI, Mexico, 1979), p. 106; MEGA II, 6, pp. 115–16. This, and hundreds of other Biblical texts [see Reinhard Buchbinder, *Bibelzitate, Bibelspielungen, Bibelparodien, Theologische Vergleiche und Analogien bei Marx und Engels* (Berlin: Erich Schnidt Verlag, 1976)] show that, for Marx, capital was the "Antichrist," Mammon, Moloch—that is, the Demon. We will show in another work that this metaphor opens, by the semantic confusion that it produces, a "new world" (as Ricoeur would say) of unexpected meaning for theology.

10

Ethical Sense of the 1994
Maya Rebellion in Chiapas

On January 1, 1994, to everyone's surprise, and just as the NAFTA Treaty with Canada and the United States went into effect, Mexico listened to news broadcasts informing of a Maya uprising in the state of Chiapas.

Later events are well known: four cities were occupied, the national army reacted, amnesty was granted, talks were proposed and took place, with thirty-two agreements signed. The members of the *Zapatista* Army of National Liberation (EZLN) returned to their communities in order to democratically discuss there what had been agreed upon in the peace talks. Meanwhile, the national government mobilized existing institutions in order to effectively and legally carry out the agreements.

Throughout this entire process a double "language game" could be noticed. The early communiqués of the EZLN used a vocabulary similar to the one employed by revolutionary movements in Latin America, Africa, or Asia. An abstract political and military language appears here, with references to "the condemned of the earth"[1]—an expression typical of Frantz Fanon, in his book by the same name:

> We are the product of five hundred years of struggles . . .; but today we say "enough!" We are the heirs of the true founders of our nationhood. We are the millions of dispossessed, and we call upon our brothers to answer our call as the only way to avoid starvation. . . . [We are against] the same people

Enrique Dussel, "Ethical Sense of the 1994 Maya Rebellion in Chiapas," *Journal of Hispanic/Latino Theology* 2, no. 3 (1995): 41–56.

who opposed Hidalgo and Morelos, those who betrayed Vicente Guerrero, and those who sold half of our land to the foreign invader. . . .[2]

Very soon the uprising received massive and deeply solidarious support from all segments of civil society, from the country's urban population, as well as from *criollos* (white Mexicans) and *mestizos*. When the entire nation echoed its protest, it seemed that the revolutionary "institution" (i.e., the EZLN) started revealing another vocabulary, no longer hiding the usual speech of the Maya people. The language of the native population, birthplace of and reason for the EZLN's struggle, could then be heard:

> For many, many years we reaped the death of our people from the Chiapas fields. Our children were killed by forces unknown to us.[3] Our men and women walked the long night of ignorance that a shadow extended over our steps. . . . The elders of our people spoke to us words that came from far away, from a time when our lives were ours, when our voice was quiet. And truth walked in the words of the elders of our people. And we learned from the words of the elders of our people that the long night of our suffering came from the hands and words of the powerful. . . .[4]

This shift in language was quickly noticed by civil society and its impact was even greater.[5] The earlier political, generic vocabulary—which is not and should not be abandoned—was changed in favour of the language of historical protest by a concrete indigenous Amerindian people. This shift also allows us to discover the new language's ethical character, which is the subject we will discuss here.

In this article we want to briefly reflect on the ethical contents or backdrop of these current events—since we are far from seeing the conclusion of this process, no one yet knowing if it will end peacefully or violently.

THE EARLIER ROOTS OF THE CONFLICT

We are in the presence of a truly historical event. There have been few serious dialogues, in Latin American history, between the original inhabitants (ill-named "Indians") and the white population (the conquering Spaniards or their *criollo* successors), and the *mestizos* (who always try to pass as whites).

The story is told of "the three *tlamatinime* of Ehécatl, of Tezcocan descent, who were eaten by dogs.[6] They had only come to turn themselves in. No one had forced them to do so. They had come bringing their paintings.[7] There had been four [*tlamatinime*], but one managed to escape; three were attacked, there in Coyoacán."[8] Today we can only imagine the humiliation, the utter lack of respect, and the tragedy of those native wise men who pretended to share the greatest treasures of their culture and of their mystical vision of existence, as their tradition demanded, with the "invaders"—Spaniards often illiterate, uneducated, and brutal.[9]

In 1524 another event occurred, perhaps the only other formal dialogue between the two cultures; and it was a complete failure. The manuscript called *Colloquios y Doctrina Cristiana*[10] is of particular value because it records that historical confrontation: for the first and last time, the few surviving *tlamatinime* were able to dialogue with educated Spaniards—the twelve recently arrived Franciscan missionaries. It was a conversation between "the reason of the Other" (the Amerindian) and "the discourse of (nascent) Modernity." There was no symmetry. It was not a "community of dialogue" in an ideal situation, since some were the vanquished and others were the victors. Besides—and contrary to what might be assumed—the knowledge of each of the interlocutors had had a different development. That of the *tlamatinime* preserved the high degree of sophistication of the *Calménac* (the Aztec philosophical school). The friars, on the other hand, although excellent religious men, did not equal the formal level attained by their Aztec counterparts. The encounter seemed a conversation in which the Amerindians were muted men, and the Spaniards were deaf (since no real "translator" was available).

The Spaniards, however, had the power of conquest and, as a result and without sufficient argumentation (as demanded by Bartolomé de Las Casas in his *De Único Modo*), the dialogue was interrupted, and "indoctrination" started. The interrupted conversation gave way to "doctrine," and to the ideological destruction of an imaginary Amerindian.

For that historical moment the *tlamatinime* had fashioned a piece of strict rhetorical art (*"flor y canto"*), filled with beauty and logic.[11] Let us see just the beginning, the actual introduction to the dialogue, as presented by these wise men: "Highly esteemed lords, our lords: You have suffered much in order to come to this land.[12] Here, before you, we contemplate you, we, ignorant people."[13] And then the rhetor formally asks, "And now, what can we say? What *must we address to your ears?*[14] Are we, perhaps, something? We are only common people. . . . "

After this brief opening (which is longer in the manuscript text), they go on to reflect on the difficulty of the dialogue itself, as response to the missionaries' proposal—a proposal that had been a brief and not very sophisticated catechism, not very acceptable even to a Christian, and totally incomprehensible to the really "Other" (as these *tlamatinime* were) in the latter's cultural, linguistic, and religious distinctiveness:

Through the translator[15] we will respond; we will return *the-breath-and-the-word*[16] to the *Lord-of-the-intimately-near-that-surrounds-us*.[17] It is because of Him that we take the risk, that we put ourselves in danger. . . . It might be that we will be led to perdition, or perhaps to destruction. But, where else should we still go?[18] We are common people; we are transitory; we are mortals.[19] *Allow us to die! Allow us to disappear!* Because *our gods have died!*[20] But calm your *heart-flesh*, our lords! We will break it a little bit now, a little we will open the *Secret*,[21] the chest of the Lord, our God.

Vanquished by the unjust and violent weapons of the Conquest, and later by those of colonization, this people was never allowed to dialogue.

Bartolomé de Las Casas arrived in Chiapas, as the new bishop, toward the end of 1544.[22] "After being somewhat coldly received by the [Spanish] inhabitants, he waited until Passion Sunday and then withdrew the permission to absolve from certain sins, reserving them to himself, among them the real enslavement of indians."[23] "The dean of the cathedral chapter absolved many *encomenderos* for holding indians, but this led to the bishops' excommunicating him and suspending his right to hear confessions. This left the bishop without a single secular priest, and with the sole support of the Dominicans who lived outside the city."[24] In 1546 Bartolomé traveled to Mexico, to a meeting of bishops, and never returned to Chiapas. He resigned his bishopric because he felt it ungovernable, given the group of the *encomenderos* who made his work nearly impossible. Bartolomé will write on this years later, in his will:

> Divine Goodness and Mercy, which had chosen me as its minister [in Chiapas], without any merit of mine, sent me to attempt to undo among those numerous peoples we call the Indies . . . the damages, evils and offenses, *as never before seen or heard*, committed by the Spaniards [against the natives] against all reason and justice.[25]

Long indeed would be the history of the injustices committed in Chiapas since the Conquest. But let us return to the present.

FIRST CRITERION OF ETHICAL VALIDITY: RESPECTING THE DIGNITY OF THE ETHICAL SUBJECT

The EZLN members speak with the language of the Maya, a millennial language older than the sixteenth-century Conquest. They speak from within their original theoretical horizon.

To start this ethical reflection, I want to address the three criteria of ethical validity that can be discovered in the communiqués the EZLN made public. First of all, it is very interesting that the rebels insist on calling our attention to *the dignity of the negated historical subject.* "Delegate Juan" often repeats the same demand: "This is why we rose . . .; we were forced to do it. We natives fight *in order to have our dignity respected.* This is what we decided to accomplish: that we *be respected.*"[26] In other communiqués we read:

> [Those who have treated us unjustly] have denied respect and dignity to those who, well before them, inhabited these lands. They have forgotten that human dignity is not only the patrimony of those who have taken care of the basic needs of life. Even those who have no material possessions have that which makes us different from things and from animals: dignity![27]
>
> Let us not allow our dignity to be treated as a commodity in the marketplace of the powerful! If we lose our dignity, we lose everything! Let our struggle be a source of joy for all our brethren, and let them join our hands and our steps on the path of truth and justice.[28]

Thus, if we were to start from an asymmetric position, the *recognition* (*re-conocimiento*) of the oppressed (Aristotle's "slave")[29] as *person* will assume: a) first of all, a knowledge (*conocimiento*) of the oppressed as function or thing (cf. A at level II in graph 1); b) as a second and already ethical act, a knowledge (*conocimiento*) of the oppressed as person[30] (cf. B at level III in graph 1); and c) a later re-cognition (*reconocimiento*)—as a reflect and turnaround act through which the human being is encountered as oppressed within a system of domination,[31] and is localized and ethically judged as negated, as a dominated and exploited indigenous person (cf. C at level III, turning to D at level II).

Merely knowing the native as a function or thing (cf. A)—or women in patriarchy as excluded or inferior, or blacks in a white society, etc.—is in a way "to offer the person (*Personen*) in sacrifice, as instruments (*Werkzeuge*) to sustain the thing (*Sache*)."[33] In other words, it is to know the native as a "functional part" of a system (colonial or capitalist).[34] The ethical moment *por excelencia*, χατ. εξοχην, consists of the "practical knowledge" that perforates mere instrumental functionality (Marx's *Werkzeug*) and constitute the Other as person (cf. B),[35] as an Other different from the

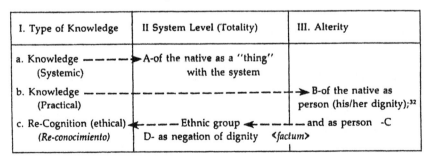

Figure 10.1.   Process of Re-Cognition (Re-Conocimiento) of the Other

system (Luhmann) as totality (Levinas). This originating-ethical rationality[36] *precedes all discourse*, and therefore precedes the process of transcendentalization and of the Apelian foundations: "A reason that precedes the beginning, that precedes the present, because my responsibility for the Other imposes itself before any decision, before any deliberation (before all argument or discourse)."[37]

If there were argument or discourse, it would be "because the Other is a person," and not the other way around. In other words, the empirical *factum*—in order to be *ethical*—demands a reflection: from the Other known as person (cf. C), the domination of the native is discovered as perverse (cf. D), as negation. This *factum* makes manifest the "function" in the "system" (totality): the Other's personhood as negated-part, or as non-autonomous subject (since the only self-referring and self-poietic structure is the very system as totality). The *factum* also makes manifest the Other's personhood as interpolating and, consequently, the very subject of knowledge (cf. A) is now situated as co-responsible[38] for the negation of the Other (i.e., solidarity vis-à-vis misery, compassion).[39] All of this constitutes the *act-of-the-recognition-of-the-Other*, which goes beyond Honneth's analysis.

SECOND CRITERION OF ETHICAL VALIDITY: FULFILLING THE REQUIREMENTS FOR THE REPRODUCTION OF LIFE

Closely tied to the first criterion is the second one: the need to fulfill the requirements for the reproduction of life, given that human life is corporeal. The discussion of poverty is a way of pointing to the nonpossibility of reproducing the native's life. All the communiqués insist on this: "It is because of this that we rose . . ., so that we would have worthy housing, and a reasonable job, and land to toil."[40] In fact, this negative situation has a cause: "All are guilty, from the highest federal officials . . ., they have all denied us health, education, land, housing, services, just work, food, justice."[41]

And also,

> Our sons and daughters have no schools, no medicine, no clothing and no food; there is no roof under which to protect our poverty. Our sons and daughters only have hard work, ignorance, and death. The land we have is good for nothing; and so we go work in powerful men's land in order to earn something for our children; but they (the powerful) pay us very little for our work. Our children must work from an early age in order to get something to eat and water, and medicine. Our children's toys are the machete, the ax, and the hoe. Playing and suffering they go out, to get firewood, to clear the brush, and to plant, as soon as they learn to walk.[42]

And yet, the following text is even more precise and frightening:

> [We understood] that our misery meant the wealth of a few; that on the bones and the dust of our ancestors and our children the powerful built their house. [We understood] that our steps could not enter that house, and that the light that brightened it was fed by the darkness [imposed on] our people. [We understood] that the abundance on the table at that house was fed by the emptiness of our stomachs, and that their children were borne by our misery. [That house's] roof and walls were built over the fragility of our bodies; and the health that filled its spaces resulted from our death; and the wisdom lived in that house nourished itself of our ignorance. The peace that sheltered it was war waged on our people.[43]

Once again we have here an attempt to tie the ethical validity of an action to the demand for bodily reproduction of the ethical subject, as a condition for ethical validity (i.e., if the subject dies there is no ethical validity possible). Furthermore, the one responsible for the impossibility of reproducing life is the perverse *por excelencia*.

In Egyptian Osiris' last judgment (c. 333 BCE), according to chapter 125 of the *Book of the Dead*, it is announced (in a manner that resembles the much later texts of Isa 58 and Matt 25): "I fed the hungry, gave drink to the thirsty, dressed the naked. . . ." These are universal, primary corporeal needs, and, therefore, a criterion of ethical validity. Based on popular wisdom, the EZLN seems to have sensed these fundamental human demands.

THIRD CRITERION OF ETHICAL VALIDITY: COMMUNAL SOLIDARITY

There is a third criterion that is fundamental, and that is "community." Every human act must be solidarious, if it wants to be considered ethically valid within the social context of its agent. Among Maya ethnic groups, the communal dimension is very ancient, foundational, and nonnegotiable. This is not, however, a natural or spontaneous community—it is institutionalized through social means conducive to consensus, agreement, and decision making.

The first and foremost among these social means is what might be called "Maya democracy." The texts we will read are not inspired on the political, "democracy" writings of Aristotle, Rousseau, or Bobbio. These texts are Maya, the creation of a millennial cultural experience as fundamental to world history as the Egyptian, Mesopotamian, Indian, Chinese, Inca, and Nahua ones. Let us now read some beautiful sample texts.

The EZLN's political, theoretical frame of reference is quite theirs. There is no imitation here:

> The terrible conditions of poverty endured by our people have but one common cause: lack of freedom and democracy. We believe that any improvement in the economic and social circumstances of our country's poor requires a truly authentic respect for the people's freedom and democratic will.[44]

An argument is developed through this political terminology: "This is why we rose . . ., so that we may have freedom of expression, and so that we may participate in *what we consider* democracy."[45] This is a Maya "democracy." Here is a text where the Maya "language" was translated into rough Spanish (still called "*castilla,*" as in the sixteenth-century):

> When the EZLN was only foggy and opaque in the mountains, and when words like "justice," "freedom," and "democracy" were only words, they were a dream[46] that had been given to us by our communities' elders—the true guardians of the *word* of our ancestors. They passed on to us the dream at the very moment when day yields its place to night. . . . But when the ages repeated themselves with no exit, without an open door, without a tomorrow, when all was that was unjust, then the true men spoke, those without face who walk in the mountains at night. And they said:[47] "It is reasonable and the will of good men and women to seek and find the best way to govern and be governed. What is good for the many is good for all. But the voices of the few may not be silenced,[48] rather let them be in their place, hoping that the thought and the heart might become shared within the will of the many and in the view of the few.[49] In that way the people, true men and women, will grow inwardly and become great, and no outwardly force can ever break them or take them along other paths."[50]

It is difficult to imagine a better way to develop general consensus in politics! The text goes on:

> It was always our path that the will of the many might be shared by the heart of the men and women who govern. This majority will was the path on which the ones who governed had to walk. If their steps diverted from the people's reason, the heart of the ones who governed had to change and become obedient. That was how our strength was born in the mountains: if the ones who governed were true, then the governed ruled through the shared heart of true men and women.[51]

Thus the text teaches what the Maya political system is and was, even from before the Conquest. This system owes nothing to contemporary political science, and we could all learn a great deal from it. The text continues: "Another word came from far away, and it[52] named this government 'democracy,' although our path had been walked long before the words."[53] And the revelation of "those without face who walk [and speak] in the mountains at night" continues:

> Those who speak at night spoke: "We see that this path of governing is not now a path for the many. We see that the few are not the ones who govern, and they govern without obedience, and they govern by power.[54] And among the few they pass power among themselves, without ever listening to the many; ruling for the few, without obeying the rule of the many. The few rule without reason. The word that came from far away[55] says that they govern without democaracy,[56] without the rule of the people, and we see that the non-reason of those who rule is what causes our pain and nourishes the pain of our ancestors. We see[57] that those who govern by power should go far away so that there may be another reason and truth on our land. And we see that there must be change, and that those who govern should govern obediently; and we see that that word that came from far away to name the manner of our government—'democracy'—is good for the many and for the few."[58]

Among the Maya, a consensus is first reached on what needs to be done, and then a person is chosen from within the community to carry out the project. In other words, the one who rules must obey the communal consensus. And the one who obeys the ruler is, in fact, the ruler. This is Maya "democracy."

The text we are citing then proceeds with a diagnosis of the present conditions:

> The people without face continued speaking:[59] "The world[60] is another world.[61] Reason does not govern anymore, nor the will of the true ones—we are now few and forgotten.[62] Over our path there is death and scorn.[63] We are small. Our word is passing away. Silence has lived for too long in our house. The hour is here for speaking our hearts out to other hearts.[64] Our ancestors must come from night[65] and soil.[66] The faceless ones, the ones who belong to the mountains must dress for war so that their voice may be heard, so that their word may later be still and they return to the night and the soil. May they speak to other men and women who walk on other lands.[67] May their word carry truth; and may it not be lost in lies. May they search for men and women who rule by obedience, and who have strength in their word and not in their fire.[68] And once they find these, may they speak to them and grant them the rod of the rules. May then the faceless ones return to the night and to the soil, they who belong to the mountains. And if reason returns to this land, may their fire be still, and may those who belong to the mountains—the faceless ones, the ones who speak in the night—finally rest in bosom of the land.[69]

The revelation had by the communities' elders concludes this way; and so does the text of the communiqué from the EZLN's General Command: "The faceless ones spoke that way.[70] There was no fire in their hands, and their word was clear and without deceit. Before the day conquered night, they left.[71] And in the land their word alone remained: enough!"[72]

The revelation has ended. Now daily reality becomes the imminent concern, and the language of the ancestors needs to be translated into the idiom of the everyday Mexican *criollo* and *ladino*:

> The men and women of the EZLN, the faceless ones,[73] the ones who walk in the night and who belong to the mountains, have sought words that other men and women could understand. And so they say: First. We demand that there be free and democratic elections. . . .[74]

CONSEQUENCES AND QUESTIONS

The texts we have briefly reviewed raise a number of crucial questions. The first of these is the very concept of the modern national state. In too many instances the *national* state was imposed on some nations by others. For example, the Castillian nation imposed the Spanish state on Catalonians, Andalucians, Basques, and Galicians. The same occurred in Germany, in Italy, in France, in the United Kingdom. In Latin America the "native nations" were never really considered nations with their own language, religion, history, and political institutions.

However, the most recent Colombian constitution, as a result of M19's work, was able to conceive of the state as plurinational—there is one state that institutionalizes the life of *many nations*. The native populations now have their own direct representation in the country's Congress, directly and without mediators. This in turn forces a reconception of the political institutions of the federal state, of the provincial states, and of the local municipal governments (where native populations could rule themselves through their own traditional institutions). The Colombian case translated into political language what the wisdom of centuries had established long before. In other words, native populations speak from their own traditions, without eurocentric imitations.

In the case of Chiapas:

> The word of truth[75] that comes from the depths of our history—from the depths of our pain, from the dead who still live with us—will fight with dignity on the lips of our chiefs. . . . There was no lie in our hearts as true men and women. Our voice[76] will carry the voice of others, of those who have nothing. Our voice will carry the voice of those who are condemned to silence and ignorance, of the ones who have been thrown out of their land and

of their history by the power of the powerful. Our voice will carry the voice of the good men and women who walk these worlds of pain and anger; and of the children and of the elderly who die of loneliness and neglect; and of the humiliated women; and of the small men. Through our voice the dead will speak—our dead, so lonely and forgotten, so dead and yet so alive in our voice and in our path. We will not plead for pardon or favor! We will not beg for alms! We will not beg for crumbs that fall from the filled tables of the powerful! We will instead go to *demand what is the right and reason of every people:*[77] *freedom, justice, and democracy!*[78]

These are the words of a people, of one of this continent's original nations, older by far than all the *mestizo* and white Latin Americans who came later. Chiapas is a very serious ethical question, demanding an answer from the history of modernity. Latin America must answer; but Europe is also bound to respond, especially mindful of the genocide it carried out in the sixteenth century—the first Holocaust of modernity! Europe must recall the fifteen million dead Amerindians, and the fourteen million Africans sold into slavery. These are ethical situations that demand a solidarious co-responsibility with the oppressed, the poor, and the excluded. We all have much to reflect upon, to analyze, and to conclude in the years that will follow the dense few weeks of 1994.

Let me conclude this article by suggesting that we read from one more communiqué, from the many that were filled with a certain utopian hope (which the poor never seem to be without—because life does not resign itself to poverty, choosing instead to fight with a passion unknown to the satisfied):

> The word that followed the path . . . of the eldest of the elders of our peoples was not a word of pain and death. In the word of the eldest of the elders there was also hope for our history. . . . Fear was buried next to our dead, and we carried our voice to the land of the powerful, and we carried our truth to the land where lies rule and we carried our dead to the city so as to show them before the blind eyes of our fellow citizens—to the good and the bad among them, to the wise and the ignorant, to the powerful and the weak. . . .[79]

Theirs is a political movement that expresses, quite articulately, the ethnicity and nationhood of one of this continent's regional peoples—similar to the *Cemanahuac* of the Aztecs, the *Abia Yala* of the Kumas, and the *Tehuantisuyo* of the Incas. We—the whites and *mestizos*, the prize-winning poets and the great university professors—still need much beauty, culture, and poetry to compare with and learn from "the eldest of the elders" of the mountains of Chiapas. May history forgive our ignorance and our pride!

NOTES

1. Cf. *Los condenados de la Sierra. Chiapas* (pamphlet printed by the EZLN on 7 February 1994) 5.

2. Cf. "Declaración de la Selva Lacandona. Hoy decimos ¡basta!," *El Despertador Mexicano* (EZLN official newspaper) 1:1 (1993) 1. After this *declaración* there are others: "Declaration of War," "Instructions for Chiefs and Officers," etc. In other words, this is the language of a recognizable revolutionary movement.

3. These seem to be diseases not recognized as such in traditional medicine.

4. "Mensaje a la Coordinadora Nacional de Acción Cívica," *La Jornada* (22 February 1994) 8.

5. This is what journalist Hermann Bellinghausen called "the semantic phase of the conflict." Cf. *La Jornada* (7 February 1994) 9.

6. In other words, the *conquistadores* threw them to dogs especially trained for this purpose in war, and these devoured the *tlamatinime*.

7. These were the famous Nahua painted codices. The main two colors employed were black (signifying the mystery of the originating night) and red (symbol of the clarity of day, of love and life, and of blood).

8. Cf. Miguel León-Portilla, *Filosofía Náhuatl* (Mexico: Fondo de Cultura Económica, 1979) 61.

9. The Aztecs had taken over the codices from Azcapotzalco (and later from other conquered towns). They first studied them, incorporated the contents into their own texts, and then destroyed the stolen codices. This is what they expected the Spaniards to do. This way, their own texts would have somehow survived within the "codices" (in the history and theory) of the *conquistadores*.

10. I will always refer to the text as edited by Walter Lehmann, *Sterbende Götter und Christliche Heilsbotschaft* (Stuttgart, 1949); and in Spanish and Nahuatl the text as edited by León-Portilla, *Filosofía Náhuatl*, 129–36. It is interesting to note that the Nahuatl text was written after the Conquest, at the "Colegio de Tlatelolco," founded by the Franciscans for the children of the *caciques* (i.e., the native nobility). One of the writers of this latter text was Antonio Valeriano, a resident of Azcapotzalco, who had to do with the Virgin of Guadalupe tradition. The text included "all the conversations, confabulations, and sermons that occurred between the twelve religious (Franciscans) and the lords, important citizens, and officials" in Mexico in 1524 (cf. W. Lehmann, *Sterbende*, 52) , in other words, just three years after the destruction of the ancient metropolis.

11. For an account of this event, see my own *1492: El encubrimiento del Otro. Hacia el origen del mito de la modernidad* (Madrid: Editorial Nueva Utopía, 1993. German translation: *Von der Erfindung Amerikas zur Entdeckung des Anderen. Ein Projetkt der Transmoderne* [Düsseldorf: Patmos Verlag, 1993]).

12. Notice that this is also how Moctezuma "receives" Cortez: the Other is respected, is allowed to a space that first establishes the "pragmatic" or "illocutionary" moment of "communicative reason." Interestingly, this moment is still very present in Mexican culture: one never goes directly to the point ("instrumental reason") or to the "propositional content." This appears to be highly improductive in the eyes of the capitalist businessman.

13. *Timacrevalti*, "ignorance" that is only gained from wisdom! Nezahualcoyotl taught it: "Do we ever speak what is *true* here, O Giver of Life? We only dream, we only awake as in a dream, all is only but a dream! No one speaks *truth* here!" In: *Cantares Mexicanos*, mss., fol. 17, r. Also in: León-Portilla, *Filosofía Náhuatl*, 60. (Translator's note: in Nahuatl the concept and glyph for "truth"/"true" are the same for "reality"/"real.")

14. These wise men of "another" culture are already aware of "distance." The recently arrived Franciscans, on the other hand, display a simplistic modern optimism that wants to "teach the Christian faith." Theirs is a rather rationalist position, honest but naïve, sincere and true . . . but that does not see the "distance" that the *tlamatinime* assume and accept as *underlying* every possible and future "conversation" or "discussion." This assumed "distance" is accepted as difficulty, as incommesurability, as pathology in communication. For them, the vanquished, this is all very evident. But for the "modern" victors, this is an obstacle that needs to be overcome in the shortest time possible, so as to then move on to "informing" about the (Christian) "propositional content." In other words, the "pragmatic, communicative" moment does not have a heavy and demanding priority in the lives of the missionaries who feel compelled to communicate the "reason (*ratio, Grund*) of the Other."

15. Again, a crucial moment. The "translator" for the Aztec wise men *could not possibly have* the necessary qualifications. There was no one at the time who could know both cultures well enough so as to *really* express or translate what each side was speaking about. In fact, this pretended "dialogue" was carried on in the language of Castile, which was the power then. Castilian was hegemonic, and its understandings and forms were considered the valid and correct ones. "The other" had to *enter* this dominant linguistic community as an outsider, if it wanted to be heard.

16. *Yn ihiio yn itlatol*. In Nahuatl this elongated expression is equivalent to "face-to-face." Elongated expressions and phrases are frequent in this highly refined rhetoric text.

17. *Tloque inNauaque*. This Nahuatl expression names Ometeótl (the Supreme Divinity) as mystic experience, penetrating the most intimate dimensions of being and present in all that surrounds us. How could these Franciscans (who were nevertheless familiar with reformed Spanish schools of mysticism) know that they should have dialogue *for weeks* on just this one experience and concept? Can one have a very quick chat with the Buddha over the concept of "nirvana"?

18. Notice how a tragic situation is being faced with courage, clear sightedness, and even heroic magnanimity. This was a "holiness" that the Franciscans did not recognize, and much less the *conquistadores* present.

19. *Tipoliuini timiquini*. An expression of Nahua wisdom signifying that all is finite "on earth" (*in Tlalticpac*). The other place where they could go is not the earth but the *Topan mictlan* ("that which is beyond," the place of the dead).

20. *Tel ca tetu in omicque*. A "world" has died, but what is life worth without that world? The Europeans were far from suspecting the dimension of the tragedy experienced by these "living dead." Perhaps the more honest course of action would have been to incorporate the native culture into the "new world." But this could not happen in the *possible* historical outcome, because this incorporation would have meant the birth of a truly "*new* world"—but this could not happen.

21. *In top in ipetlacal.* Another elongated Nahuatl expression to indicate what is hidden, what is not revealed, what *cannot* be revealed due to the incapacity of the recipient. This is another crucially important "pragmatic" moment: the inner life experience of this culture that can only express itself through the experience of a communal historical praxis. In other words, an extended period of "shared living" is necessary in order to start "understanding" that which is revealed. "Revelation" (*Offenbarung*) is not the same as "manifestation" or "appearance" (*Erscheinung*). I thoroughly discussed this theme in my *Filosofía de la liberación* (Mexico: Edicol, 1977), and in my *Para una ética de la liberación latinoamericana* (Buenos Aires: Siglo XXI, 1973), vol. I, ch. 3; as well as in my contribution to the discussion with K. O. Apel ("*La interpelación como acto-de-habla*") in my recent book *Apel, Ricoeur, Rorty y la filosofía de la liberación* (Guadalajara: Editora de la Universidad de Guadalajara, 1993).

22. See my *El episcopado hispanoamericano. Institución misionera en defensa del indio (1504–1620)* (Cuernavaca: CIDOC, 1970), vol. IV, 249ff. This is part of my doctoral dissertation presented at the Sorbonne. In nine volumes, this work includes documents from Seville's Archives of the Indies.

23. Ibid., vol. IV, 248.

24. Ibid., vol. IV, 249.

25. "Cláusula del testamento," *Colección de documentos inéditos para la historia de México*, ed. J. García Izcazbalceta (Mexico: n.ed., 1866) 2:511.

26. "Delegado Juan: 'Luchamos para que se nos respete como indígenas,'" *La Jornada* (25 January 1994) 6.

27. "Carta a tres periódicos," *La Jornada* (18 January 1994) 2.

28. "Cartas al Frente Cívico de Mapastepec," *La Jornada* (12 February 1994) 14.

29. Aristotle thought that true friendship could not be established with someone "inferior," with the other as "other." In his words: "With regard to the slave (δουλος), there can be no friendship with him," because one would degrade oneself otherwise. There is nothing here resembling compassion, solidarity, or mercy. Cf. *Nicomachean Ethics*, VIII, 11, 1161 b a.

30. Aristotle touches on this by saying that the slave "as human" (cf. Ibid.) can be an object of friendship "because a certain justice seems to exist, in reference to every human, in all relations that the latter enters into because of law or of contract" (cf. Ibid.).

31. The "re-(*an*-)" in "re-cognition (*An-erkennung*)" indicates the returning, the reflecting, and the mirroring of "C" in "D."

32. See the three levels studied by Honneth: the emotional (love, *Liebe*), the cognitive (rights, *Rechte*), and the social recognition (dignity, *Würde*). Cf. A. Honneth, *Kampf zum Anerkennung. Zur moralischen Grammatik sozialer Konflikte* (Frankfurt: Suhrkamp, 1992) 211.

33. K. Marx, "Bemerkungen über die neueste preussische Zensurinstruktion," (1842) *WEB*, 1:3–27. See E. Dussel, *Apel, Ricoeur, Rorty y la filosofía de la liberación*, cit.

34. "System" is used here in the same sense as by Niklas Luhmann: "Our thesis that there are systems can now be expressed with greater precision. These are self-referent systems." Cf. N. Luhmann, *Soziale Systeme* (Frankfurt: Suhrkamp, 1984) 31. In this system, the individual acts as a "function."

35. In São Leopoldo (Rio Grande do Sul, Brazil), Hans J. Sandkühler asked me for an explanation of this constituting of the other as person. The answer

will be discusssed in chapter four, section two, of my forthcoming *Etica de la liberación*.

36. This will be the subject of chapter five, section seven, of the above-mentioned *Etica de la liberación*, where we will study the "types of rationality."

37. Cf. Emmanuel Levinas, *Autrement qu'être ou au-delà de l'essence* (The Hague: Nijhoff, 1974) 212.

38. This is "re-sponsibility" (from the Latin *spondere*, "to-commit-oneself-to-take-care-of-the-[defenseless]-other"). It is prior to the "responsibility" of H. Jonas or of K. Apel.

39. Reyes Mate (in *La razón de los vencidos* [Barcelona: Ed. Anthropos, 1991] 143) poses the question correctly, citing Horkheimer's perspective: "This love cannot be understood without an orientation toward a future of human happiness. This orientation does not come from a revelation but from the *misery* of the present" (cf. M. Horkheimer, "Materialismus und Moral," *Traditionelle und kritische Theorie* [Frankfurt: Fischer, 1970] 94). However, Horkheimer is of the opinion that compassion is a *"moral feeling;"* on the other hand, I believe that it is the first moment of the "originating ethical *reason."* This is a fundamental difference since I do not support an ambiguous compassionate "sentimentalism." See also, H. Schnädelbach, "Max Horkheimer und die Moralphilosophie des deutschen Idealismus," *Max Horkheimer heute*, ed. A. Schmidt and N. Altwickler (Frankfurt, 1983) 52–79.

40. "Delegado Juan: Luchamos . . .," 6.

41. "Carta a tres periódicos," 2.

42. "Buscamos caminos de paz y sólo encontramos burla," *La Jornada* (12 February 1994) 15.

43. "Mensaje a la Coordinadora Nacional de Acción Cívica," 8.

44. "Comunicado del 6 de enero," *La Jornada* (11 January 1994) 10.

45. "Delegado Juan: Luchamos . . .," 6.

46. Dreams have always been channels for the "revelation" of "truth" among Amerindian populations. This has certainly been the case among the Mapuche of Chile, the Guarani of Paraguay, the Inuit of the Arctic, and the Aztec of Mexico. The interpretation of dreams was one of the major skills to be developed by Aztec *tlamatinime* in the *calmecac* of Tenochtitlán.

47. Clearly implied is that this is a "message" from the ancestors who speak through dreams.

48. For this type of government minorities have the *same* rights as the majority.

49. In other words, it is necessary that consensus or unanimity be encouraged, and not just the attainment of a majority. This requires time—the time for reflection, for arguments, and for consensus building.

50. "Comunicado de la Comandancia General: Elecciones democráticas," *La Jornada* (27 February 1994) 11.

51. Ibid.

52. They are aware that it is another name for something *similar but not the same.*

53. "Comunicado de la Comandancia General . . .," 11.

54. A reference to the modern state.

55. Once again, the ancient "revealing" word that manifests itself through dreams, and through the eldest of the elders.

56. What "the few" call democracy is not observed even by them.

57. With a prophetic and wise glance that comes from ages past.

58. "Comunicado de la Comandancia General . . .," 11.

59. In other words, the "revelation" continues.

60. This current world.

61. Not the ideal world desired and hoped for by the eldest of the elders.

62. The Chiapas Maya themselves.

63. Once again the experience of dignity being trampled on.

64. This heart-to-heart conversation is based on the idea that the heart is the seat of reason, of humanness, of intelligence, of love, of sincerity, and of dignity.

65. From the place where the ancestors live.

66. From the place where the ancestors are buried.

67. Probably the country's *criollos* and *ladinos*.

68. This is a beautiful and clear pragmatic expression of rationality, in the manner of Habermas or of Apel, whereby strength is granted to the word and not to violence or to weapons. These are men and women of reason, who only wish to be reasonable.

69. "Comunicado de la Comandancia General . . . ," 11.

70. The "faceless ones" are the ancestors who speak through dreams, or through the eldest of the elders. But since the EZLN members also cover their faces, there might be a reference here to their disappearing into the mountains (in imitation of their ancestors) after their mission of peace and justice has been fulfilled.

71. Similar to the struggle that occurs every dawn, according to Aztec mythology, between the Moon and her four hundred brothers, and the Sun (Huitzilopochtli).

72. "Comunicado de la Comandancia General . . .," 11.

73. Members of political parties and of religious organizations have said that they would not dialogue with people who cover their faces. They seem to forget that the Amerindians we see walking down country roads or city streets have always been treated as "faceless." They also seem to forget that they have at best perceived the natives as part of a picturesque rural scene, a part of a tourist trip. On the other hand, the people who have been faceless for the white *criollos* and for the *ladinos* now cover their faces to precisely emphasize their being deprived of dignity for five hundred years. The natives remind us that we have stolen their faces, and now claim them by consciously exposing their facelessness.

74. "Comunicado de la Comandancia General . . .," 11.

75. See the Maya and Aztec sense of "truth" in my work, *1492: El encubrimiento* . . . , chapter 7, especially note 17.

76. This is the voice of "interpellation." See the pertinent chapter in my *Apel, Ricoeur, Rorty y la filosofía de la liberación*.

77. See my article in: E. Dussel, ed., *Fundamentación de la ética y la filosofía de la liberación* (Mexico: Siglo XXI, 1992).

78. Ejército Zapatista de Liberación Nacional, "Comunicado dirigido al pueblo," *La Jornada* (20 February 1994) 14.

79. "Entramos otra vez a la historia de México: EZLN," *La Jornada* (22 February 1994) 8. It seems that we are again hearing from the (Maya literary and religious classic) *Book of the Books of Chalam Balan*: "The ninth of *Ahuau Katun* is the second

one to be counted. *Ichcaansihó*, the 'Face-of-the-Birth-of-Heaven,' will be their seat. In time tribute will be paid to the foreigners who will come to this land, at the time of the arrival of the owners of our souls, when they will gather the people and teach the holy faith of Christianity. . . . Very heavy will be the work and weight of the *katun* because this will be the beginning of the lynching, and of the explosions of fire at the end of the arm of the whites. . . ." (*Libro de los Libros de Chalam Balan* [Mexico: Fondo de Cultura Económica, 1991] 70–71). This did happen in the sixteenth century. This is how they now say it: "Our land was covered with war, our steps armed themselves and began walking, and fear was buried next to our dead. . . ." ("Comunicado dirigido al pueblo," 8).

IV

HISTORY

11

From Secularization to Secularism: Science from the Renaissance to the Enlightenment

The secularization of science from the Renaissance to the Enlightenment is a process to which one can put an artificial beginning with Nicholas of Cusa's *De Docta Ignorantia* of 1440, and end with Immanuel Kant's *Kritik der reinen Vernunft* of 1781, which links the Enlightenment to Romanticism. Modern secularization, beginning as a political movement, scored its first success with the *Golden Bull* of 1356, in the empire of Charles IV, the culmination of a tradition that inspired Luis of Bavaria in his struggles against John XXII, following the theories of Marsilio of Padua or William of Ockham. The movement was to reach its apogee after the limit of the present study, the Feuerbach's *Das Wesen des Christentums* of 1841 and Nietzsche's *Also sprach Zarathrustra* of 1883. I propose to concentrate on the period between Nicholas V (1447–1455), the first humanist pope, and Pius VI (1775–1799), the pope at the time of the French Revolution. This period is essential for an understanding of the "death of God" question that is so much at the forefront of modern theological speculation.[1]

I. SECULARISM OR CHRISTIANITY: A FALSE ALTERNATIVE

It is impossible to talk of the secularization of science without being clear as to the meaning of the term. Pierre Duhem rightly said that the Fathers

Enrique Dussel, "From Secularization to Secularism: Science from the Renaissance to the Enlightenment," *Concilium* 47 (1969): 93–119.

of the Church, "in the name of Christian doctrine, opposed the pagan philosophers on matters that we would now consider more metaphysical than physical, but which formed the cornerstone of classical physics."[2] In fact, it was first the biblical theologians, and then the apologists and the Fathers themselves, who criticized the basic thought patterns or ethico-mythical nucleus[3] of Greco-Roman culture in the light of the basic patterns of Judaeo-Christian thought. The doctrine of creation, the denial that events on earth were dictated by the stars, the destruction of belief in the eternal return and the disappearance of the classical Pantheon opened up a new world for the Christian, a world *created*, in contradiction of the adage that "everything is full of gods."[4]

This collision, cultural as well as doctrinal, between Judaeo-Christianity and Hellenism in the 2nd century, also produced a secularization, an *Entgottlichung* (de-divinization), of the cosmos, a genuine a-theization of the divine world of the Greeks and Romans, which led to Christians being justly accused of being atheists in regard to the ancestral gods. This de-mythologization opened up a new world in astronomy and physics, and a new world to the sciences,[5] which had not previously achieved a sufficient degree of independence from theology, nor a consistency which would enable science to be practiced outside a framework of Christianity.

In metaphysical terms, to consider the world as *created* was not yet an adequate springboard for the new science. A radical sort of "making mundane," desacralizing or profaning had to take place for the cosmos to be considered on the basis of its physical makeup. It is one thing to see the world as not-God and created, but still thinkable only in terms of faith, theology and the theocentric structures of Christianity; it is quite another to see a world existing before one's eyes, absolute[6] and autonomous when considered in terms of its physical structure, on the basis of its essence.

For modern man the question of whether the world is created or not is of little interest (this would be to study its contingent metaphysical condition); he wants to learn about the very structure of the world, on the basis of an examination of them in themselves. If this absolute consideration inclines toward pantheism, atheism or deism, this is not secularization of science but *secularism*; recourse to the foundation, to the God of Israel or of Christianity, is not permitted.

In any form, consideration of the non-divine and now profane world is something quite new in history. Man had never before faced the cosmos with the assumption that it rested on nothing other than its own structures, which were to be described scientifically, independently from theology. The world seen as absolute is a product of evolution of ideas about God and about nature, an evolution which, as history shows us, has passed from secularization to militant secularism. Science was to become the chief instrument of this mode of confronting reality. It was not to be mainly the metaphysical approach that was most concerned with the original and final foundation of the world, nor the theological; only science, particularly mathematics (as Niccolo Tartaglia, 1499–1577, saw), would enable man to penetrate the confused secrets of his world. As science advanced, so theology recovered its healthy transcendence over cultural patterns.

The Church, or rather many theologians and the more influential schools, gradually fell into the following opposing scheme of ideas:

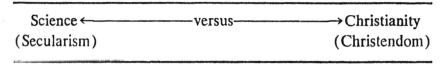

Science ←——————————versus——————————→ Christianity
(Secularism) (Christendom)

Figure 11.1.

Whenever a scientist of the new school discovered an unknown element in the makeup of the cosmos, there followed an immediate conflict with the tradition of Latin-Western culture. I shall examine the cases of Galileo and Richard Simon in due course. Copernicus, encouraged by Clement VII in his youth when he published the *Commentariolus* (1514), only avoided condemnation for the *De revolutionibus orbium coelestium* (1543) through the astute intervention of Andreas Osiander, who put his ideas forward as mere "hypotheses." The work was in any case condemned in 1616 as being contrary to the Bible.

The Church was in fact in a difficult situation. On the one side a whole scientific culture was in the air, largely originating in Rome itself; on the other, the results of its investigations were not accepted. Why this apparent contradiction? It arose through a confusion between the supracultural values of faith and the cultural values of a particular culture—the Latin-Mediterranean culture of medieval Christendom. *Christendom*, in both its Byzantine and Latin forms, arose in the 4th century after the triumph of Constantine. It took many of the cultural values of the Greco-Roman world at face value—those based on the Bible and tradition which had withstood the criticism of the Fathers. But it failed to notice that those traditions, even those based on the Bible, formed a whole cultural conditioning which, though necessary, was not the only one possible. Thus along with the language came a whole host of astronomical, ethnological, physical, geographical, medical, historical, psychological and political hypotheses that, difficult to disengage from the general background, came to constitute the cultural a priori, the basic *idée reçu*,[7] of Christendom.

II. THE CORRECT ALTERNATIVE

The great scientific discoveries of the Renaissance and the Enlightenment were to produce a crisis, a great barrage of criticism directed against the cultural bases of Christendom. These basic cultural values had grown through the thousand years of Mesopotamian and Egyptian civilization, on which the world of the Bible was nourished; they spread along the Mediterranean through Greek civilization in the East and Roman civilization in the West, and consequently through Europe with the Latinization that followed the Roman conquests. Christianity evangelized this world and, without realizing it, became confused with it at a certain cultural level.

The new science, starting with the demythologization begun by the Fathers, questioned certain principles that had come to be "considered" as of faith. Examples of these were: the astronomical descriptions of the Bible, with the earth as the center of the universe and a spherical structure for the heavens; the belief that Moses was the direct author of the law; the acceptance of the demonaical origin of sickness; the direct creation by God of each star and each species of animal; the miraculous appearance of comets in the sky. The new discoveries made the suppositions of old schemes that conflicted with them no longer tenable.

For some churchmen, this was tantamount to questioning the very principles of faith: the world of Christian faith, essentially *trans*cultural, had become united and confused with the values of a culture—that of Latin Christendom. Hence there resulted an antinomy that should never have been: science versus Christianity. It should rather have been pointed in the following terms:

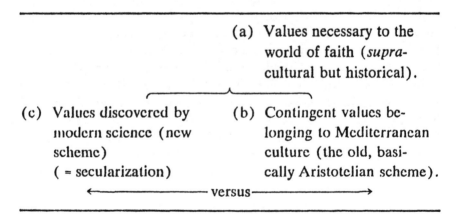

Figure 11.2.

Theology and Christianity should have realized that the conclusions could not be in opposition to the values necessary to faith. Yet many theologians, and the most influential ones, held that such discoveries cast doubt on the whole of Christianity. They had mistakenly brought together the (a) and (b) of figure 11.2. Science became tinged with an air of lack of faith, heresy, or just plain error. This was not merely a Catholic phenomenon: in the Copernicus-Galileo case, for example, Luther and Calvin took the same attitude as the Inquisition.

The scientists, for their part, who were nearly all originally churchmen, found themselves forced into one of two inevitable errors: either to fall into "concordism"—twisting the Bible or tradition to make it fit in with their scientific conclusions, or to turn from secularization into secularism, setting themselves up against the Church, or at least against many of its theologians. This lack of understanding produced a scientific world which at first grew alongside the Church, but then gradually grew away from it, seeking the autonomy it needed but which was denied it. Modern science was only opposed to the old patterns of Latin culture. Christendom pushed it into secularism. But science itself contained its own impetus toward a new concept of nature and, correspondingly, of God. The general lines along which this impetus evolved will show us the metaphysical basis of modern secularism.

III. FROM SECULARIZATION TO SECULARISM: THE AUTONOMY AND ABSOLUTIZATION OF NATURE

For the Greeks, nature was a vast divine organism consisting of bodies extending in space and moving in time, the whole endowed with life since the celestial powers moved by themselves; there was a teleology and a divine order or *logos*. The whole polytheistic understanding of the cosmos disappeared with the patristic era and the Middle Ages, but only to be replaced by the angelology and demonology we see reflected in the paintings and other manifestations of medieval culture. Humanism and the Renaissance imposed another pattern. Nature gradually began to take on the pattern of a machine (*natura naturata*) which functions by virtue of certain fixed laws laid down by nature itself (*natura naturans*). This change naturally did not come about overnight, but took centuries.[8]

Flight from the Turks brought the Byzantine sage Plethon (1355–1452) to Italy, where in 1440 he wrote his famous "On the Differences between the Philosophies of Plato and Aristotle,"[9] which was to be the spark that set off many a blazing dispute. His disciple Bessarion (1395–1472) defended him in his *De natura et arte*.[10] About this time the young Nicholas of Cusa (1401–1464) was sent to Constantinople. The immense evil and refined science of the Byzantine civilization of the time brought about a deep conversion in him. *De docta ignorantia* was the fruit of his morose contemplation of this civilization. His system was clearly inspired by the neo-Platonists. Although he asserted the creation of the universe ex nihilo, one can already see the birth of the modern tradition: "The world is like a book written by the finger of God."[11] The universe is the *maximum contracto* of everything that is possible, the *explicatio Dei* that preexisted in God as *complicatio*. This was not yet an absolute view of the universe,[12] but Cusa does abandon Aristotelian cosmology. The earth is no longer the center of the system; the center is now God in all things; the earth is of the same substance as the spheres and could be seen shining like a star if we could get out of the "the region of fire"[13] to look back at it. Marsilio Ficino himself (1433–1499) affirmed: "Deus per esse suum quod est simplicissimum quoddam rerum centrum a quo reliqua tamquam lineas deducuntur."[14]

It was the achievement of Nicholas Copernicus (1473–1543) to apply this new view of nature to astronomy. This lay not so much in having dethroned the earth from its central position as in having denied that the universe had a center. Studying our own system, the sun can be considered as its center, but the whole system is made of the same matter and the same astronomical laws govern all parts of the cosmos. The earth is a star just like any other. The whole universe is a vast machine whose structure can be worked out by mathematics. Thus Johann Kepler (1571–1630) could say: "Ubi materia, ibi geometria." Giordano Bruno (1545–1600), even more than Nicholas of Cusa, propounded a neo-Platonic and Renaissance view of nature: God is the *fons emanationis* rather than the creator; "productio rei" is a better term than "creatio." As an enthusiastic follower of Copernicus, he held that there is an active divine force present in nature (*natura naturans*) and also in the world as *complicatio explicationis* (*natura naturata*).[15] On February 17, 1600 he was burned alive in Rome, condemned by the Inquisition.

It was with Galileo Galilei (1564–1642) that the new view of nature received its first classical scientific expression: "Philosophy has been written in this immense book which is continually open before our eyes (I am referring to the universe), but which cannot be understood without first knowing the language and recognizing the signs with which it is written. It is written in the language of mathematics and its characters are triangles, circles and other geometric figures, without which it is impossible for me to have a human understanding of these words, and without which I would be wandering vaguely in a dark maze."[16] And he ends by saying that all this has been done "for the benefit of us, Catholics."[17]

Nature is pure quantity, and on these grounds Galileo criticizes and discounts the existence of qualities.[18] This nature, inert matter, must however suppose some cause outside itself. But this cause will henceforth be a *Deus ex machina*. Descartes (1596–1650) pushed this view of the world as a vast machine of matter still further.

It was Baruch Spinoza (1632–1677) who had the courage to give the definitive expression to the idea of nature that began to emerge in the 14th century and that was to make secularism possible. Science claimed that the world was absolute and autonomous in regard to theology. Spinoza formalized this by saying: "By self-causing I understand that whose essence includes its existence."[19] God is his own cause, the only substance, *natura naturans* and *naturata*. Nature is God himself, the expression of his attributes and modes. In this the Dutch Jewish philosopher summed up the whole of the nominalist, humanist and Renaissance tradition of the 16th and 17th centuries. Science now contemplates the universe as pure extent and movement, an absolute that can be worked out by mathematics.[20] This is an absolute immanentism containing its own idealism: *Deus sive natura*.

In England, meanwhile, Bacon had formulated the experimental scientific method. But Isaac Newton (1642–1727) typifies the Anglo-Saxon scientific approach. Nature is a total phenomenon,[21] organized in absolute[22] and in absolute space;[23] it is the *sensorium Dei* set in motion by absolute movement.[24]

Through idealism, following the Cartesian tradition but also that of Berkeley ("Esse est percipi") and English empiricism, Immanuel Kant (1724–1804) conceived nature as the object (*Gegenstand*) of scientific knowledge. Newton's absolute space and time become the a priori of understanding, ordering the chaotic world of the *noúmenon*: nature is a phenomenon. Nature is thought by the a priori forms of understanding and cannot be understood metaphysically, but only scientifically,[25] whereas things in themselves, neither God nor the "I" on its ontological level, can be known scientifically. Nature is a transcendental absolute which has ended by losing its own reality. We are now very far from the spheres of the 13th century, but very close to the crisis of modern science. The idealist mechanism of this view was to be criticized by the vitalist- and biologist-inspired philosophies of the later 19th century.

Goethe expressed the enthusiasm of modern man when he exclaimed: "Nature! She surrounds us and embraces us, incapable as we are of escaping from her, and unable as we are to penetrate her more deeply. Without our asking or noticing, she catches us up in the cycle of her dance and carries us with her until we fall back exhausted into her arms again."[26]

IV. PANTHEISM, DEISM, AND ATHEISM

As we have seen, the idea of an absolute nature always and logically posits a certain idea of God, a God who gradually fades away until he has practically disappeared from view, in the visions of Holbach, Feuerbach, and Nietzsche.[27]

From the thinkers of the 14th century up to Campanella (1568–1639), the idea of God always resembles either the first *ousía* of the neo-Platonists, the God of Duns Scotus or that of Meister Eckhart, the first moment preceding all emanations, always with a hidden leaning toward pantheism. In the great mechanist systems, God is the organizing architect, the origin of movement and the end of all matter. Copernicus, Kepler and Galileo all see him in this way. Descartes himself makes this idea of God the key to his whole system. But in this new scheme it is in fact an *idea* of God that carries out the function of subjectivity. It is no longer the living, transcendent, provident God of Israel. It is a *Deus ex machina*, put there for the convenience, viability and rational and mathematical understanding of the theoretical structure of modern science and idealist subjectivity. This tradition culminates in Spinoza's philosophical fusion of God and nature. Nature here becomes definitely all; the rest is nothing. The creator and provider has been displaced, but before reaching the stage of declared atheism God was reduced to the idea of a being—a supreme being, admittedly—in the variant known as deism.

In France it was Pierre Bayle (1647–1706) who initiated the process.[28] All the dogmas of positive religion had to submit themselves for examination before the tribunal of reason.[29] In *Pensées diverses sur la comète qui parut en 1680* (1683), his aim was to show that there was no connection between science and revealed religion. He proves that the comet (Haley's) which was seen in December 1680 had no miraculous or providential origin, that it was not an indication of the wrath of God, but simply a natural astronomic happening. His god is not a god of providence; miracles are impossible. He goes on to make the first apologia for atheism in Western culture.[30]

In England Lord Herbert of Cherbury (1582–1648) first sketched out the deism that was to receive its fullest expression with Hobbes (1588–1679). The Earl of Shaftesbury (1671–1713) made a distinction between the theism of believers (including Christians) and the deism of those who preach or accept only a natural religion. He had already criticized positive religion in *An Inquiry Concerning Virtue or Merit* (1699), in which he propounded a natural autonomous morality independent of any revealed religion. The moral philosophy of Hutcheson, Adam Smith, Diderot, and even Herder and Kant was to owe much to him.

In his *Christianity not mysterious* (1696) John Toland (1670–1722) paved the way for the religious skepticism of Hume (1711–1776), who in his *Dialogues Concerning Natural Religion* (1751–1755) denies revealed religion and provides the bases of the natural religion of the philosophers of the French Revolution. Denying the God of revealed religion became constantly more acceptable, particularly with the initial shocks provided by the developing sciences of history and philology. The Bible appeared to have little chance of standing up to the attacks made on it by the new sciences of the mind.

The deism expressed by Diderot in the *Encyclopédie* (1751) turned into a naturalist pantheism, which Baron Holbach (1723–1789) used in his *Le système de la nature* (1770) to set out the first frankly materialist modern concept of nature. He attacks the God of natural religion as well as the God of revealed religion, and his atheism leads directly to that of Feuerbach: "O nature, sovereign of all beings! And you her adorable daughters: virtue, reason, truth! Be our only divinities forever; it is to you that the incense and praises of earth are due. Show us then, O nature, what man must do to obtain the happiness you make him desire? . . . Reason! Lead his uncertain steps on the ways of life. . . ."[31]

This is the replacement of God by nature, pure matter. Modern man, having gone through the nominalist and Renaissance neo-Platonist phases, is defined by Descartes as *cogito*. For the thinking consciousness the world and God fade away as *ideas*. It is a process of anthropology taking the place of everything else. For Kant the world is representation (*Vorstellung*) organized by the transcendental "I." Things (*tà ónta*) and God have vanished from the horizon of the knowable. Only objects systematically organized as nature remain. The subject constitutes himself originating subjectivity; *man is the measure of all things*.[32] This is now the situation of secularism.

V. GALILEO'S PROPHETIC VIEW

From the Renaissance to the Enlightenment, science produced a complete, autonomous, and absolute view of the world, independent of theology or revelation. Why did this happen? There are many factors to account for it, but not the least important was the attitude taken by the Church in conflicts whose repercussions were certainly resounding at the time. Having taken the option of figure 11.1, science *versus* Christianity, it made the process of secularization into a secularism. Science, which was a fruit of the Church's age-long attempt at demythologizing the world, turned against its progenitor, whereas it should have been the Church itself that encouraged secularization, not as absolutization but as the due autonomy of political, economic, cultural and scientific life, of a civilization come of age.

As it is impossible in this article to follow all the conflicts between the Church and science step by step, let us take some prototypical examples. The age of humanism and the Renaissance admired achievements in the realms of geography, astronomy and physics; the age of the Enlightenment discovered history, philology and other sciences of the mind, which presented Christianity with even greater problems.

It is easy today to show the contributions made by many churchmen to the development of science. There are the Humanists such as Marsilio Ficino, Pico della Mirandola, Lefèbre d'Etaples, Erasmus, Luis Vives, Thomas More, and so many others. What concerns us here is rather the process of secularization itself, the slowly growing autonomy of the sciences from theology and the Church; the *conflicts* created show the particular reactions of two ways of consciously being Christian—figure 11.1 for some, and figure 11.2 intuitively adopted to a sufficient degree by others, unfortunately not in positions of sufficient authority within the institutional Church.

Christopher Columbus' voyages were based on the fact that the earth was round. This hypotheses was accepted as possible by the theologians of Salamanca and La Rábida. Magellan first sailed round the world in 1519. Therefore the geographical description in Psalm 104 had to be set aside. Is the earth then a star like the other stars in the sky? Geography posed questions of astronomy. Copernicus proposed the sun as center of the system. Tycho Brahe (1546–1601) opposed this "hypothesis." It was only with Galileo, who possessed a great capacity for expressing himself and for theorizing, as well as great theological intuition, that the conflict became public, universal, and immediate. From 1610 to his death in 1642, one of the clearest examples of the secularization of science was acted out.[33] When he was forty-six he published *Sidereus nuntius magna longeque mirabilia spectacula pandens*. In a letter of May 12, 1612 he wrote that his discoveries "were the funeral rites, or rather the end and last judgment of pseudo-philosophy. . . . What will they of the Peripatos not say in order to defend the immutability of the heavens."[34] Note that for Galileo his opponents were the defenders of the "old scheme" (of figure 11.2). For our purposes the letter he sent to one of his disciples, the Benedictine monk Castelli, on December 21, 1613, is vital. It was later to be the cause of his delation to the Roman Inquisition and the Congregation of the Index by Frs. Caccini and Lorini, O.P. This letter shows that for Galileo the Sacred Scriptures cannot err in any way,[35] but their interpreters can be mistaken.[36] Galileo, firm in his Catholic orthodoxy, regarded the Scriptures and nature as the works of God, who cannot contradict himself.[37]

He set out his thought with greater length, clarity and precision in the letter he wrote to Christine de Lorraine in 1615. He repeats his fundamental principle that the Scriptures cannot lie to us;[38] they contain certain principles of faith (*de fide*) which are beyond man's natural comprehension, and science can have nothing to say about these; they have to be received with faith in revelation. But the Scriptures also contain natural truths, some of which cannot at the present time be proved either way (such as, for example, the question of whether there is life on the stars); some, on the other hand, have been proved with indisputable evidence.[40] In these latter cases, if there is some apparent contradiction between science and the texts of Scripture, then the real meaning of the scriptural passage must be studied carefully, without haste, making the doubtful texts conform with others that are clearer.[41] Galileo inevitably falls into "concordism," but despite this his sure Christian faith and feeling of solidarity with the Church are quite apparent.

He adds that the Scriptures contain some principles which are of faith, but others which are only put forward to make revelation intelligible to a particular culture, such as the Hebrew.[42] Every culture contains patterns which are obvious to it, accepted by general opinion and social consensus.[43] These patterns are different from those described by science, but necessary for the understanding and expression of revelation. "But the mobility or stillness of the earth or the sun are not [principles] of faith."[44] The Fathers of the Church appear to be opposed to the astronomical principles recently discovered, but in reality this is only because they did not examine the question seriously or scientifically. Their unanimity on the subject has no force in the scientific field, in which Christians of the new age to which Galileo belongs are doing what the Fathers were unable to do.[45]

It can be seen that Galileo had a perfectly developed Christian understanding of the questions of his age, as well as a theological intuition perhaps surprising in one untrained in the subject. He opted automatically for the right alternative in overcoming the crisis between Christianity and science by showing the transcultural dimension of faith while rigorously opposing the "old system." If this path had been followed, the passage from Christendom to a Christianity understood and expressed within the new modern cultural framework would have been achieved without struggles, misunderstandings and, worse, the alienation of the Church from the world of science.

Without Galileo being able to defend his thesis before the Tribunal of the Inquisition, the doctrine of heliocentrism and the movement of the earth was condemned as "senseless, philosophically absurd, and formally heretical" on February 24, 1616. Two days later, Bellarmine told Galileo the verdict. Bellarmine, for his part, had written a fairly revealing letter to Foscarini on April 12, 1615, in which he said that if Galileo had defended the principle of heliocentrism as Copernicus had done, hypothetically,[46] saying that it was presumed that the earth moved,[47] but without claiming that this *really* happened,[48] there would be no trouble. To claim the reality of such a doctrine seemed to him highly dangerous, since it attacked philosophy, theology, and Sacred Scripture.[49] Bellarmine, as can be seen, identifies faith—(a) in figure 11.2—with cultural frameworks—(b) in the same figure. He lives in an integral and indivisible framework of Christianity.

This is clear from the fact that he argues that Galileo's hypotheses call into question everything that has been said by the Greek and Latin authors on the subject.[50] What they would have done was throw doubt on and show the lack of foundation of many of the cultural systems of the Mesopotamian and Mediterranean worlds, cultural beliefs that had been held for forty centuries. Bellarmine could not accept that any element of these could be questioned, thereby in some sense confusing faith with a particular culture. This led him to propose a distinction by which the entire cultural baggage of primitive Hebrew-Christian culture would become *de fide*: "It cannot be said that this [the matter under debate] is not a question of faith, because even if it is not a matter of faith *ex parte obiecti*, it is a matter of faith *ex parte dicentis*."[51] As a result whatever is written in the Bible becomes, word for word, literal truth for all men of all cultures. Bellarmine leaves no place for secularization, and so, without realizing it, launches science on the road of secularism.

He himself was not particularly interested in the value of the sciences in themselves. He was waiting for a proof of the centrality of the sun or the movement of the earth from arguments drawn from Scripture alone, and so he could exclaim: "They have not proved it to me."[52] Therefore the subsequent course of events should not surprise us. For decades and decades Catholic theologians went on maintaining that the earth was the center of the solar system.

VI. THE APPEARANCE OF PHILOLOGY

The Bible, which means the very bases of faith, also seemed to be under attack at a much deeper level. As early as 1506 the leading Hebrew scholar of his day, Johann Reuchlin (1455–1522) had published his *Rudimenta linguae hebraicae*, and *De Verbo mirifico* had appeared even earlier, in 1496. For pointing out numerous mistranslations in the Vulgate he was condemned by the Inquisition of Mainz in 1513, a condemnation approved by the universities of Cologne, Louvain, Mainz, and Paris in 1514, and finally by Leo

X himself in 1520. But it was to be in France, considerably later, in the days of Bossuet (1627–1704), Louis Quatorze and the Edict of Nantes, that this debate was to come to a head with really serious repercussions.[53] The chronological discoveries of scientific historical investigation and the advances made in the study of the history of language could not leave the Bible on one side. In the West Indies, the studies of the Inca civilization made by José de Acosta had showed how narrow the views of universal history based solely on a European viewpoint were, while Saint-Evremond in his *Réflexions sur les divers génies du peuple romain* first questioned the mythical accounts of the origins of Greece and Rome. Romulus was reduced to a mythological figure. But Bossuet objected to this hypothesis which questioned the established patterns of Mediterranean culture, and so of Christianity: "The first age shows you in the beginning a great spectacle: God creates the heavens and the earth by his word (year 1 of the world: 4004 B.C.)."[54] Then scientific chronology showed, with Paul Berzon in his *L'antiquité des temps rétablie* (1687), that the Egyptian dynasties began before the dates assigned to the flood, and continued without interruption.

Now it was the turn of the "past" to start moving, the earth, thanks to Galileo, having lost its immobility some time before. More serious was the appearance of the philological works of Richard Simon (1638–1712), a Catholic priest of the Oratory and a loyal son of the Church to his death, with sharp and penetrating intelligence, fantastic memory and unshakable tenacity. Studying in the Oratory, this early philologist was able to consult Hebrew manuscripts of the Bible.[55]

He knew Greek, Hebrew, Syriac, and Arabic well and was a tireless reader of the Fathers, particularly of Jerome, from whom no doubt he received his combative spirit. His first work shows his knowledge of the tradition of the Eastern Church.[56] Shortly before, he had defended the Jewish community of Metz against a false charge of murder, in a spirit that we would now call ecumenical.[57] He tried to undertake a joint translation of the Bible with Protestants, which earned him the following reproach from Bossuet: "Ten years ago, a group of gentlemen from Charenton resolved to embark on a new translation of Scripture; Justel, a Protestant whose learning is well known, proposed to Simon that he join the project; Simon himself drew up the plan of this new version; all together jointly decided to give the public a French translation *that would not favor any side* and that would be equally useful to Catholics and Protestants alike. . . . Doubtless [he adds ironically] this is a fine undertaking for a Catholic priest!"[58] So Simon, perhaps, is the forgotten founder, without immediate followers, of Catholic ecumenism.

Simon wrote many other works of an ecumenical tenor.[59] Finally there appeared his major work, *Histoire critique du Vieux Testament* (Paris, 1678).

The aim of the whole argument is apologetic: the Bible is "not sufficiently clear in itself to establish the truth of faith independent from tradition."[60] Simon shows that the texts have a long and complex history from the scribes and prophets to his own day: "Des revolutions du texte hebreu de Moïse jusqu'a nos jours." God did not speak Hebrew to Adam; Moses is not the sole author of the Pentateuch; the Samaritan Pentateuch can be authentic; Esdras must have been one of those principally responsible for the composition of the Bible as we have it; the Septuagint introduces important variations, and so does the Vulgate.

All his criticism is opposed to the rationalism of Spinoza and the anti-traditionalism of Luther and Calvin. Simon's aim is to defend orthodoxy and so he extends infallible inspiration to the authors, scribes, compilers and composers of the Bible.[61] What happened was that Protestants, Jansenists, and Catholics in general, starting with Bossuet, were scandalized by his use of the new philology, by this sort of secularization of the Bible through making it the object of scientific investigation. At the instigation of Bossuet, the police, by order of the Conseil du Roi, withdrew the 1,300 copies that had been printed from the market. A few got through to London and Amsterdam, and were passed avidly from hand to hand.

Simon produced several other exegetical works.[62] He wrote: "He who seeks to see truths of physicals, mathematics, astrology, or any other part of philosophy (*sic*) in certain passages of the Scriptures, which do not treat of these matters except in passing and in terms common among the [Hebrew] people, is committing an act unworthy of a theologian and a philosopher."[63]

Simon distinguished clearly (see figure 11.2) between the cultural, changeable patterns of the Bible and transcultural faith. As a scientist and philologist he overthrew many cultural patterns in order to demonstrate the universal transcendence of faith. Bossuet, on the other hand, as a Defender of Christendom, failed to make this basic distinction. A letter to him written by Capperonnier in 1702 tells him that before criticizing Simon he has to have a very good knowledge of the science of philology. Bossuet has failed to observe this rule and so has been led into important errors.[64] Bossuet thought that Simon's" literary criticism overthrew the whole of theology and tradition.[65] He confused tradition with a "traditionalist" exegesis, and this is why, when Simon showed that the Fathers did not possess sufficient equipment to discover the full meaning of the texts from the Hebrew version, he exclaimed that Simon had the "dark design to destroy the bases of religion."[66] In his view, the science of philology invalidated the Bible.[67] By a decree of December 1, 1682, Simon's main work was placed on the Index, where most of his other works were, and were to remain until this instrument went into its last edition.

VII. CONCLUSIONS

History is the mistress of life because she shows that what happened in the past goes on happening in the present. Bossuet in this dispute took the same position as Bellarmine in the Galileo crisis. He confused, in fact if not in design, the necessary patterns of faith with certain relative patterns of a particular culture. The critical viewpoint of science, from the Renaissance to the Enlightenment, and far more afterward, required a differentiation between faith, the essential, and cultural patterns. Modern science displaced many mythical expressions—the centrality and immobility of the earth, the Hebrew or Roman chronologies, etc. And yet the great institutions rejected the astronomy of Galileo, the philology of Richard Simon, the geography of de Clave, Bitaud, and Villon (condemned by the Sorbonne), the chemistry that from the time of Paracelsus (1493–1561) was suspect because it was confused with alchemy and magic, Priestley (by the Anglicans), the first doctors (either on account of dissection or vaccination—Boyer condemned by the Sorbonne), and many, many more. . . . Their rejection could not help but transform a healthy secularization into an anti-Christian secularism. At the very least it was one of the causes of this, and not a minor one. Christendom was protected for a time by the efforts of some of its protagonists such as Bossuet, but the price paid was a further opening of the gates of incredulity, indifference and secularism in the Europe of the 18th century. Montesquieu, Voltaire, Rousseau, and the French Revolution could have been a positive movement instead of one of anti-Catholic secularism. The Church failed to welcome science wholeheartedly as a daughter, and only did so jealously and against its will. The false antinomy science-Christendom prevented a growth to maturity. Only those who recognized the supracultural transcendence of faith in the very rout of the "old system" achieved a dispassionate understanding of the positive value of secularization. This secularization-become-secularism now presents us with a culture *etsi Deus non daretur.*

NOTES

1. Cf. A. Auer, "Säkularisierung," in *LTK* IX (1964), p. 253; C. Ratschow, "Säkularismus," in *RGG* V (1961), pp. 1288–96; A. Dondeyne, "Sécularisation et foi," in *Lumen Vitae* 3 (1968), pp. 415–30; A. Durand, "Sécularisation et sens de Dieu," in *Lumière et Vie* 89 (1968), pp. 61ff.; F. Gogarten, *Verhängnis und Hollnung der Neuzeit. Die Säkularisierung als theologisches Problem* (Stuttgart, 1953); A. Auer, "Gestaltwandel des christlichen Weltverständnisses," in *Gott in Welt, Festgabe für K. Rahner* I (Freiburg, 1964), pp. 338–65; J. B. Metz, "Weltverständnis im Glauben, Christliche Orientierung in der Weltlichkeit der Welt heute," in *Geist und Leben* 35

(1962), pp. 172ff.; F. K. Schumann, *Zur Ueberwindung des Säkularismus in der Wissenschaft* (Munich, 1950); E. Cassirer, *Individuum und Kosmos in der Philosophie des Renaissance* (Berlin, 1927); idem, *Das Erkenntnisproblem in der Philosophie und Wissenschaft der neueren Zeit* (Berlin, 1920); W. Dilthey, *Weltanschauung und Analyse des Menschen seit Renaissance und Reformation* (Berlin, 1914); A. D. White, *A History of the Warfare of Science with Theology in Christendom* (New York, 1896); G. Bachelard, *Le nouvel esprit scientifique* (Paris, 1941); S. van Mierlo, *La science, la raison et la foi* (Paris, 1948); J. Daujat, *Physique moderne et philosophie traditionelle* (Tournai, 1958); A. Rich, *Die Weltlichkeit des Glaubens* (Stuttgart, 1966). A. Maier, *An der Grenzen von Scholastik und Naturwissenschaft. Studien zur Naturphilosophie des 14. Jahrhundert* (Essen, 1943); C. Michalski, *La physique nouvelle et les différents courants philosophiques au XIV° siècle* (Cracow, 1928); R. Guardini, *Das Ende der Neuzeit* (Würzburg, 1950); D. De Lagarde, *La naissance de l'esprit laïque au déclin du moyen âge* (Louvain, 1962). To this should be added various histories of the Church (Fliche-martin, Lorca-Garcia Villoslada, Bihlmeyer-Tuechle, etc.) and histories of science (Lain-Entralgo-Lopez Pinero, Mieli, Taton, etc.).

2. "Au nom de la doctrine chrétienne, les Pères de l'Eglise frappent les philosophies païennes en des points que nous jugeons, aujourd'hui, plus métaphysiques que physiques, mais où se trouvent les pierres d'angle de la Physique antique": P. Duhem, *Le système du monde, Histoire des doctrines cosmologiques de Platon à Copernic* II (Paris, 1914), p. 408. Cf. G. Ebeling, "Die nicht-religiöse Interpretation biblischer Begriffe," in ZThK 52 (1955), pp. 296–360.

3. On the "noyau éthico-mythique d'une culture" cf. P. Ricoeur, *Histoire et vérité* (Paris, 1955), pp. 274–88; C. Tresmontant, *La métaphysique du Christianisme et la naissance de la philosophie chrétienne* (Paris, 1961), pp. 9–85.

4. *Fragmento A 22* and *A 1* (Diels-Kranz, 1964), pp 79 and 68.

5. "Sciences" here means both natural sciences and sciences of the mind.

6. Absolute is the metaphysical condition of unbased notes. "Absolute, then, is self-sufficient. . . . Essences are in the line of the formation of the ultimate foundations on which the whole world, with its [archaic] physical principles, rests": X. Zubiri, *Sobre la esencia* (Madrid, 1963), pp. 208–9.

7. "Ist die Lebenswelt als solche nicht das Allerbekannteste, das in allem menschlichen Leben immer schon Selbstverständliche, in ihrer Typik immer schon durch Erfahrung uns vertraut?": E. Husserl, *Die Krisis der europäischen Wissenschaften* (Haag, 1962), p. 126

8. R. Collingwood, *The Idea of Nature* (Oxford, 1945); A. Whitehead, *Science and the Modern World* (Cambridge, 1927); E. Burtt, *The Metaphysical Foundations of Modern Physical Science* (New York, 1932); E. Cassirer, op. cit.; K. Loewith, *Der Weltbegriff der neuzeitlichen Philosophie* (Heidelberg, 1960).

9. *PG* CLX, cols. 889–934.

10. Rome, 1469.

11. "Est enim mundus quasi liber digito Dei scriptus": *Serm. 10;* cf. *Opera* (Basel, 1565).

12. "Est enim Deus quidditas absoluta mundi seu universi; universum vero est ipsa quidditas contracta": *D. ign.* II, p. 4.

13. "Si quis foret extra regionem ignis, terra ista in circunferentia regionis per medium ignis lucida stella appareret, sicut nobis, qui sumus circa circunferentiam regionis solis, sol lucidissimus apparet": Ibid., p. 12.

14. *Theol. plat.* II, p. 6; cf. H. Blumenberg, *Die kopernikanische Wende* (Frankfurt, 1965).

15. "Omnia in uno, omnia in omnibus, unus et omnia, unus in omnibus." "Natura est sempiterna et individua essentia": *Acrotismus Camoeracensis; De Natura.*

16. "La filosofia è scritta in questo grandissimo libro che continuamente ci sta aperto innanzi a gli occhi (io dico l'universo), ma non si può intendere se prima non s'impara a intender la lingua, e conoscer i caratteri, ne'quali è scritto in lingua mathematica, e i caratteri son triangoli, cerchi, ed altre figure geometriche, senza i quali mezi è impossibile a intenderne unanamente parola; senza questi è un aggirarsi vanamente per un oscuro laberinto": "Il Saggiatore," in *Le opere di Galileo Galilei* VI (Florence, 1933), p. 232.

17. ". . . per beneficio di noi Cattolici": ibid., p. 233.

18. ". . . ch'ella [la materia] debba essere bianca o rossa, amara o dolce, sonora o muta . . . non sento farmi forza alla mente di doverla apprendere a cotali condizioni necessariamente accompagnata. . . . Non siano altro che puri nomi"; "Annichilate tutte queste qualità." Cf. G. Galli, *L'idea di materia e di scienza fisica da Talete a Galileo* (Turin, 1963).

19. "Per causam sui intelligo id, cuius essentia involvit existentiam": *Ethica* I, def. 1.

20. "Totam naturam unum esse Individuum, cuius partes, hoc est omnia corpora, infinitis modis variant, absque ulla totius Individui mutatione": ibid. II, prop. 13, lemma 7, sch.

21. "Philosophiae naturalis id revera principium est, et officium, et finis, *ut ex phaenomenis*, sine fictis hypothesibus, arguamus": *Optices* III, q. 28/.

22. "Tempus absolutum, verum et mathematicum": *Principia Mathematica*, def. VIII, sch.

23. "Spatium absolutum . . .": ibid.

24. "Motus absolutus est translatio corporis de loco absoluto in locum absolutum": ibid.

25. Cf. *Kritik der reinen Vernunft: Transzendentale Elementarlehre* (A 19, B 33) and *Die transzendentale Logik* (A 50, B 74).

26. "Natur! Wir sind von ihr umgeben and umschlugen unvermögend, aus ihr herauszutreten, und unvermögend, tiefer in si hineinzukommen. Ungebeten und ungewarnt nimmt sie uns in den Krieslauft ibres Tanzes auf und treibt sich mit uns fort, bis wir ermüdet sind und ihrem Arme entfallen": *Die Natur*, fragment, 1782: *Naturwissenschaftliche Schriften* I (Leipzig, Inselverlag), p. 9.

27. Cf. W. Scholz, *Der Gott der neuzeitlichen Metaphysik* (Pfullingen, 1957); C. Fabro, *Introduzione all'ateismo moderno* (Rome, 1964); idem, "Genesi storica dell'ateismo contemporaneo," in *L'ateismo contemporaneo* (Turin, 1968), pp. 3–54: "Questa dissoluzione dell'idealismo nell'ateismo avviene in due tappe: prima l'assunzione del panteismo di Spinoza da parte di Lessing (*lo Spinozastreit*) e poi l'elevazione dell'Io kantiano ad Assoluto nell'idealism (*lo Atheismusstreit*) di Fichte" (p. 14).

28. Cf. B. Magnino, *Illuminismo e Christianismo*, (Brescia, 1959); P. Hazard, *La crise de la conscience européenne* (Paris, 1935); Preclin-Jarry, "Les luttes politiques et doctrinales aux XVIIe et XVIIIe siècles," in Fliche-Martin, *Hist. de l'Egl.*, t. XIX, 1 (1955).

29. *Réponse aux questions d'un provincial*, cap. CXXVIII.

30. "Que ce qui nous persuade que l'athéisme est le plus abominable état ou l'on se puisse trouver, n'est qu'un faux préjugé que l'on se forme touchant les lumières de la conscience, que l'on s'imagine être la regle de nos actions, faute de bien examiner les veritables ressorts qui nous font agir": *Pensés diverses*, n. 233.

31. "O nature! Souveraine de tous êtres! et vous ses filles adorables, vertu, raison, vérité; soyez à jamais nos seules divinités, c'est-à-vous que son dûs l'encens et les hommages de la terre. Montre-nous donc, O nature! ce que l'homme doit faire pour obtenir le bonheur que tu lui fais désirer. . . . Raison! Conduis ses pas incertains dans les routes de la vie. . . .": *Le Système* II, ch. XIV.

32. Protagoras, *Fragment B 1* (Diels-Kranz II, p. 263). It is clear that the Sophist's text has no idealist sense.

33. Cf. M. Virgano, "Fede e scienza in Galileo," in *La Civiltà Cattolica* 116 (1965): I, pp. 33–45; 228–39; II, pp. 35–47; 447–55; A. Dubarle, "Les principes exégétiques et théologiques de Galilée concernant la science de la nature," in *Rech. Sc. Ph. et Th.* I (1966), pp. 67–87; A. Koyré, *Galilé et la révolution scientifique du XVII siècle* (Paris, 1955); G. Di Santillana, *The Crime of Galileo* (Chicago, 1955); Gemelli et al., *Nel terzo centenario della morte di Galileo Galilei* (Milan, 1942); J. Yela Utrilla, "Galileo el ortodoxo," in *Rev. Fil.* I (1942), pp. 99–125; J. Ortega y Gasset, "Ideas en torno a las generaciones decisivas en la evolución del pensamiento europeo," in *Obras completas* V (Madrid), pp. 9–164.

34. ". . . la quale novità dubito che voglia essere il funerale o più tosto l'estremo et ultimo giuditio della pseudofilosofia . . . e sto aspettando di sentir scaturire gran cose dal Peripato per mantenimento della immutabilità de i celi": Letter to the Count of Sesi, May 12, 1612, in *Le Opere* XI, p. 296.

35. ". . . non poter mai la Scrittura Sacra mentire o errari": Letter to Benedetto Castelli from Florence, December 21, 1613, in *Le Opere* V, p. 282.

36. "Se bene la Scrittura non può errare, potrebbe nondimeno talvolta errare alcuno de'suoi interpreti ed espositori . . . quando volessero fermarse sempre nel puro significato delle parole . . . è necessario che i saggi espositori produchino i veri sensi": ibid.

37. ". . . perchè, procedendo di pari dal Verbo divino la Scrittura Sacra e la natura, quella come dettatura dello Spirito Santo. . . .": ibid.

38. Non poter mai la Sacra Scrittura mentire": Letter to Madame Cristina de Lorena, Grand Duchess of Tuscany, in 1615: *Le Opere* V, p. 315. Cf. F. Russo, "Lettre de Galilée à Christine de Lorraine," in *Rev. Hist. Soc.* 17 (1964), pp. 330–66.

39. "Io non dubito punto che dove gli umani discorsi non possono arrivare, e che di esse per consequenza non può avere scienza, ma solamente opinione e fede, piamente convenga conformarsi assolutamente col puro senso della Scrittura": ibid., p. 330.

40. "Indubitata certezza": ibid.

41. ". . . concordi col fatto dimostrata. . . . Concordare un luogo della Scrittura con una proposizione naturale demostrata": ibid., pp. 330–31.

42. "Che dunque fosse necessario attribuire al Sole il moto, e la quiete alla Terra, per non confonder la poca capacità del vulgo e renderlo renitentee contumace nel prestar fede a gli articoli principali e che sono assolutamente *de Fide*": ibid., p. 333.

43. "Ma più durò, che non solamente il rispeto dell'incapacità del vulgo, ma la *corrente opinione* di quei tempi, fece che gli scrittori sacri nelle cose non necessarie

alla beatitudein più si accommodorno all'uso ricevuto che alla essenza del fato. . . . L'assenso de gli uomini tutti, concordi nell'istesso parere, senza che si sentisse la contradizione di alcuno": ibid., pp. 333–36.

44. "Ma la mobilità o stabilità della Terra o del Sole non son *de Fide* nè contro a i costumi [Galileo is clearly referring to the decisions of Trent], nè vi è chi voglia scontoro luoghi della Scrittura per contrariare a la Santa Chiesa o i Patri": ibid., p. 337.

45. ". . . che tal particolar disquisizione non si trova esse stata fatta da i Padri antichi, potrà esser fatta da i sapienti della nostra età, li quali, ascoltate prima l'esperienze, l'osservazioni, la ragioni e le dimostrazioni, de'filosofi ed astronomi": ibid., p. 388.

46. "*Ex suppositione* e non assolutamente": Letter of Robert Bellarmine to Paolo Fascorini from Rome, April 12, 1615: *Le opere di Galileo* XII, p. 171.

47. "Che supposto che la terra si muova et il sole stia fermo si salvano tutte l'apparenze . . . e questo basta al mathematico": ibid.

48. "Ma volere affermare che realmente il sole stia nel centro del mondo . . .": ibid.

49. "E cosa molto pericolosa non solo d'irritare tutti i filosofi e theologi scholastici, ma anco di nuocere alla Sacra Fede con rendere false le Scritture Sante": ibid.

50. ". . . et a tutti li espositori greci et latini": ibid., p. 17.

51. "Nèsi può rispondere che questa non sia materia di fede, perchè se non è materia di fede *ex parte obiecti*, è materia di fede *ex parte dicentis*": ibid.

52. "Ma io non crederò che ci sia tal dimostratione, fin che non mi sia mostrata": ibid.

53. Cf. P Hazard, op. cit.; G. Schnueer, *Katholische Kirche und Kultur im 18. Jahrhundert* (Paderborn, 1941); W. Dilthey, *Friedrich der Grosse und die Aufklärung, Gesam. Schriften* II (1921); E. Cassirer, *Die Philosophie der Aufklärung* (Tübingen, 1932); E. Guyenot, *L'évolution de la pensée scientifique, les sciences et la vie aux XVIIe et XVIIIe siècles* (Paris, 1941); Latreille-Palenque, *Histoire du catholicisme en France* II-III (Paris, 1962).

54. "La première époque vous présente d'abord un grand spectacle; Dieu qui crée la ciel et la terre par sa parole (an du monde 1; dev. J. C. 4004) . . .": "Histoire Universelle," in *Oeuvres complètes de Bossuet* X (Paris, 1866), col. 687.

55. *Ms. hebreo 1295*, Bibliot. Nat. Paris. Cf. F. Strummer, *Die Bedeutung Richard Simon für die Pentateuchkritik* (Münster, 1912); R. de la Broise, *Bossuet et la Bible* (Paris, 1891); A. Monod, "La controverse de Bossuet et de Richard Simon au sujet de la version de Trévoux," in *Cahiers Rev. Hist. Et Phil. Rel.* (1922); A. Molien, "Richard Simon," in *DTC* XIV (1941), pp. 2094–2118.

56. *Gabrielis metropolitae Philadelphiensis . . .* (Paris, 1671).

57. *Factum servant de réponse au livre intitulé: Abrégé du procès fait aux juifs de Metz* (Paris, 1670).

58. *Critiques de la version du N.T.* VI; *Oeuvres complètes* X, col. 604.

59. *Cérémonies et coutumes des juifs* (Paris, 1674); *Voyage du Mont Liban traduit de l'italien* (Paris, 1675); *Factum contre les bénédictins de Fécamp* (Paris, 1675).

60. ". . . claire d'elle-même et suffisante pour établir seule la vérité de la foi et indépendente de la tradition": *Preface*.

61. "Le Saint-Esprit les a conduits d'une manière qu'ils ne sont jamais trompès dans ce qu'ils ont écrit": Prologue to *Lettre à M. l'Abbé P. touchant l'inspiration des Livres sacrés* (Rotterdam, 1699).

62. Among the more important are: *Novorum Bibliorum polyglotorum synopsis* (Utrecht, 1684); *Histoire critique du texte du N.T.* (Rotterdam, 1689); *Historire critique des versions du N.T.* (Rotterdam, 1690); particularly *Histoire critique des principaux commentateurs du N.T. depuis le commencement du christianisme* (Rotterdam, 1693). Here Simon says: 'Il es difficile de tirer des conclusions de l'Ecriture, comme d'un principe clair et évident" (p. 94). Bossuet regards this as a disqualification of Scripture: (". . . pour montrer qu'on ne gagne rien avec l'Ecriture": *Defense de la tradition et des Saints Pères* II, 1; *Oeuvres complètes de Bossuet* X, p. 175), but he fails to see that Simon is only indicating the difficulties posed by philology and history, which cannot be avoided in biblical studies. He was still to write *Le Nouveau Test, de J.C. traduit sur l'ancienne édition Latine* (Trévoux, 1702), in which he states: "Notre version Latine érant obscure et équivoque en quelques endroits, il n'y a point d'autre remède pour être ces obscurités que d'avoir recours aux originaux. . . . Ce n'est pas que je blâme ceux qui publient des réflexions morales sur l'Ecriture, mais je souhaiterais qu'elles fussent toujours jointes à des interprétations littérales" (*Preface*); and finally, *Moyens de réunir les protestants à l'Eglise romaine* (Paris, 1703).

63. "Celui qui voudrait établir les vérités de la physique, des mathématiques, de l'astrologie, et de toute autre partie de la philosophie, sur de certains passages de l'Ecriture, qui n'en font mention qu'en passant et en des termes usités parmi le peuple, ferait une chose indigne et d'un théologien et d'un philosophe": *Bibliothèque critique* IV (Basle, 1710), p. 96.

64. "Comme M. Simon veut triompher en fait de grec et d'hebreu . . . il faut apporter un grande exactitude . . . cette importante règle n'a point été observée [par vous même]": *Oeuvres* XI, col. 1077.

65. "Selon ce critique, on ne doit suivre que les règles de la grammaire, et non pas la théologie de la tradition, pour bien expliquer le Nouveau Testament. Si l'on fait autrement, ce n'est pas le sens de saint Paul que l'on donne; c'est celui que l'on s'est formé sur ses propres prejugés": "Lettre CCX de M. Arnauld," July 1693, in *Oeuvres complètes de Bossuet* XI, col. 1066. Arnauld expresses Bossuet's thought precisely, with an unthinking opposition between science (philology) and traditional theology (i.e., that of Christendom).

66. ". . . un sourd dessein de saper les fondements de la religion": Letter to Nicole, December 7, 1691, in *Oeuvres* XI, col. 998. But it cannot be denied that Simon sometimes went too far. Cf. H. de Lubac, *Histoire et Esprit* (Paris, 1950), pp. 425–26.

67. "Et l'on va voir que le résultat est précisément ce que j'ai dit, que l'Ecriture et ensuite la tradition, ne prouvent rien de part et d'autre": *Défense de la tradition* II, 1; *Oeuvres* X, col. 172.

12

Modern Christianity in Face
of the "Other" (from the "Rude"
Indian to the "Noble Savage")

Man possesses "dignity" intrinsically, through being a human person;
there is nothing in all creation more dignified than the human person. However, throughout history all systems of oppression have deprived of "dignity" all those who are either the oppressed "within" the
system, or enemies, barbarians, *goim*, the "senseless," those "outside" the
system: those who are not. Everywhere outside the system reigns "civilisation's" night, the shapeless mass which, for the system, represents im-
pending danger, the demoniacal. This pattern has always been presented
in history, but now we must analyse it briefly as it is to be seen in the
process of European expansion from the fifteenth century onwards, since
America was discovered in 1492 and the Pilgrim Fathers reached the
shores of North America in 1620. The subject is a highly topical one.

1. THE FACTS OF THE CASE

In 1577, before Italy, Germany, France or England had seen beyond the
merely European horizon, José de Acosta published in Lima (Peru), in the
introduction to his work *De procuranda indorum salute* (or *Predicación del
Evangelio en las Indias*), a typology of three categories of "barbarians": "Although these peoples are of many different provinces, nations and qualities,

Enrique Dussel, "Modern Christianity in Face of the 'Other' (from the 'Rude' Indian to the
'Noble Savage'," *Concilium* 130 (1979): 49–59.

yet it seems to me, after long and careful consideration, that they can be reduced to three very diverse classes or categories, which embrace all barbarian nations."[1]

In a general sense, "barbarians" means[2] "those who reject true reason and the way of life commonly accepted among men, and who thus display barbarian *roughness* (*rudeza*), barbarian savagery."[3] Of course, for every European down to the present day, "true reason" and "the commonly accepted way of life" are *his own*, by which others are judged and condemned as less than human, as we shall see shortly. José de Acosta suggests that the Chinese, the Japanese and the peoples of other parts of the East Indies, though they are barbarians, should be treated "in much the same way as the apostles treated the Greeks and Romans in preaching to them."[4] So far as these "stable republics, with public laws and fortified towns" are concerned, says Acosta, "if one tried to bring them into submission to Christ by force and with arms, one would only succeed in rendering them exceedingly hostile to the name of Christian."[5]

A second type of barbarian consists of such as the Aztecs or Incas, who though they are well known for their political and religious institutions, "have not attained to the use of writing or to the knowledge of philosophy."[6] These are, as it were, in the middle of the road.

Finally we come to "the third category of barbarians." "This is composed of savages resembling wild beasts. . . . And in the New World there are countless herds of them. . . . They differ very little from animals. . . . It is necessary to teach these people who are hardly men, or who are half men, how to become men, and to instruct them like children. . . . They must be held down by force . . . and, in a way, even against their will, they must be compelled (Acosta quotes Luke 14:23) to enter the kingdom of heaven."[7]

All this in spite of the fact that José de Acosta was a defender of the Indians and a famous theologian who did not accept the thesis of Ginés de Sepúlveda. Even so he was unable to avoid contamination by the ideology of his time, unable to free himself from a humanistic Eurocentrism. The temporal Messianism of Spain and Portugal led on to those of Holland in the seventeenth century, of France and England from the eighteenth century onwards, of Germany in the nineteenth century and of North America in recent decades.

Feudal Europe made its firsts attempt at expansion by conquest with the crusades, but the Arab world resisted this first act of European aggression perpetrated in the name of Christianity. The second expansion, also in the name of Christianity, began in the fifteenth century, not in the Eastern Mediterranean but across the Atlantic and Indian Oceans. Pierre Chaunu even says that "the sixteenth century brought about, from our point of view, the greatest mutation in the human species."[8] From that moment on, the citizen—who for Aristotle was "political man"—is the one who inhabits the European city; the *civis*, or civilised person, displayed *civilitas*, or "conduct becoming to the citizen"—*civilisation*. "Man" is, for the European, the European citizen, just as he was for the aristocrat Aristotle under a system which practised slavery. Gonzalo Fernández de Oviedo (1478–1557), writing more as a European than as a Spaniard, said in his *Historia General y natural de las Indias*: "These people of the Indies, though they are rational and descended from the same stock that came out of Noah's sacred ark, have become *irrational and bestial* by reason of their idolatries, sacrifices and infernal ceremonies."[9]

And along the same lines Ginés de Sepúlveda explains: "The fact of having cities and some sort of rational manner of life and some kind of commerce is something brought about by natural necessity, and it only serves to prove that they are not bears or monkeys, and that they are not totally lacking in reason."[10]

For Europeans, for Spaniards, "the other," the native, was a *rudo*. The word is derived from the Latin *rudis* (in the rough, not having been worked on), from the verb *rudo* (to bray, to roar). It is the opposite to "erudite" and erudition (which indicate the one who has no roughness, brutishness, lack of cultivation). Even the best Europeans thought of the Indian as a "rudo," a "child," a piece of educable, evangelisable "material." "Christendom" was beginning its glorious expansion, and papal bulls gave theological justification to the plundering of the peoples of the Third World.

2. THEOLOGICAL PREMISSES

Every theology becomes a "theology of domination" when it expresses theoretically, with the support of theological arguments, the interests of the dominant class of a nation which practises oppression. Such a "theology of domination" can argue its case logically with great coherence. In the first place, the system, the totality (the "flesh," *basar* in Hebrew) is made into a fetish, becomes totalitarian, comes to see itself as an absolute, as the ultimate, before which the Utopia of a later and better system is judged to be demoniacal, illegitimate, atheistic. The Israelites themselves, whether as a result of ideological contamination from neighbouring nations and empires, or as a development occurring during the period of the monarchy, use the category of *goim*[11] to indicate those peoples who are barbarian, foreign, inferior. "Hellenicity," *romanitas*, Christendom, European *civilisation* are concepts which involve the same fetishistic absolutising of the totality, of the system. These concepts are the top layer of the theology of domination. In essence this process of making into a fetish the dominant class of the nation which practices oppression is based on the denial of "exterior-ity"[12] on the relegation of the *other* as such to a position where he is seen only as relative to the system. And it is in this that sin ultimately consists. To deprive the Other of the "dignity" which is essentially and naturally his (*dignus* is the one who by being a person, whether "Other" or not, is de-serving of the highest respect: he is *someone* distinct), means, primarily, to plunder him of his alterity (otherhood), of his liberty, of his humanity. Once the Other has been deprived of his divine exteriority (by means of the arti-fice of judging him to be a barbarian, non-man, a mere beast, the Enemy[13] par excellence) he can be manipulated, controlled, dominated, tortured, as-sassinated—and all this in the name of "Being" (as old Schelling would say), or of "civilisation," or of "Christendom," of the totality elevated into a fetish. It is obvious that this negative judgment on the Other will lead im-mediately, because of the political and practical power of those who make it, to a limitation of his *material* possibilities in life. It is at the economic level—which still forms part of what is offered to God in worship, as in the Catholic *Offertorium*, which says: "Through your goodness, we have this bread to offer, which earth has given and human hands have made"—that the deprivation of the Other is consummated. It is at this point that it be-comes a *reality*. The Indian will not only be regarded as a "beast," but he will be free manpower for a colonial tributary system which will be one of the main contributory factors to the original accumulation of European cap-ital, beginning in the sixteenth century.

This is why, in times of prophetic activity or messianic expectation, this burden of negativity resting upon the *goim*, the pagans, the "nations," is immediately lifted: "I have put my spirit upon him, he will bring forth justice to the nations (*goim*)" (Isa. 42:1); "When the Son of man comes in his glory . . . then he will sit on his glorious throne. Before him will be gathered all the nations (*ēthnē*)" (Matt. 25:31–32).[14]

A theology of domination fixes the "frontiers" ("that my salvation may reach to the *end* (frontiers) of the earth," Isa. 49:6),[15] and declares the Other "beyond" salvation, beyond being, beyond dignity. Liberation, on the other hand, goes beyond the horizon of the system and includes the Other as an equal, a brother, a member of the eschatological community.

3. THE DISPUTE OVER THE
STATUS OF THE NATURE OF THE INDIAN

Theologically the dispute of 1550 in Valladolid between Juan Ginés de Sepúlveda and Bartolomé de las Casas is the most important that has ever taken place in Europe on the subject of the nature of man and cultures of the

Third World, in terms of what a man is ontologically and what he is in the light of faith. Thereafter the question would not be re-opened until the theology of liberation appeared, well on into the twentieth century. We have to understand that theologically the Indians were helped, paradoxically, by a certain interplay of *classes* (although in practice they were to be oppressed politically and economically to the point of complete alienation). In effect the "encomendero class" (those who received the tribute contributed by the Indians in the form of work) was organising itself into a powerful oligarchy in Spanish America (as was the slave-owning class in Brazil). The king could not lend his support to this "encomendero class," because they had a tendency towards separatism—as the conquistadors had shown in Peru. Thus, paradoxically the king would not permit the publication of the works of Ginés de Sepúlveda (which offered justification for the oppression of the Indian by the "encomenderos" in America), and on the other hand would permit the publication of the works of Bartolomé de las Casas, which denied that the conquest had any proper foundation and established the Indian's right to freedom. The king needed to weaken the growing American oligarchy in order to buttress his own power. At this juncture, Bartolomé came out in criticism of the "encomenderos" and sought the support of the king for the liberation of the Indians. "For the first—and probably the last—time," says a North American author, "a colonialist nation set up a genuine investigation into the justice of the methods employed to extend its domination."[16] In fact, the Council of the Fourteen, the "Council of the Indies," listened to the judgment of theologians before giving its opinions on the justice of the conquest.

Ginés de Sepúlveda based his theological arguments on many authors, among them Aristotle, John Major, Fernández de Oviedo, the Bull of Alexander VI, etc. Bartolomé argued passionately against the same authors.

Aristotle had affirmed that "he who is a man not in virtue of his own nature but in virtue of that of another is by nature a slave. . . . Those who find obedience to authority advantageous to them are slaves by nature (*physei douloi*). . . . The usefulness of slaves differ little from that of animals."[17] Ginés applied this doctrine to his theology of domination: "There are other grounds for a just war against the Indians . . . and one of them is to subdue by arms, if no other way is possible, those who by reason of their natural condition ought to obey others but reject their rule."[18]

The Scottish theologian John Major, for his part, had published in 1510 some *Commentaries on the Second Book of Sentences*, in which he referred to the territories recently discovered. Having said: "If a certain people has embraced the faith of Christ, and has done so wholeheartedly, it is to be hoped that its rulers will be deposed from power if they persist in their paganism,"[19] he went on to write: "There is something more to say. These peoples live as though they were beasts on both sides of the equator, and between the poles men live like wild beasts. And today all this has been discovered by experience."[20]

To which Bartolomé de las Casas replies: "Away, then, with John Major, seeing that he knows nothing at all of the law or of the facts! We have the ridiculous situation that this Scottish theologian comes and tells us that a king, even before he understands the Spanish language and even before he understands the reason why the Spaniards are building fortifications, should be deprived of his kingdom."[21]

To Fernández de Oviedo, who argued that the Indians had fallen into "bestial customs" and so found themselves incapable of receiving faith, Bartolomé replied: "Since Oviedo was a member of these perverse expeditions, what will he not say about the Indians? . . . Because of these brutal crimes God has blinded his eyes,[22] along with those of the other plunderers, . . . so that he should not be able by the Grace of God to know that these naked peoples were simple, good, and pious."[23]

So far as the Bulls of Alexander VI are concerned, Bartolomé analyses the question and shows that the pope never justified war or violence as a means of propagating the faith in the Indies. Queen Isabel herself defended the Indians, and ordered that they should not "be made to suffer any kind of harm to their persons or their belongings."[24]

It was in this way that in August and September 1550 Ginés and Bartolomé were in confrontation with each other over the ability of the Indians to receive the faith.

4. POSITION OF BARTOLOMÉ DE LAS CASAS

First as a conquistador, then as a young cleric, Bartolomé had a particular respect for the Indian, whom he regarded as *"other"*: "God created each one of these widely scattered and innumerable people to be of the utmost simplicity, without wickedness or duplicity, most obedient and most loyal to their natural rulers and to the Christians whom they serve. They are the most humble, most patient, most peaceful and docile, and the most free from quarrels and bickering, to be found anywhere in the world. Similarly they are extremely delicate peoples, slender and frail in build, little able to support heavy labours and readily dying from almost any illness."[25]

It must be borne in mind that when Bartolomé exalts the Indian in this manner he is in no way giving expression to the later myth of the *bon sauvage*, the noble savage, much of which might well have had its inspiration in the *Brevísima relación* itself. Bartolomé respected the Indian in his *exteriority*. His language is at times stereotyped, as when he writes of the Indians as "so mild, so humble, so peaceful," but such an expression shows precisely his ability to cross the frontier of the system and make himself open to the *exteriority of the other as other*.

The arrival of the Spaniards in America was the first experience of the "face-to-face" encounter: "The Admiral (Columbus) and the others . . . who now made the acquaintance of" the Indians[26] were confronting them for the first time.

But immediately the Europeans attacked the Indians: "As soon as they made their acquaintance, they hurled themselves upon them (the Indians), like the most cruel wolves,[27] tigers, and lions, which had not eaten for many days. And for forty years from then until now (1552), they have done nothing but tear them to pieces, kill them, distress, afflict, torment and destroy them by strange, new, diverse forms of cruelty, the like of which have never been seen, read of, or heard of."[28]

Our prophetic *theologian of liberation* goes on building up his case against the alienation of the "other." He continues his discourse with a frontal attack on the *totality* of European system of oppressive expansion: "Convinced by the truth itself, he (the cleric Bartolomé de las Casas, in his autobiographical narrative) came to the conclusion that *everything* which was being done to the Indians in the Indies was unjust and tyranical."[29]

To Bartolomé, the greatest theologian of the sixteenth century, the whole system was unjust, starting with its basic intention: "A hundred thousand victims have died and disappeared because of the labours which they (the Spaniards) out of their *lust for gold* imposed upon them."[30] "Out of their desire to have gold and wealth."[31]

The God gold, the new fetish or idol of developing capitalism, was criticised by Bartolomé even when it was still in its cradle, when it had just been born. His critique of the modern European world—pre-capitalist, mercantile, capitalist, imperialist—had already begun. Along with Portugal and Spain he was criticising in anticipation Holland, England, France, and in our own time the "Trilateral Empire" of the United States, Germany, and Japan. The unjust notion of national prosperity was beginning its idolatrous reign: "During the seventy years that have passed since they began to scandalise, rob, kill, and extirpate those nations, *nobody to this day has pointed out* that so many things which are a scandal and shame to our holy faith, such robberies, injustices, ravages, killings, taking of captives, usurpation of the rights of nations, and of others' right to rule, and, finally, such universal devastation and depopulation, *have been sinful and the greatest possible injustice*."[32]

This explicit theologian of liberation was, in addition, an ideological theologian. Very intelligently he drew attention to the relation between theory and practice ("nobody to this day has pointed out," nobody has seen, discovered), and, above all, to the sin which was being committed with European expansion and oppression of other peoples. This is a theology of liberation which lays bare the ethico-theological perversity of colonialism and of the tributary economic system of the *encomienda*. To the present day European theology has ignored all this theology. It is time to revise history and remake it.

Bartolomé understood and expressed the dialectic of master and slave—two centuries before Rousseau and three before Hegel or Marx—on a global scale. This is to be seen when he tells us that after the invaders had murdered all those who "could long for, or sigh for, or think of liberty," a colonial order was set up "which *oppressed them* with the most severe, horrible and harsh *servitude*." In his *Testamento*, shortly before his death Bartolomé writes:

> God thought it right to choose me for his service though I did not deserve it, to campaign for all those peoples of the region we call the Indies . . . to *liberate them* (in the fine Spanish of the sixteenth century) from the violent death which they are still suffering.[33]

5. THE QUESTION OF THE "NOBLE SAVAGE" IN TRIUMPHANT CAPITALISM

It was important to decide whether or not the Indian was capable of receiving the faith in order to justify or otherwise Spanish rule, and that of the "encomendero" (the Creole who exploited the Indian as manpower), over the peoples of America. The discussion was set within the framework of capitalism in its early form, pre-industrial and mercantile. On the other hand, the question of the noble savage, at the end of the seventeenth and during the eighteenth centuries, was concerned with the right of Europeans (mainly the English and the French) to dominate the new colonies, but now within the framework of a capitalist system which was soon to be industrial (and, from the end of the nineteenth century, imperial). From a recent study we can see that "Eurocentrism" and contempt for other peoples go hand-in-hand:

> Although Europe is the smallest of the three parts of our continent, it has nevertheless certain advantages which make it preferable to the *others*. Its air is extremely temperate and its provinces very fertile. . . . It excels by reason of its good properties and its peoples, who are normally mild, honest, civilised, and

much given to science and the arts. . . . The peoples of Europe, by reason of their education and their valour, have brought into submission *other* parts of the world. Their spirit is apparent in their works, their wisdom in their systems of government, their power in their arms, their standards of conduct in their commerce, and their magnificence in their cities. Thus in every respect Europe surpasses the *other* parts of the world. . . . In *our* view it is only right that the name of Europe should frequently be confused with that of Christianity.[34]

What is "ours" means what is European, civilised, Christian; it means honest, strong people, gifted in science and the arts. The "others" are pagans, foreigners, barbarians, without proper government and without faith. Bernard Duchene, going through the various articles in the *Dictionary* to which we have referred one by one, discovers, in the end, that "not only does the sense of *the other* as such never appear in Moreri and his readers, but on the contrary, by means of colonialism, the dream is merging into reality: the dream of making the whole earth co-extensive with *us* (*chez nous*), and thus unifying the globe under the banner of Christian Europe."[35]

Two views of primitive man continued to exist side by side, as they were to be found in José de Acosta. He was seen either as a brutish, cruel, fierce, wild barbarian,[36] or as an innocent, mild, docile, gentle savage, of good disposition, virtuous, happy.[37] In the eighteenth century, to provide ideological backing for a triumphant bourgeoisie, Rousseau was to present the *bon sauvage* as distinct from the "natural state" and the "civil state" (or feudal, monarchical, medieval civilisation). Thus he said that "we must take care neither to confuse the natural state with the savage state (*l'état sauvage*), nor, on the other hand, the natural state with the civil state (*l'état civil*).[38] The *bon sauvage* (or primitive man with positive characteristics—as in the first and second of de Acosta's categories, or the second of the two types mentioned above) stands as a criticism of the "civil state," or feudal, monarchical culture. In fact the "state of nature" is that of the bourgeois subject emerging in a pure and free condition in order to create a new world (capitalist Europe from the eighteenth century onwards).[39] In this case the *bon sauvage* is the positive view the triumphant bourgeoisie takes of the peoples of the Third World as possible subjects for exploitation, now secularised (the question is no longer whether they can perceive the faith, as with the rough (*rudos*) Indians of the Spanish conquest; nor yet whether they are disbelieving pagans as seen by French Christianity in the seventeenth century), and thus available as cheap manpower or as possible markets for its industrial merchandise: "Such a (bourgeois) society is led to seek new consumers, outside itself, and so it will seek means of subsisting among other peoples who are its inferiors in the matter of the resources of which it has a superfluity, or in terms of industry in general."[40]

The countries of the Third World, who represent the *bon sauvage*, are thus considered as a *tabula rasa*, an extra and cheap productive force, a potential market for over-production, the *raw material* of civilisation. The great "theologian" of Europe's domination in the world actually says in his "modern" *Summa theologiae*: "The material existence of England is based on trade (*Handel*) and industry (*Industrie*), and the English have accepted for themselves the role of *missionaries* (*die Missionarien*; notice the religious connotation) of *civilisation* throughout the world. Thus their commercial spirit (*Handelsgeist*, the Holy Spirit of capitalism?) impels them to explore all seas and all lands, to make alliances with barbarian peoples (*barbarischen Völkern*), to arouse in them new needs and industries, and, above all, to create in them the conditions necessary for engaging in human relations, that is, the renunciation of acts of violence, respect for poverty(!) and "hospitality" (towards capital, Hegel forgot to add!).[41]

We Latin Americans, the first "barbarians" of Europe's Modern Age—the Africans and Asians were to follow us in due course—have been acquainted with this "theology" for five centuries, but in our time it has become more tragic. The actual number of *rudos*, noble savages, barbarians, is today the number of "underdeveloped countries," countries of the Third World, poor countries.

This *civil religion* is, as ever, the ideological justification which salves the conscience of capitalism as it exploits the new *rudos*, *sauvages*, barbarians: the peoples of the Third World. Moreover, the difference between worthy (*dignos*) "men" and unworthy (*indignos*) "barbarians" is said to have its origin in the "divine plan" or in "nature": "Disparities in conditions between political entities are natural."[42]

How far removed we are from that Christian doctrine which Peter taught Cornelius, the pagan, the barbarian, one of the *goim*:

Stand up; I too am a man (*autos anthrōpos*). . . . Truly I perceive that God shows no partiality (*ouk estin prosopolēmptēs*), but in any nation anyone who fears him and does what is right (*dikaiosynēn*) is acceptance to him (Acts 10:26, 34–35).

NOTES

This selection was translated by G. W. S. Knowles.

1. *Obras del padre José de Acosta* (BAE Madrid 1954) p. 392a.
2. The author bases himself on Thomas In *Epist. ad Rom.*, c.l., lect. 5; and *I ad Cor.*, c. 14, lect. 2.
3. J. de Acosta *De procuranda*.
4. Op. cit. P. 392b.
5. Loc. Cit.

6. Loc. Cit.

7. Ibid. p. 393b.

8. *Conquête et exploitation des nouveaux mondes* (PUF Paris 1969) p. 7.

9. Op. cit. (BAE Madrid 1959) III p. 60. See Lewis Hanke *Uno es el género humano* (Chiapas 1974) pp. 54 ff.

10. *Democrates Alter* (CSIC Madrid 1957) p. 15.

11. See Kittel *TWNT* II pp. 362 ff, art. "ethnos."

12. "Exteriority" (*Aeusserlichkeit*) is for Hegel "existence" (*Dasein*): what is farthest removed from "being" (springing originally from the division (*Entzweiung*) of being). For us (see *Filosofía ética latinoamericana* [Edicol Mexico 1977]) "exteriority" is the sphere from which *the other*, the poor insofar as he is unconditioned by the oppressing system and *outside* our world, demands justice.

13. "Mobilisation against the Enemy acts as a powerful impulse to production and employment, and thus maintains a high standard of living. . . . The alienation of the totality absorbs particular alienations and converts crimes against humanity into a rational undertaking" (H. Marcuse *One Dimensional Man*, 2 [Spanish edition Mortiz, Mexico 1969] pp. 43, 73).

14. In the preaching of Jesus as a whole we observe an openness to the one who is "other than" the Jewish people. See J. Jeremias *Jésus et les paiens* (Neuchâtel, Delachaux, 1956).

15. Kittel *TWNT* V p. 453.

16. Lewis Hanke *Uno es* p. 9.

17. *Pol.* I 5 1254a 14–16, 1254b 19–24.

18. *Sobre las justas causas de la guerra contra los indios* (Fondo de Cultura Económica, Mexico 1941) p. 81.

19. Stafford Poole *Bartolomé de las Casas. Defense against the Persecutors and Slanderers for the People of the New World* (De Kalb, Illinois 1974) p. 333.

20. Ibid. p. 338.

21. Ibid. p. 329.

22. The "blinded eyes" are precisely the *blind* ethical conscience (*Gewissen*). D. von Hildebrand would say. See his *Die Idee der sittlichen Handlung* (Damstadt 1969).

23. S. Poole *Bartolomé de las Casas* pp. 345–46.

24. Ibid. p. 353.

25. *Brevisma relación de la destrucción de las Indias* (BAE Madrid) V p. 136a.

26. *Historia de las Indias* I ch. 40 p. 142a.

27. This is how Hobbes defined European man, the product of bourgeois capitalism: "*Homo homini lupus.*"

28. *Brevísima relación* p. 136b.

29. *Historia de las Indias* III ch. 79 II p. 357a.

30. *Representación a los regentes Cisneros y Adriano* V p. 3a.

31. *Memorial de remedios* V p. 120a.

32. *Cláusula del testamento* V p. 540a.

33. *Cláusula del testamento* V p. 540a, b.

34. Article "Europe" in *The Grand dictionnaire historique* ed. L. Moreri (Provence 1643). See Bernard Duchene "Un exemple d'univers mental au XVIIIe. siècle" in *Civilisation chrétienne* (Paris) pp. 29–30.

35. Ibid. p. 44.

36. Ibid. p. 35.

37. Loc. Cit.

38. *Emile ou de l'éducation* (Paris 1964) p. 514.

39. See my work *Ética filosófica latinoamericana* (Mexico 1977) III pp. 136 ff.

40. Hegel *Rechtsphilosophie* p. 246.

41. Idem. *Philosophie der Geschichte* (Frankfurt 1970) XII p. 538.

42. R. Cooper, K. Kaiser and M. Kosaka *Towards a Renovated International System* (1977) (typewritten text of the Trilateral Commission) p. 21.

13

Was America Discovered or Invaded?

The quincentenary of the arrival of Christopher Columbus in the West Indies in 1492 will soon be celebrated. In a spirit of triumphalism which is
completely at odds with the historical facts, the Church has already started
preparing for these celebrations at the highest level. On 11 February 1988,
the *Asociación Indígena Salvadoreña* (Salvadoran Indian Association) published *I Encuentro espiritual y cultural* (Spiritual and Cultural Encounter I) in
which it repudiated the foreign invasion of America and called a halt to the
genocide and ethnocide of its peoples and culture and also demanded a
complete rejection of the celebration of 500 years of that *foreign invasion*.[1] The
fact is that the first Europeans reached these lands towards the end of the fifteenth century—the Spaniards came first, followed by the Portuguese and
then the Dutch, English, French, etc.; and it is claimed that they "discovered"
(they revealed what was covered) that these lands formed a continent. It is
further claimed that they "evangelised" the indigenous peoples of the continent. There is not much awareness of the fact that both of these terms already indicate an interpretation which con-ceals (which hides or covers
over) the historical event. From the European point of view (from above),
something was dis-covered; from the point of view of the inhabitants of the
continent (from below), what we are really dealing with is an invasion by
foreigners, by aliens, and by people from outside; people who murdered the
menfolk, educated the orphans and went to bed with ("lived with" was the
sixteenth century Spanish euphemism) Indian women. "After killing off all

Enrique Dussel, "Was America Discovered or Invaded?," *Concilium* 200 (1988): 126–34.

those who wanted, yearned for, or even thought about liberty, or to be relieved of the torments they suffered, as all *native leaders and adult males did* (because they normally allow only youngsters and women to survive these wars)," then those who are left alive are "subjected to the hardest, most horrific and harshest servitude that man or beast could ever endure."[2]

1. THE INVENTION OF AMERICA

Incredible as it may seem, it is now more than 30 years since the historian Edmundo O'Gorman presented the thesis which became the title of his famous book *La invención de América* (The Invention of America).[3] Inspired by Heidegger, his thesis is a masterly ontological analysis which far exceeds the limits of perfunctory anecdotal material. Taking as a point of departure the European concept of "being in the world" of the likes of Columbus or of Amerigo Vespucio, then the notional "American being" is generated from the idea of "Asian being" since the islands of the Caribbean were understood to be properly situated in the great ocean adjacent to the continent of Asia, just like the archipelagos of Japan or of the Philippines. As far as Europe was concerned, there only existed Africa to the south and Asia to the east. America simply was not there. "When it is claimed" writes O'Gorman, "that America was invented, we are dealing with an attempt to explain a *being* (*Dasein*) whose existence depends on the way that it is understood by Western culture. The coming into being of America is an event that depends on the form of its appearance."[4] Accordingly Western culture has the "creative capacity of giving its own existence to a being which that culture understands to be different and alien."[5]

This vision which to a certain extent is creative *ex nihilo* of being or of the meaning of entity is the way in which many historians conceive what is essentially South American; this also applies to Church history. The native American was seen as a mere material being, devoid of feeling, of history, and of humanity—even his name, "Indian," was of Asian origin since it was believed that he was a Hindu from India; he was merely a potential *recipient* of evangelisation who could not and was not expected to make any contribution of any kind—an invented non-being. This is an extreme, Eurocentric point of view which has, nevertheless, been postulated by a South American historian—an extraordinarily absurd piece of self-deception!

2. THE DIS-COVERY OF AMERICA

Theologically, dis-covery seems at least slightly more positive to an American than mere invention. Dis-covery at least presumes the prior existence of something which was covered and was not created from a vacuum. However, the use of the term "dis-cover" implies that the point of departure in this process is the European ego which is a constituent element of the historical event: "I discover," "I conquer," "I evangelise" (in the missionary sense) and "I think" (in the ontological sense). The European ego turns the newly dis-covered primitive native into a mere object—a thing which acquires meaning only when it enters the world of the European. Fernánez de Ovideo wondered if native Americans were even human and he stated: "These people of the (West) Indies, although rational and of the same race as those of the holy ark of Noah have become irrational and bestial because of their idolatries, sacrifices and devilish ceremonies." [6] Thus, the European ego (of conquistador, missionary or merchant) considered the other as something which only acquired meaning because it had been discovered (revealed): what it had already been was of no consequence.

Accordingly, any discussion about dis-covery inevitably limits parameters to one perspective which is incomplete, is in favour of those who dominate and is from above. In the same way, mission or evangelisation, the basic activity of the missionary, only takes into account the ecclesial ego which, along with the conquistador from Spain or the merchant from Holland or England, preaches the doctrines of Christianity to the newly dis-covered "for the greater glory of God" (*ad maiorem Dei gloriam*).

Nearly every history of the Church describes events in the mission areas of South America, Africa and Asia from the sixteenth to the end of the nineteenth century as a glorious expansion of Christianity. As Hegel stated: "Europe became the missionary agent for civilisation throughout the world." [7] In this process, one has to note both the deification of civilisation and the secularisation of mission; in fact, both amount to the same thing and Euro-centralism is basic to both.

3. FOREIGN INVASION (A COPERNICAN UPSET FOR AMERICAN SUBJECTIVITY)

The notions of invention and dis-covery, as well as those of conquest and evangelisation are centered on Europeans as constituent egos. But if we take a Copernican leap and abandon our accepted world view of the European ego to look around and try to understand things from the perspective of the primitive American native where the American Indian ego becomes the core of this new solar system, everything takes on a new significance. Tupac Amaru was an Inca and a rebel; he was put to death by being pulled apart by four horses at Cuzco in Peru in 1781 because he had tried to gain freedom for his own oppressed Indian people. In a statement found in his pocket when he was imprisoned, he wrote: "For that reason, and because of the voices which have cried to Heaven" (as in Exodus),[8] "in the name of the Almighty God, we ordain and order, that not one of these said people, render any payment to or obey in any way these intruding European agents."[9]

The world "intrusion," from the latin *intrusio* (a violent entering), means an entry into someone else's world which is uninvited and without permission. Amaru, a great rebel and popular liberation theologian, [10] saw Europeans as intruders into our continent; intruders who had invaded, occupied, and taken over a particular space: the space in which the world, the culture, the religion, and the history of American man belonged. Faced with the unfamiliar European, the first reaction of the native inhabitant was one of bewilderment: an inability to know what to think or what to do. As has already been pointed out, the native American was given the Asian misnomer Indian which had no bearing on his world; and, within terms of that world, his only natural solution to the extraordinary problem of his encounter with Europeans, with their fair skin and fair hair, with their horses and dogs which he had never seen before, with their cannons and gunpowder and their metal armour, was to see them as gods: "They really inspired fear when they arrived. Their faces were so unfamiliar. The Mayans took them to be gods. Tunatiuh[11] slept in the house of Tzumpam."[12]

The emperor Montezuma of Mexico experienced the same wonder when he met the invader Hernán Cortés, since "having already consulted his own people," as José de Acosta writes, "they all assured him that without doubt his ancient and great master Quezalcoatl[13] had returned as he said he would and that that was why he had come from the East."[14] The aboriginal American neither invented nor dis-covered the new arrivals. He admired them with a sacred respect as they invaded his land; he found his own understanding for them which was quite different from that of the European invaders. At first, Europeans interpreted what they found in terms of an Asian being and then in terms of an American being when it was understood that America formed a fourth part of the known world along with Europe, Africa and Asia. The invaders were understood with the same kind of limitations by the native Americans[15] who saw them as gods who had appeared amongst them. This understanding, in its turn, demanded answers to such questions as why the divine beings had come, whether they had come to demand their rights and to punish or whether they had come to bless and endow. This initial encounter created feelings of expectation, of unease, of admiration:

The admiral and others noted their simplicity—as Bartholomé de las Casas told us on 12 October 1492—and how they took great pleasure in and enjoyed everything; the Spaniards took careful note of the Indians (sic) and how much gentleness, simplicity and trust they showed towards people they had never seen. They seemed to have returned to a state of innocence such that it seemed a matter of a mere six hours or so since our common father Adam himself had lived.[16]

4. THE VISION OF THOSE WHO WERE CONQUERED (A DESTROYED SUBJECTIVITY)

The original face-to-face encounter did not last very long and the American Indians soon discovered why these gods had come: "They soon found out what they were really like and that they were the most cruel and hungry wolves, tigers and lions who threw themselves at them. For the last forty years and including this very day, they have done nothing but tear them apart, kill them off, cause them distress, hurt them, torment them and destroy them by every conceivable and unimaginable form of cruelty."[17]

In actual fact, from within his own world, the native American lived in great terror through the invasion by these divine beings: "Ahuau Katún 11[18] the first one in the story, is the original katún . . . it was during this katún that the red-bearded foreigners, the children of the sun, the fair skinned ones, arrived. Woe! Let us lament because they arrived! They came from the east, these messengers of the sign of the divinity, these foreigners of the earth. Woe! Let us lament because they came, the great builders of stone piles;[19] the false gods of the earth who can make fire burst from the ends of their arms.[20] Woe! Heavy is the weight of the katún in which Christianity first appears! This is what is going to happen: there will be an enslaving power, men will become slaves, a slavery that will include even the Chiefs of the Thrones."[21] "The hearts of the Lords of the people will tremble and be full of fear because of the signs of this katún: an empire of war, an epoch of war, words of war, food of war, drink of war, a journey of war, a government of war. It will be a time for old men and old women to wage war, for children and brave men to wage war, for young men to wage war on behalf of our honoured gods."[22]

This glorious conquest and even the accompanying evangelisation will always be closely linked to that perverse ethical activity: a generative evil and a structural oppression which still weigh so heavily on our lives even as we approach the end of the twentieth century. Accordingly, the original inhabitants, within terms of their own world, had a very personal perception of the events which followed the discovery. The world of the foreign oppressor saw things in terms of a discovery *cum* conquest while within our subjective American world it was a process of bewilderment, servitude, and death. The same events, therefore, generated two quite different sets of feelings and effects.

5. THE CREATIVE RECEPTION OF THE GOSPEL AND AN HISTORICAL INDEMNIFICATION

In this Testament (1564), Bartolomé has written an explicit piece of liberation theology:

> God saw fit to choose me to try to make good to all these peoples we call Indians, owners of these countries and lands, some of the insults, the wrongs and the injuries of a kind unseen and unheard of, which, contrary to all reason and justice, they have received at the hands of us Spaniards, to restore them to their *first liberty* of which they have been so unjustly deprived and to *liberate them* from the violent death they still suffer.[23]

"These peoples"—the Indians—were free and were masters of these lands. They were invaded and dispossessed, oppressed and impoverished. However, they did get the Gospel message, even if that occurred frequently in spite of the missionaries. Christ crucified and bleeding (more a feature of the South American baroque style than of the contemporary Spanish style).[24] made the Indians aware of their identity with the Son who had been put to death. They lived out in their own bodies, in their complete poverty, in their absolute nakedness, impoverished in the fullest sense of the word, the cross which the missionaries preached about. It was no mere passive apprenticeship or a learning by rote of Christian doctrine by those who had been conquered, but a creative acceptance of the Gospel from below. Can the fifth centenary of that kind of evangelisation be properly celebrated? Would that not be yet another insult of the kind indicated by Bartolomé de las Casas?

The word insult implies an offence against the honour and reputation of someone's rights. In actual fact, the dis-covery and the conquest were not only insults but forms of practical oppression and structured servitude, involving the killing off of a people and the destruction of a culture and a religion. The process involved more than insult; it was an offence, a humiliation, an assassination, and the gravest sin against the dignity of others.

For these reasons, what has to occur in 1992 is an *historical indemnification* made to the American Indians. Although, I do believe that the one great protagonist who will be absent from the preparations for the commemoration of 12 October 1492 will be the *Indian himself*.

Indemnification surely involves, at the very least and even if it is so late, the making good of the offence committed against another person, fully satisfying the humiliated party and making compensation for the prejudice which has been inflicted. Can we do that? Is it too idealistic to restore all that has been taken away from the Indian? How can indemnification be made for the irreparable damage which has been done and is still being done?

In any case, the American Indian was never conquered. Hundreds of rebellions occurred during the period of colonial rule from the sixteenth to the nineteenth century and nowadays revolt is occurring in the struggles of the "Second Emancipation,"[25] in the *processes of liberation* being lived out at this very time in Guatemala, in El Salvador, and in Nicaragua and in the whole of South America, wherever there is any problem or suffering. With Mariátegui[26] I believe that the Indian problem is most closely linked with the future of South America. An *historical indemnification* in 1992 would be a sign, a milestone on the road towards the Kingdom, leading to the freedom of the Indian in a liberated South America. A clear awareness of all this can come to us only from an historical conspectus which emerges from below.

NOTES

This selection was translated by John Angus Macdonald.

1. See *El Dia* (Mexico, 12 February 1988) p. 6. On the theme of "discovery," see P. Chaunu *Conquête et exploitation des Nouveaux Mondes* (Paris 1977); E. Schmitt ed. *Die grossen Entdeckungen* (Munich 1984); I. P. Maguidovich *Historia del descubrimiento y exploración de Latinoamérica* (Moscow 1972); Z. Todorov *The Conquest of America* (New York 1985) in which my own hypothesis of viewing the Indian as "other" is taken up in a Levinasian theory which I first postulated in 1972.

2. See E. Dussel *Filosofía ética de la liberación* (Buenos Aires 1987) vol. 1 p. 5. For further explanation of this text see my own articles: "Histoire de la foi chrétienne et changement sociale en Amèrique Latine" *Les luttes de liberation bousculent la théologie* (Paris 1975) pp. 39–99; "Expansion de la cristiandad y su crisis" *Concilium* 164 (1981) pp. 80–89. For general information about the period see my "Introducción General" to the colonial period in *Historia General de la Iglesia en América Latina* (Salamanca 1983) and *History of the Church in Latin America* (Grand Rapids 1981).

3. *FCE* Mexico 1957.

4. Ibid. p. 91.

5. Ibid. p. 97.

6. See E. Dussel "La cristiandad moderna ante el otro" *Concilium* 150 (1979) p. 499.

7. See E. Dussel "One Ethic and Many Moralities" *Concilium* 170 (1981) pp. 54–55.

8. See E. Dussel "Paradigma del Exodo en la teología de la liberación," *Concilium* 209 (1987) pp. 99–114. In this book see chapter 6, p. 115 ff.

9. B. Lewis *La rebelión de Tupac Amaru* (Buenos Aires 1967) p. 421. For information about other Indian rebellions see J. Golte *Repartos y rebeliones* (Lima 1980); S. M. Yañez *Sublevaciones indígenas en la Audiencia de Quito* (Quito 1978); M. T. Huerta and P. Palacios *Rebeliones indigenas de la epoca colonial* (Mexico 1976).

10. See E. Dussel *Hipótesis para una historia de la teología en América Latina* (Bogota 1986) p. 33.

11. In the Mayan language "tunatiuh" means the Sun God. They gave this name to the Spanish conquistador Álvarado, a brutal fair-haired soldier whose locks were taken by the natives to be the very rays of the sun.

12. See *Memorial de Sololá. Anales de los Cakchiqueles* 11, 148 (Mexico 1950) p. 126; N. Wachtel *La vision des vaincus. Les Indiens du Perou devant la Conquéte espagnole* (Paris 1971); On American religions see W. Krickeberg. H. Trimborn, W. Mueller and O. Zerries *Die Religionen des Alten Amerika* (Stuttgard 1961); also M. L. Portillo *El reverso de la conquista* (Mexico 1964); F. Mires *En nombre de la cruz* (San Jose 1986) includes very fine pieces of writing "Discusiones teológicas y politicas frente al holocausto de los indios (periodo de conquista)"; S. Zavala *Filosofía de la conquista* (Mexico 1977); J. O. Beozzo "Visão indigena da conquista ē da evangelizacão," *Inculturacão e libertacão* (Sao Paulo 1986) pp. 79–116.

13. A "god" of the peoples ruled over by the Aztecs (like the Greek Zeus vis a vis the Romans). The overlord had a "bad conscience" and believed that the god of the underlings was coming to take his revenge for the oppression of his faithful. Cortés left from Tlaxcala, from the temple where Quezalcoatl was adored; the name means the "divine duality" or "the feathered serpent;" *coatl* means dualism and *quezal* refers to the splendid feathers of the quetzal bird which was itself a sign of the divinity.

14. *Historia Natural* vol. VII; Chap. 16; (Madrid 1954) p. 277.

15. Even the name "American" is foreign and dominating and properly belongs to an Italian geographer and not to an "American" as such.

16. *Historia de las Indias* vol. L. Chap. 40 (Madrid 1957) p. 142.

17. B. de las Casas *Brevisima relacion de la destruccion de las Indias*; ibid. p. 137.

18. The proper name for an epoch, a "kairos" of fear.

19. The reference is to the Spaniards' building of Churches in the sixteenth century.

20. *El libro de los libros de Chilam Balam* Part II. (Mexico 1948) pp. 124–25. The reference is to gunpowder and shotguns used by the Spaniards.

21. Ibid. p. 126.

22. Ibid. p. 137.

23. See *Obras* op. cit. p. 539.

24. See E. Dussel "L'art chrètien de l'oprimé en Amérique Latine. Hypotèse pour caractériser une esthétique de la liberation" *Concilium* 152 (1980) pp. 55–70.

25. The "First Emancipation" took place against Spain and Portugal from 1809. The "Second Emancipation" began in 1959, but today the neocolonial metropolises are the industrialised countries on the "centre."

26. See his *Siete ensayos sobre la realidad peruana* (Lima 1954).

Index

About the Author

Enrique Dussel is professor of philosophy at the Universidad Autónoma Metropolitana-Iztapalapa and the Universidad Nacional Autonóma de México. He has doctorates from the Universidad Complutense in Madrid, and the Sorbonne in Paris, and has been awarded *honoris causa* doctorates from the Freiburg University and La Paz. He has written over fifty books and three hundred articles, many of which have been translated into English, including *The Underside of Modernity* (1996), *The Invention of the Americas* (1995), *Ethics and Community* (1988), *Philosophy of Liberation* (1985), and *Ethics and the Theology of Liberation* (1978). His last book was *Ética de la Liberación en la edad de la globalización y de la exclusión* (1998). The recent work by Linda Martín Alcoff and Eduardo Mendieta, eds., *Thinking from the Underside of History: Enrique Dussel's Philosophy of Liberation* (2000) deals with the philosophical aspects of his work. He is currently at work on a political sequel to *Beyond Philosophy* tentatively titled *Critique of Political Reason*.

About the Editor

Eduardo Mendieta is associate professor of philosophy at Stony Brook University. He is the editor and translator of Enrique Dussel's *The Underside of Modernity* (1996). He is also coeditor of *Liberation Theologies, Postmodernity, and the Americas* (1997), and *Identities: Race, Class, Gender, and Nationality* (2003). He edited *Latin American Philosophy: Currents, Issues, and Debates* (2003), and is the author of *The Adventures of Transcendental Philosophy: Karl-Otto Apel's Semiotics and Discourse Ethics* (2002).